Against Obscenity

Reconfiguring American Political History

Ronald P. Formisano, Paul Bourke, Donald DeBats, and Paula M. Baker, Series Founders

Against Obscenity

Reform and the Politics of Womanhood in
America, 1873–1935

Leigh Ann Wheeler

The Johns Hopkins University Press
Baltimore and London

©2004 The Johns Hopkins University Press
All rights reserved. Published 2004
Printed in the United States of America on acid-free paper
9 8 7 6 5 4 3 2 1

The Johns Hopkins University Press
2715 North Charles Street
Baltimore, Maryland 21218-4363
www.press.jhu.edu

Library of Congress Cataloging-in-Publication Data

Wheeler, Leigh Ann, 1967–
Against obscenity : reform and the politics of womanhood in America,
1873–1935 / Leigh Ann Wheeler.
    p.   cm. — (Reconfiguring American political history)
Includes bibliographical references and index.
    ISBN 0-8018-7802-0 (alk. paper)
    1. Women social reformers—United States—History—19th century.
2. Women social reformers—United States—History—20th century.
3. Obscenity (Law)—United States—History—19th century.
4. Obscenity (Law)—United States—History—20th century.   5. United
States—Moral conditions—History—19th century.   6. United States—
Moral conditions—History—20th century.   I. Title.   II. Series.
HQ1419W45 2004
303.48'4'0973—dc21

                          2003006240

A catalog record for this book is available from the British Library.

For Don

Contents

Preface and Acknowledgments

My intellectual and political coming-of-age took place against the backdrop of the so-called feminist sex wars of the 1980s. One of the earliest battles occurred at a national conference held at Barnard College in 1982, entitled "Toward a Politics of Sexuality." Conference organizers hoped to create a forum for discussing sexual pleasure as a route to women's empowerment, but many women in attendance, representing feminist anti-pornography groups, circulated leaflets accusing conference organizers of excluding their perspective, and celebrating pornography, "patriarchal sexuality," and "sadomasochism." Several women so charged called the anti-porn group a "phony" organization of "prudes" and "moralists" that used "McCarthyite tactics" to silence other points of view. The following year, Catharine MacKinnon and Andrea Dworkin declared a "new day for women's equality" when they persuaded the Minneapolis City Council to pass a pioneering anti-pornography ordinance. But many women mobilized against the ordinance on the grounds that it imposed censorship and policed sexual pleasure in the name of feminism. And so it went. The confrontations mounted until, when I entered Kansas State University in 1985, each side had dug in, prepared for a protracted confrontation.

Unaware of the feminist war raging around me, I registered for my first women's studies class and rejoiced to find language and support for beliefs and questions I had thought were mine alone. Classmates led me to the local chapter of the National Organization for Women, where I discovered a vision of politics that made women and gender central. Proudly, I announced to my family that I was a feminist. But confusion and disappointment soon set in. Rather than the nurturing and rigorous intellectual environment I sought, women's studies classes and NOW meetings resembled battlegrounds where women attacked each other over issues of sexuality.

These years of seemingly unprecedented internecine warfare among feminists left me with persistent questions about women, politics, and sexuality. Why did women who agreed on most issues attack each other so viciously? How did matters of sexuality become so polarizing? What did these bitter fights imply for the future of women's political efforts? I knew that I needed to explore these questions from the distance that history allows, but I did not initially consider studying female anti-obscenity activists in the early twentieth century. The scant secondary literature characterized these women as female versions of the notoriously repressive vice crusader Anthony Comstock, making me think they would be of little help in my quest. Fortunately, I investigated a bit before moving on, and what I found surprised and intrigued me. Women's anti-obscenity reform in the early part of the century proved more complex and interesting in its own right—and more illuminating of the broader sweep of women's history, including women's political participation and recent feminist fights—than I could ever have imagined.

I join historians who search for a "usable past"—one that helps us comprehend and cope with our present. This book relates such a past, not by rushing to find contemporary relevance, but by understanding people from the past on their own terms and in their own context and using that carefully contextualized understanding to illuminate the present. The subjects of this book lived in a world very different from ours, and only after carefully sifting through mounds of correspondence and volumes of primary and secondary literature have I attained a level of understanding and empathy necessary to one who writes the history of people. Still, as I have written and revised this book, I have wrestled to resolve the tension between explaining female anti-obscenity reformers in their own context and evaluating them in mine. I suspect that some readers will think that I have erred in one direction, while others will find the error elsewhere. Certainly, this work is profoundly shaped by the deeply held values and concerns that led me to the topic, infusing with anticipation the arduous tasks of researching and writing. Like any good scholar, though, I have tried to let my personal passions inform the questions I ask but not the answers I find. This invaluable advice, and many of the tools to implement it, came to me through my dissertation adviser, Sara Evans. Her patience, caring, and confidence in me, combined with her superior intellect, deep knowledge of women's history, and commitment to making history accessible to nonspecialists have made this a better book and me a better historian. Readers will also appreciate Sara's imprint on the book's style—especially her insistence that I avoid subordinating the narrative to my scholarly agenda and instead allow my arguments to unfold with the story.

Sara Evans is only one of the many treasures I found at the University of Minnesota. Other faculty who helped me get this project under way and chart its course to becoming a book include George Green, the late Paul Murphy, Lisa Norling, and Naomi Scheman. I thank all of my graduate student colleagues who offered invaluable assistance, both emotional and intellectual. In particular, Katherine Meerse, Michelle Mouton, and Mari Trine read and commented on the entire manuscript, and all three continue to enrich my life with the sort of precious and lasting friendship that, despite physical distance and months without contact, deepens and grows.

I have been fortunate to pursue my profession at several supportive institutions of higher education. Although I was only a temporary sabbatical replacement at Concordia College in Moorhead, Minnesota, faculty there—especially Carroll Engelhardt and Joy Lintelman—warmly welcomed and invested in me while helping me land my first tenure-track job. At Rollins College in Winter Park, Florida, I found incredibly nurturing colleagues who inspired my teaching and my scholarship. Thank you Steven Briggs, Barbara Carson, Charlie Edmundson, Rick Fogelsong, Laura Greyson, Jack Lane, Barry Levis, Austa Weaver, Gary Williams, and Yusheng Yao; you all made leaving so difficult. I have found, at Bowling Green State University, a new community of scholars and friends. Thanks especially to Tina Amos, Rachel Buff, Ed Danziger, and Jan Finn, for their warmth, friendship, and enthusiasm for students, to Gary Hess and Fuji Kawashima for their caring mentorship, and to Liette Gidlow, for all kinds of things, including her encouraging and provocative comments on several chapters of the book.

This book has benefited enormously from the incisive criticism of leading scholars in the field of women's history. Conference commentators whose responses have improved my work include Leila Rupp, Ruth Rosen, Sharon Ullman, and Lisa Bowers. Anonymous reviewers for the *Michigan Historical Review*, *Frontiers*, and the *Journal of Women's History* all offered suggestions for revision that improved individual chapters, and Helen Lefkowitz Horowitz, who reviewed the book for Johns Hopkins University Press, offered helpful advice that pushed me to sharpen the book's analysis. The most useful guidance came from two other scholars of women's anti-obscenity activism; Andrea Friedman (whom I had not met prior to sending her the manuscript) and Alison Parker (whom, at the time, I had encountered only once) have been unbelievably generous, reading and commenting thoroughly on the entire book manuscript and helping me strengthen arguments that, in some cases, challenge their own. Wendy Gamber also read the entire manuscript, providing invaluable insights and encouraging me at crucial moments, and Robyn Rosen helped with the introduction and bolstered my morale. Paula Baker contributed to this project in ways that went well beyond what anyone should expect of a series editor, reading the book carefully, helping me to think more deeply, articulate more precisely, and contextualize more broadly, all while bolstering my confidence.

Several people actually conducted research for me, locating key documents that were, for various reasons, beyond my reach. Caroline Loken, President of the Woman's Club of Minneapolis, waded through decades of club bulletins and minutes, and, within a short time, mailed me a packet of meticulously collected materials that proved essential to my first two chapters. Kathleen Laughlin took time away from her own research at the Catholic University of America in Washington, D.C., to find and copy a file on women's motion picture reform in the 1930s. Several letters in that file turned out to be pivotal. Ruth Vasey, whom I've met only by e-mail, searched through her personal, microfilmed copy of the Motion Picture Producers and Distributors of America records, and mailed, from Australia, an envelope full of vital correspondence and notes.

Many people whose jobs are to help researchers have gone well beyond their duties, providing me with exceptional assistance. I thank Dallas Lindgren and Steve Nielsen, at the Minnesota Historical Society—Dallas, for introducing me to the Catheryne Cooke Gilman collection and Steve, for quickly locating illustrations and arranging to have them reproduced. Jill Costill, at the Indiana State Library, Maggie Sloss, at the Minneapolis Public Library, and Linda Bernard, at the Hoover Institution Archives, guided me expertly through their collections, making my short time at each site more efficient. The interlibrary loan staff at the University of Minnesota, Rollins College, and Bowling Green State University—especially Kausalya Padmaraj—procured countless obscure materials, quickly and efficiently. My four graduate research assistants exercised admirable initiative and tenacity: Jim Weeks located an excellent soft-ware program and assembled my bibliography with it; Seneca Vaught perused many microfilm reels from the Will Hays collection and discovered several pertinent documents in the process; Lorna Sippo unearthed a particularly exciting source that I had overlooked; and Rachel Ayers assisted with proofreading.

Several institutions provided financial assistance that allowed me to visit archives, photocopy sources, attend conferences, and devote uninterrupted time to this project. Annually, since my arrival, the Bowling Green State University History Department has provided funds that have taken me to the National Archives in College Park, Maryland; the Hoover Institution Archives at Stanford University; the Academy of Motion Picture Arts and Sciences in Beverly

Hills, California; the Indiana State Library; and the New York Public Library. Two Jack B. Critchfield research grants from Rollins College financed travel to conferences in Chicago, Connecticut, and the United Kingdom. Several fellowships and travel grants from the University of Minnesota jump-started my research, buying me time and photocopies.

The Johns Hopkins University Press has provided me with attentive and skilled editors. By reading early drafts closely and commenting profusely, Robert J. Brugger made my writing both more efficient and colorful, even as he communicated his investment in my work. Melody Herr has been just the sort of cheerful and dependable source of encouragement and information that every new author craves. Thank you, Melody, for helping me navigate the intricate publication process. Thanks, too, to Marie Blanchard for copy-editing the manuscript respectfully, expertly, and expeditiously.

My family must wonder why this book has taken me so long to complete. My mother, Shirley Hoden, and brother, Todd Wheeler, have listened to me complain about book woes and celebrate book triumphs on a weekly, sometimes daily, basis. Thank you, Mom and Todd, for continuing to care and for letting me know that you believed I would finish it and that it would be good—but that you'd still love and respect me even if I didn't finish it and it weren't so good after all.

"Thank you" can sound so inadequate, especially when offering it to someone who is and has been everything to me, from my teacher, mentor, and colleague, to my friend, lover, and husband. Don Nieman doesn't just occupy these roles—he excels in all of them. And despite his busy life as a dean, Don knows this book nearly as well as I do; he has pored over archival sources with me, discussed ways to interpret them, read the manuscript repeatedly, combed and styled the prose, debated the arguments with me, gently suggested revisions, praised my accomplishments, and taken on more than his share of household chores so that I could write. Without Don, this book would not exist. More important, without Don, my life would not be filled with poetry, passion, and unspeakable joy— and I would not understand just how woefully insufficient "thank you" can be. By the time you read this, Don, you will be the father of our child, another role you'll fill with your characteristic tenderness, humor, and love. And, as with everything we do together, I know this new relationship with each other and with our son will be magical in ways we cannot yet imagine. With bright hopes for the future and deep, deep appreciation for the past, I dedicate this book to you.

Against Obscenity

Crossing the Great Divide

Women, Politics, and Anti-obscenity Reform

"What is the matter with women?" Mrs. Richmond Wheeler demanded to know in 1934. Like her correspondent, Catheryne Cooke Gilman, Wheeler had expected woman suffrage to usher in a moral renaissance. But neither Wheeler nor Gilman saw much evidence that women, as a group, had any moral convictions left. Men had warned of this, Wheeler pointed out. They had advised women to protect their purity, declaring that women would not reform politics or commercial vice; rather, politics and commercial vice would sully women. In Wheeler's estimation, men's worst predictions had come true. "If ordinary mothers and clubwomen cannot tell right from wrong—at least for children—or have not enough character to put up a fight for right," she concluded unhappily, "it looks as if the pessimistic brothers are justified in their foreboding."[1] Wheeler and Gilman's assessment of women may have been shortsighted, but it captured a basic truth: American women's political participation and relationships to commercial entertainment had changed dramatically in the previous twenty years.

During these decades, when the country experienced the Great War, a booming postwar economy, and the onset of the Great Depression, American women provoked great political and cultural change—to uncertain ends. Temperance activists won, then lost Prohibition. Welfare reformers built, then dismantled the Children's Bureau. Suffragists cheered their own victory, then quarreled over its meaning. Simultaneously, young women helped to nudge America's timepiece toward "sex o'clock," ringing in a more sexually permissive society.[2] By shortening their hair and dresses, they sent a mixed but clearly transgressive message of boyishness and femininity, independence and sexual availability.

The emergence of this increasingly commercial, sexual, youth-oriented consumer culture incited the opposition of many politically active middle- and upper-class women, including clubwomen, temperance activists, suffragists, and others. Their immediate and telling response was to mobilize against public amusements they considered obscene. By bringing women into the arena of anti-obscenity reform, which men had dominated for several decades, female reformers challenged men's leadership in a peaceful coup that placed women at the helm of the anti-obscenity movement for the next quarter century. Between 1910 and 1935, female anti-obscenity activists used their new political power to reshape the meaning and regulation of obscenity. This book tells their story, exploring how women's anti-obscenity leadership molded American attitudes toward sexual material even as it charted a new era in women's politics.

Female anti-obscenity activists employed what I call a politics of womanhood, one rooted in Victorian notions of true womanhood that characterized women as innately pure and domestic.[3] On the assumption that women shared a superior moral sensibility that would unite them to protect children by condemning obscenity and commending sex education, women wrested control of the anti-obscenity movement from men in the 1910s. Their story pivots on struggles with men over who would define and regulate obscenity, but it is not a simple tale of women versus men. Indeed, the symbolic politics of womanhood crashed against reality when women of different classes and persuasions disagreed passionately over these issues, battling each other over whether to ban a touring stage show, close a local burlesque theater, disseminate explicit sex education pamphlets, support state censorship, or create a federal agency to regulate the motion picture industry. Thus this book examines how issues of identity, sexuality, and partisanship divided organized women, exposed "womanhood" as a chimera, and disarmed an important contingent of female reformers early in the twentieth century.

Men played vital roles in this drama. Many feared what female anti-obscenity activists believed—that women shared an essential womanhood that would unite them politically on issues of morality and, with the vote, help them remake American society in their image. Anticipating that racy movies and burlesque shows would be early victims of a woman's voting bloc, men in the commercial entertainment world quickly crafted strategies to defend themselves. Some men courted organized women, shamelessly flattering and bestowing favors on them; others aimed to divide organized women, provoking and publicizing disagreements among them; still others—the most effective ones—employed both approaches simultaneously.

Several questions propel this study. Why did women play such minor roles in anti-obscenity reform before 1910 but ascend to national leadership thereafter? How did women's and men's approaches to the issue differ? How did women understand and use the political process in the wake of suffrage? What impact did women's leadership have on cultural and judicial definitions of obscenity? Why, by the middle of the 1930s, did women lose their place in anti-obscenity reform? Answers to these questions shed new light on the history of obscenity regulation, deepen our understanding of women's political activism, and reveal key consequences of woman suffrage—consequences that extended well beyond electoral politics to encompass the wider realm of enfranchised politics, the world of white women's reform after 1920.

Investigating how and to what effect men as well as women manipulated the politics of womanhood illuminates several interesting conceptual and historiographical problems. The year of suffragist victory, 1920, for example, has produced a "great divide" in women's history, with most scholars beginning or ending their studies at, but rarely extending across, that momentous year. Those who first bridged the divide focused on electoral politics and radical feminism, finding that in the twenties and thirties women voted like men when they bothered to vote at all, "feminism" declined, and women did little that could be considered historically or politically noteworthy.[4] Three recent approaches challenge this rather pessimistic view. One shows how newly enfranchised women made their mark on the electoral system by easing the shift from party-based to interest- and pressure-group politics.[5] Another examines women's participation in political parties, revealing that female partisanship began well before 1920.[6] The third casts a wider definitional net, employing a meaning of politics broad enough to encompass activism motivated less by electoral ambitions or feminist aspirations than concern for public policy regarding mothers and children. To date, most of this work focuses on the role of women in shaping the American welfare state.[7] This book joins the third body of scholarship. However, by taking us across the great divide of 1920 in a new vehicle, women's anti-obscenity activism, it discovers an instructively different female reform experience.

Although female anti-obscenity leaders enjoyed the loyalty of millions of American women and the attentions of U.S. presidents, congressmen, and Hollywood executives, few women's historians even know their names; until recently, women's historians have focused on "liberal" women, or women whose agendas—welfare reform and sexual liberation, for example—resonate with contemporary feminism.[8] Knowing little about female anti-obscenity activists, most historians have ignored them. In fact, many of these reformers resembled their counterparts in welfare reform: they were middle-class white women who trained in the settlement house movement, focused on child welfare, employed rhetoric and strategies that historians would call maternalist, challenged private industry, endeavored to influence public policy, experienced a temporary surge of success with the passage of woman suffrage, eventually watched men take over their work, and later wondered at the unintended consequences of their activism. Compared to female welfare reformers, however, whose work can be traced back to women's early-nineteenth-century benevolent associations, women came late to anti-obscenity activism, and they arrived to find a movement already in place. Thus, in contrast to women in welfare reform—who used their rich experience in maternal and child welfare to create a new field of expertise and develop a female-dominated federal bureaucracy, the Children's Bureau (1912)—female anti-obscenity reformers confronted a male-dominated system that relegated jurisdiction over obscenity to the courts and the postal department, institutions within which women had little influence. In response, women who took charge of anti-obscenity reform employed a host of grassroots voluntary associations, hoping to effect change by bringing the moral authority of American womanhood to bear on entrepreneurs and the state.

Female welfare reformers and anti-obscenity activists entered enfranchised politics with very different preparation and institutional support. Welfare reformers knew how to build coalitions, use their positions in government bureaucracies to achieve incremental change, and manage differences among women. *Against Obscenity* examines female leaders of a much younger movement, showing how they raced to catch up with their sisters in maternal and child welfare, rapidly forming and just as rapidly abandoning coalitions, exploiting men's fear of newly enfranchised women's political power, and demanding dramatic and instant bureaucratic change, all in the name of womanhood. Unsurprisingly, female anti-obscenity activists ultimately fell short where welfare reformers succeeded, failing to erect an effective reform "dominion," gain a foothold within the federal bureaucracy, or establish themselves as professionals and experts. Nevertheless, they generated a number of notable successes, persuading entertainment entrepreneurs to modify their shows, placing female representatives in prominent posts, and precipitating the rise of an even more influential anti-obscenity movement. More important than their fleeting failures and successes, however, their story offers a cautionary tale about the possibilities and limits of the politics of womanhood between 1910 and 1935.

Most students of anti-obscenity movements have neglected female activists because of their relative invisibility. Male anti-obscenity activists have captured historians' attention; they show up in court records and highly publicized obscenity trials where they inveigh against "immoral rubber goods," *Medical Com-*

mon Sense, and *Leaves of Grass.* In contrast, female anti-obscenity activists rarely appear in court documents, and they seldom, if ever, condemned contraception, medical texts, or literature. Women's anti-obscenity work differed from men's in ways that historians of women failed to anticipate and most scholars of anti-obscenity activism have simply overlooked.

Male anti-obscenity activists and United States law defined obscenity as sexual material that could "deprave and corrupt" a vulnerable viewer—defined, since the 1870s, as a woman, a "feeble-minded" man, or a child.[9] For the next several decades, judicial obscenity decisions and male anti-obscenity activists continued to focus their *rhetoric* ever more narrowly on the child as the vulnerable viewer, even as, *in practice,* they confiscated birth control devices, educational texts, and risqué novels and other materials that children would not encounter, understand, or desire. Significantly, female anti-obscenity activists, who also declared children their primary concern, ignored such items, considering them of little risk to children. Indecent magazines, movies, and burlesque shows were another matter entirely. Such materials did appeal to children, and they became the focus of women's anti-obscenity work.

Reform directed at popular culture has traditionally received less attention than reform involving high culture, in the form of novels, paintings, and plays. The latter's very suppression has led later generations to revere it as classic and offer it to their own youth, making the history of its repression especially intriguing. The venerated positions obtained by banned books contrast starkly with the few remaining traces of the racy burlesque shows, pulp magazines, and motion pictures targeted by female reformers. Few people know enough about these items even to wonder why they were suppressed. Moreover, women's offensives against them almost never entered the courtroom—a favorite research site for many historians—in part because the transitory nature of magazines, movies, and burlesque shows inhibited litigation. By the time an obscenity case regarding one of these could make it to trial, the magazine in question would have disappeared from the newsstand, the film vanished from the marquee, and the burlesque show left the stage, only to be replaced by others, equally offensive to reformers, and equally short-lived. The cultural and commercial life of books, paintings, and plays, however, extended indefinitely, so efforts to censor them frequently entered the court system. Female anti-obscenity reformers also avoided pursuing their agenda through the courts and the postal department because they recognized these arenas as male preserves where the politics of womanhood would hold little sway. Thus scholars' conventional focus on litigation and adjudication has kept them occupied with reform that rarely concerned items appealing to children and seldom directly involved women.

Growing attention to women's history, fascination with the study of popular culture, concern about the proliferation of sexual imagery, and debates over censorship have begun to inspire historical research on women's activism against obscenity. The two pioneers in this field, Alison Parker and Andrea Friedman, both place gender and culture at the analytical center of their work, demonstrating that women's organizations formulated unique reform strategies to overcome obstacles to their activism.[10] Because neither, however, focuses on individual women or investigates how suffrage changed women's reform politics, their insightful books cannot fully explain how and why women's anti-obscenity work waxed then waned—nor can they comprehend the implications of this for middle-class women's political activism.

In using women's anti-obscenity activism to explore the wide-ranging impact of suffrage on women's politics, *Against Obscenity* helps us understand the seismic shifts that realigned and undermined organized women in the 1920s and 1930s. Unlike earlier work on women's anti-obscenity reform, it investigates political dynamics internal and external to women's organizations, showing how and why organized women, as a group, lost their once potent ability to speak for womanhood even as individuals among them catapulted into positions of influence in politics and the entertainment industry. By following the movement's national leaders and focusing on individual women and their relationships—as they worked together and against one another in local and national reform politics—it distinguishes between people and associations, treating reformers as individuals rather than using their words and deeds as proxies for the organizations they represented.[11] As a result, many fascinating personalities shape the story; these include the central characters, Catheryne Cooke Gilman, an indomitable middle-class white woman who fought doggedly against obscenity at the local and national level, and Alice Ames Winter, Gilman's elite rival, whose political connections and club work led to her controversial appointment as "woman's ambassador" to the motion picture industry. Both women became politically active while living in Minneapolis, Minnesota, and, in the course of their work, they lead us back and forth between the local and national levels. Thus, unlike scholarship with an exclusively local focus or national sweep, this study underscores linkages between the two arenas, suggesting how, why, and to what effect activists pursued their agendas on each level. In the process, it reveals that Minneapolis—the city in which feminists first tested anti-pornography legislation in the 1980s—gave rise to a much earlier women's movement around sexual material, a movement that caused as much division and rancor among women as its successor would more than half a century later.

Against Obscenity takes a historical approach to language, letting its subjects define their own terms and, in the process, excavating a lost world that helps us understand reformers in their own context rather than simply judge them in ours. In the United States between 1873 and 1935, most people did not think it censorship to prohibit nudity on stage; few would have considered the possibility that the First Amendment might embrace motion pictures; and fringe radicals had a fairly uncontested monopoly on the notion of a "right" to sexual expression. Whereas obscenity issues have become central to contemporary debates over the scope and meaning of the First Amendment, the First Amendment was not central to debates over obscenity in the early twentieth century, despite the efforts of several radical libertarians to make it so. Disagreement regarding how to define and whether to employ censorship flourished, and dissenting voices could be heard from a variety of constituencies, including free speech advocates, "free love" devotees, commercial entertainment entrepreneurs, and labor organizers, as well as women's organizations. In court, defendants in obscenity cases—especially those who relied on First Amendment arguments—usually lost, even though today most historians celebrate them as free speech trailblazers who exposed puritanical repression and championed freedom of expression. Thus those who lost legal battles over obscenity in their day have won the historical war. This study offers a different perspective, one attentive to the unique intellectual, cultural, and political milieu of the early twentieth century. As it examines the widely divergent definitions and values underlying debates over obscenity, it recovers the voices of female anti-obscenity activists and, in attempting to understand them on their own terms, restores them to a history currently dominated by free speech pioneers. The book also strips the term *obscenity* of its strictly legal import, using it, instead, as female reformers used it—as a catch-all for the material they found sexually "indecent," "immoral," "objectionable," or "offensive." Most of this material would not have been considered obscene under the law, and female reformers knew it. Even so, their activism intersected with obscenity law at a number of points that helped to reshape cultural, political, and judicial responses to sexual material.

It is common to caricature women who objected to obscenity as buttoned-up schoolmarms who considered sex a distasteful necessity and open discussion of it offensive and dangerous.[12] But most female anti-obscenity leaders did not hate sex. Many, in fact, rather enjoyed it, even using contraceptives to minimize the procreative consequences of their pleasure. They did, however, consider sex a powerful force capable of great destruction if left in the hands of entrepreneurs, who exploited sex for commercial gain, or self-righteous prudes, whose prohibitions on sex education created an unhealthy aura of mystery. These middle-class women wanted to maintain control over shaping children's sexual development, hoping, in the process, to develop a generation whose joyful sexuality would enhance rather than impair relations between women and men. As we will see, they endeavored, with mixed results, to use the politics of womanhood to rescue sex from Victorian prudery and modern prurience at a time when doing both, simultaneously, still seemed possible.

CHAPTER ONE

"Protect the Innocent!"

Men, Women, and Anti-obscenity Reform, 1873–1911

"I can imagine nothing," Julia Ward Howe declared in 1873, "more important than the careful and rigid enforcement of the laws" against obscenity. Her address accompanied exhortations by an array of speakers assembled in New York to inspire a revival in women's rights activism. Proclaiming disappointment in male reformers who had failed to halt the proliferation of objectionable sexual material, Howe implored her female listeners to take up the anti-obscenity cause. Women would "be more strict and scrupulous than the average of the other sex," she avowed.[1] The urgent call of this beloved leader of clubwomen and suffragists went largely unanswered. Twelve years later, anti-obscenity campaigns remained dominated and led by men. Moreover, the day's premier anti-obscenity organization, the New York Society for the Suppression of Vice, continued to exclude women, restricting its meetings to "gentlemen only."[2]

At the same time, Victorian women created sex-segregated organizations of their own, including women's clubs, temperance societies, and benevolent associations, treating such activity as an extension of their roles as chaste, pious, domestic, and submissive helpmates. Howe hoped that these same characteristics, collectively referred to as true womanhood, would steer women into anti-obscenity work. But women played relatively minor roles in the anti-obscenity movement between 1873 and 1911. Women's later prominence as leaders on the issue in the 1920s and 1930s makes all the more puzzling their scarcity in earlier movements. A close look at some of the sources of women's anti-obscenity reform—male anti-obscenity activism and women's clubs—helps to make sense of women's initial low participation and their later emergence as leaders by exposing the dynamics of nineteenth-century middle-class gender ideals.

Anthony Comstock and Victorian Vice Crusades

Nineteenth-century anti-obscenity movements emerged alongside the rapid growth in industry, urbanization, and immigration that followed the Civil War.

Advances in printing and transportation technology encouraged development of a mass culture bound by no community moral code. Increases in leisure time and disposable income afforded many the opportunity to attend public prizefights, burlesque shows, and ballets, while cheap mass-circulation magazines and story papers provided at-home entertainment through crime reports and other sensational tales, many bordering on the salacious. New printing technologies allowed inexpensive reproductions of paintings—a disturbing development to those who believed that a museum-ensconced artistic nude metamorphosed into obscenity on a cheap postcard. At the same time, progress in medical technology led to widespread dissemination of contraceptive information and devices. Reformers worried that, together, modern entertainments and birth control would weaken the moral fiber of the community and the individual by simultaneously encouraging and concealing illicit sexual behavior. Birth control, in other words, threatened to make sexual transgressions undetectable. If cities generated temptations to immorality, they offered relatively few sources of moral guidance. Family, church, and community influence seemed to dwindle in the increasingly anonymous urban setting. Growing numbers of single men and women populated metropolitan centers, the former creating a potential market and the latter a product for sexual commerce. New arrivals from southern and eastern Europe brought cultural practices and values divergent from the Yankee mainstream. The inducements to sexual deviance in modern cities seemed to multiply every day, provoking protests from many late-nineteenth-century Americans.

Experiences during the Civil War itself inspired some of the most legendary vice crusaders, most notably Anthony Comstock—whose very name still connotes prudery—and members of the Young Men's Christian Association (YMCA). Twenty-year-old Comstock's many months as a soldier in the Union Army proved painful to his New England Protestant sensibilities. Presented with regular army rations of whiskey and urged by his fellow soldiers to join them in gambling, chewing tobacco, and indulging their sexual appetites, Comstock resisted their taunts, clinging to his evangelical Christian practices and entreating his countrymen to join him in prayer, worship, and abstinence. Comstock found solace in the YMCA, an organization founded in 1852 by New York merchants determined to protect their young male clerks from the city's immoral influences. Like Comstock, YMCA leaders recognized the military's inducements to debauchery. During the war, they channeled their resources into saving soldiers from corruption by dispatching Christian ministers, Bibles, and literature among the troops and sponsoring a rider to the Postal Act of 1865 that forbade the mailing of sexually explicit matter to soldiers. After the war, Comstock continued his reform efforts, along with his volunteer affiliation with the YMCA. With the help of his YMCA allies, by 1873 he had obtained passage of a federal statute to prohibit sending obscenity through the mails, accepted the position of special agent of the United States Post Office charged with enforcing the new law, and become a well-paid, full-time employee of the YMCA's spin-off organization, the New York Society for the Suppression of Vice (NYSSV).[3] For the next forty-two years, Comstock would retain these positions of power and use postal regulations to apprehend and prosecute purveyors of obscenity.

Comstock had his critics, but even those whom historians classify as free speech advocates agreed that obscenity existed and needed to be suppressed. They reproached Comstock for defining obscenity broadly and refusing to distinguish between material designed to arouse sexual feelings and material created to educate about sexual matters. Few individuals whom Comstock prosecuted in the nineteenth century incorporated First Amendment arguments into their legal defenses, but those who did relied more heavily on other claims and made no headway with constitutional arguments. Even De Robigne Mortimer Bennett, a zealous free speech advocate whom Comstock arrested multiple times, castigated Comstock in 1878, not for repressing obscenity, but for equating "those who were really guilty of issuing vile publications—whose only object was to inflame the baser passions" with "those who published and sold books for the purpose of educating and improving mankind."[4] As his critics attested, Comstock exercised greater discernment when dealing with materials available primarily to elites. He ignored paintings of nude women, for example, as long as they remained sequestered in museums, but arrested street peddlers who presented the same images to the unrestricted public through newspapers, postcards, or other forms of open display.[5] Comstock's vulnerability to the critics of his day derived not from the First Amendment—which remained, until the middle of the next century, peripheral at best to the issue of obscenity—but from his choices regarding what material and purveyors to target.

Comstock and other vice crusaders pronounced children's protection their primary goal. Obscene materials, they claimed, would "inflame the passions of youth," arousing irrepressible desires and inducing masturbation or other forms of equally illicit but less solitary sexual gratification. Comstock's message resonated with middle-class Victorian parents who may have felt especially protective of their children's sexual innocence; because their children served as conduits of family status, a youth's sexual indiscretion could jeopardize the family position, destroying links to important social networks and degrading marital choices.[6] In this context, given the middle- and upper-class identities of Comstock and his fellow anti-obscenity reformers, their concern about children's sexual purity was hardly surprising.

But the types of material that Comstock and his allies targeted suggest that they pursued a much broader agenda. The federal anti-obscenity law adopted at Comstock's urging in 1873 encompassed items unlikely to be available, appealing, or comprehensible to children. For example, the law forbade using the postal system to distribute obscene materials, including devices and information about contraception and abortion. Of all prosecutions under the Comstock Law in Chicago's federal court, 32 percent concerned private correspondence and 25 percent involved abortifacients and contraceptives. None had fallen into the hands of children. Nineteenth-century critics made similar observations, noting that although Comstock declared children his primary concern, he doggedly pursued items circulated exclusively among adults.[7]

Comstock and his fellow reformers took great pains to shield adult women, in particular, from material they considered obscene, especially contraceptive information and devices. Their determination to protect women from exposure to such material extended to excluding women categorically from anti-obscenity work. The two major vice societies—the New England Watch and Ward Society and the New York Society for the Suppression of Vice—asked organized women for "moral support," but barred women from meetings until the very end of the century, justifying this as a measure for protecting female purity.[8]

Several nineteenth-century women's organizations offered the anti-obscenity movement more than prayers and good wishes. In 1879, for example, the national Women's Christian Temperance Union began to develop a "Do Everything" policy, broadening its activist agenda beyond alcohol to include other forms of vice, including obscenity. Its Department for the Suppression of Impure Literature, formed in 1883, sought to protect children from salacious material by organizing letter-writing campaigns, circulating petitions, drafting legislation, and even destroying public advertisements. The WCTU, the National Congress of Mothers, and women's clubs all invited Comstock to speak at their meetings. In turn, Comstock assured the women and his male colleagues that he would tailor his speeches to a female audience, removing any references to obscenity that might jeopardize the purity of his feminine audience. And not until 1891, nearly twenty years after its founding and following a prolonged debate, did Comstock's New York Society admit women to meetings.[9] While admission alone constituted an important step for women, it did not clear the way for their ascension into leadership positions. Nor did it stop men from invoking women's vulnerability and delicacy as a rationale for anti-obscenity work. Thus the vice societies reinforced a paternalistic masculinity that posited men as the guardians of women and children. Late in the nineteenth century, this paternalism began to crack slightly—especially in response to organized women's efforts on behalf of the anti-obscenity movement—but it survived well into the twentieth, emerging with a vengeance in municipal efforts to regulate the new motion picture theaters.

Men, Progressive Reform, and Minneapolis Theaters

Like most American cities around the turn of the century, residents of Minneapolis, Minnesota, launched successive waves of Progressive reform. But reform-minded midwesterners, unlike their eastern counterparts, confronted a very new urban scene. Minnesota remained a sparsely settled territory, boasting a total population of fewer than fifteen thousand residents in 1849 but developing rapidly thereafter. Rich natural resources attracted farmers, miners, and lumbermen from the East and abroad, and construction of the Great Northern railway expedited travel to, from, and throughout the state. By the end of the century, the Northwest's fertile soil made it the "wheat market of the world," with Minneapolis the region's industrial, financial, and transportation hub. Between 1880 and 1890 Minneapolis's population increased by some 250 percent, from 66,000 to 165,000 residents, making the city the nation's eighteenth largest. Thus, by the beginning of the new century, an economic and demographic boom transformed Minneapolis into a flourishing metropolis.[10]

Minneapolis businessmen organized to protect their collective interests early in the state's history, forming the Chamber of Commerce in 1881 to facilitate trade and advance members' business pursuits. By 1903, leading businessmen, beginning to fear organized labor, created associations to promote "industrial peace" by discouraging strikes and labor unions. Founded by such prominent citizens as Martin B. Koon, a prominent state judge, and Charles D. Velie, of Deere and Webber Company (later John Deere), the Citizens Alliance easily recruited the area's most powerful men. Many also belonged to the Minneapolis Club or the Minikahda Club, organizations that provided cultural and social advantages to members of the elite while cultivating institutions for the cultural and educational benefit of the wider public. Through these clubs, businessmen developed the city's industrial and cultural base, breaking strikes, securing pro-business legislation, and maintaining an open-shop town even as they built public libraries, art museums, and vocational schools.[11]

Minnesotans marginalized by the emerging business elite began to organize between 1870 and 1890. Farmers resisting capitalist control of agricultural marketing and distribution fomented a wave of agrarian protest that coalesced in the Granger and Populist movements. Industrial workers seeking greater control over working conditions and compensation began to unionize and strike, forming the Minneapolis Trades and Labor Assembly in 1883, the Minnesota Federation of Labor in 1890, and joining such radical labor organizations as the Western Federation of Miners and the International Workers of the World (IWW). Minnesota women formed local branches of the Women's Christian Temperance Union and the Woman Suffrage Association in 1877 and 1881, respectively. Even more popular were the women's clubs that proliferated in the 1890s, attracting white middle-class women who sought sisterly community but eschewed the more oppositional pursuits of temperance or suffrage reform. Within a decade, Minneapolis alone boasted thirty-five women's clubs. Progressive politicians in Minnesota built upon the foundation laid by groups of farmers, workers, and women, incorporating into law reforms that addressed some of their concerns. They responded to the needs of agrarian reformers with railroad and insurance regulation (1905 and 1907), tax reform (1906), and the statewide primary (1913), and the demands of urban workers and women with factory inspection (1907), municipal ownership of public utilities (1907), minimum wage and maximum hour legislation for women (1911), and workers' compensation (1913). Several of these laws passed over Citizens Alliance resistance; others made it through only after the Citizens Alliance lobby had weakened them, and most labor legislation, including the eight-hour day for all workers, never had a chance, due largely to Citizens Alliance opposition. With regard to the new motion picture theaters, the Citizens Alliance weighed in, predictably, on the side of owners, but paid little attention to the new amusements until labor problems surfaced in 1917.[12]

The motion picture made its Minneapolis debut in 1894, when a local department store, owned by Norwegian immigrant Seaver Olson, hosted the city's first Edison Kinetoscope exhibit. Owners of museums, opera houses, and vaudeville theaters quickly realized the profit-making potential of the new medium and, only one year later, began to project moving picture images onto screens. Between 1906 and 1909, thirty theaters exhibited motion pictures; half continued to stage live performances but the other half devoted their entire business to the new entertainment medium. The fifteen or so proprietors who showed motion pictures exclusively came from a range of occupations, including a jeweler, a slot machine vendor, and a tea and coffee merchant. A few emigrated from other countries, but most were native-born citizens. Nearly all, beginning with little capital, hastily transformed clapboard structures, often storefronts, into makeshift auditoriums by purchasing a projector, hanging a screen, and setting up rows of folding chairs. Constructed of combustible cheap timber and designed for retail purposes, many of these buildings ill suited their new purpose as motion picture theaters. Nitrate stock, an industry standard for early motion pictures, made films highly flammable, and the combination of wooden buildings, ignitable film, and hot motion picture lamps created fire hazards in motion picture theaters around the nation. The deadliest theater fire on record occurred in 1904 at Chicago's Iroquois Theater, killing no fewer than six hundred people, most of whom perished in a blazing stampede as fire rapidly consumed the flimsy facility.[13]

The Chicago theater tragedy radiated waves of fear that sent residents of distant cities scurrying to inspect their own theaters. Between 1904 and 1911, reformers in Minneapolis followed suit, aided by a local press war. Adopting the style of the day's muckraking journalism, investigative reporters for the *Minneapolis Tribune* used their findings to tug at the emotions of readers, accusing local theater owners of operating "veritable death traps" by "packing" children into dark theaters, sacrificing safety for profits. Shortly after this particular article appeared, a theater fire in neighboring Anoka, Minnesota, fanned the flames of reformers' protest. The *Tribune* took full advantage of the incident, recounting the harrowing story of young Mary Pratt, who succumbed, momentarily, to the stampede of panicked fans.[14] Even as the *Tribune* celebrated little Mary's escape, it warned readers that their children might not be so lucky. Responding to the public outcry provoked by the *Tribune*, aldermen launched their own investigation and began to consider a new ordinance for theaters that exhibited motion pictures.

In 1911, these theaters charged a low ten-cent admission fee that catered to a diverse working-class audience, providing a public entertainment experience that many scholars have characterized as unusually democratic. Most urban dwellers lived near a theater, could afford an occasional ticket, enjoyed open seating restricted only by race, and viewed many films written and produced by people not so unlike themselves—female, immigrant, and working-class entrepreneurs who made films that reflected their interests and values. For example,

What Happened to Mary (1912) and *Hazards of Helen* (1914) celebrated adventurous and independent women; *The Ghetto Seamstress* (1910) portrayed immigrant workers sympathetically, and *The Coal Strike* (1905) and *The Egg Trust* (1910) valorized strikers and demonized corporate monopolists.[15] In cost, style, and content, cheap motion picture theaters challenged middle-class values and standards.

Even so, many motion picture theater owners aspired to attract a middle-class audience, and those with access to capital renovated their buildings, upgraded their entertainment, and used the reform movement to showcase their accomplishments. Samuel Rothapfel, later known as the impresario "Roxy," pioneered this approach in 1911 by transforming the Lyric Theater into an elegant movie palace and hiring singers and members of the city's symphony to accompany his silent films. When aldermen visited his theater, Rothapfel proudly displayed his emergency plans, demonstrating an actual fire drill for good measure.[16] But few proprietors who showed motion pictures exclusively could afford such renovations, and they felt especially vulnerable under the city council's scrutiny. As small motion picture theater owners suspected, some of their more established rivals—proprietors of the so-called "first-class theaters" that featured plays as well as motion pictures—supported the safety crusade, hoping that new regulations would drive marginal competitors out of business. Indeed, proposals to mandate that theaters use the new "non-ignitable film" could raise the cost of a motion picture from $5.00 to $50.00. Prohibitions on motion picture theaters in one-story, frame buildings would force many small theaters to close. Mandating that all motion picture exhibitors install new "daylight pictures" technology—which allowed house lights to remain on during the movie—would impose significant expenses on struggling enterprises. Moreover, holding theater owners responsible for enforcing a juvenile curfew seemed an unfair burden when the police had failed to make the juvenile curfew ordinance effective. Appointing municipal inspectors to examine motion picture theaters every month would disrupt business, limit owners' freedom, and raise licensing fees. Requiring that all projectionists obtain licenses would cut into profits immediately and, in the long term, encourage projectionists to unionize and demand even higher wages. Censorship of films judged immoral might limit what proprietors could show, compromising their ability to use sex to sell tickets. Any one of these new expenses could close the doors of many start-up motion picture houses.[17]

Because motion picture theater owners in Minneapolis confronted threats of municipal regulation slightly later than their peers in eastern cities, they benefited from the experiences of predecessors. Initially more concerned with moral than physical safety issues, New York City's mayor revoked all motion picture theater licenses in 1908, threatening to reopen theaters only under official censorship. In response, exhibitors organized a massive public relations campaign and recruited local reformers to help them develop a system of self-regulation. The product of these efforts, the National Board of Censorship, arranged to preview the films of individual motion picture producers in exchange for a National Board rating of "Passed," "Condemned," or "Passed with Changes Specified." Any producer who failed to submit all of his films for previewing, or neglected to make the suggested changes or cuts before releasing a film, would be publicly expelled from the National Board. The National Board placed its seal of approval on films it passed and mailed its reviews and ratings to motion picture exhibitors, public welfare boards, police departments, and social and civic organizations around the country, requesting their assistance in monitoring producers' cooperation. Meanwhile, exhibitors counted on the National Board to protect their profits by placating pro-censorship forces and providing them with some leverage against producers.[18]

Minneapolis exhibitors learned from their New York City predecessors and immediately pooled resources to defend themselves against what they called "unwarranted and unjust" attacks on their business. With a fund of $450, they ran advertisements in the *Tribune*'s competing newspapers, the *Minneapolis Journal* and the *Minneapolis Daily News.* A bold, two-page heading—"THE TRUTH ABOUT MINNEAPOLIS MOVING PICTURE THEATRES"—introduced testimonials by a building inspector, a fire marshal, and a city electrician, as well as articles entitled "Moving Picture Houses Safe" and "Photo Plays Are Social Necessity." Anticipating, rightly, that the local theater reform movement would soon shift to moral concerns, they published a two-column article written by the National Board of Censorship, suggesting that Minneapolis exhibitors showed only motion pictures that the National Board approved.[19]

Like the New York exhibitors who founded the National Board, Minneapolis exhibitors employed a language of democracy that highlighted the potential for class-based oppression. They claimed that their more established competitors wanted to regulate them out of business—a possibility that seemed genuinely to concern several aldermen. Owners of the new motion picture theaters also argued, rightly, that cheap theaters served a working-class clientele, one that could not afford the more expensive entertainment patronized by the "well to do class." On a more personal front, a man whose application for a theater license was rejected by the city council accused Alderman Platt Walker of approving licenses only for businesses that would benefit his uncle's vast property holdings. Walker retorted that mothers' clubs and neighborhood residents, not his uncle—Thomas B. Walker, Citizens Alliance member, lumber magnate, and patron of the Walker Art Center—had influenced his vote, convincing him that a motion picture theater in the proposed location would disrupt their community and endanger their children. When C. A. Smith, another lumberman and Citizens Alliance member, weighed in on the side of regulation, small theater owners and aspiring ones must have felt squeezed between established theaters, influential elites, grassroots pressure groups, and the city council; all threatened to encroach on motion picture show proprietors' autonomy.[20]

The class antagonism that emerged in early motion picture regulation did not diminish the real fire hazards that motion picture theater patrons—especially working-class patrons of cheap theaters—confronted. The worst fire catastrophes occurred very early in the history of these theaters, but throughout the decade, Minneapolis movie houses periodically burst into flames. In 1918, for example, William Koenig—a long-time theater worker who overcame a failed 1911 license application to become manager of several theaters—reported a delay in the opening of his theater due to a second fire in the building. "Never in all my experiences as a theatre employee have I seen such a terrible condition of a theatre," he wrote. Luckily, this fire occurred in an empty house, but such fires usually broke out with the projector running and the auditorium full. The internal architecture of many cheap theaters increased casualty rates; a single entrance and aisle frequently provided the only escape route, and even such inadequate exits were often clogged with overflow seating. As Koenig admitted: "I took chances of going to jail by putting chairs right down the aisle all week and the Fire Marshall never got wise to it."[21] To make matters worse, most theaters lacked fire-fighting equipment.

The physical conditions of movie theaters in the 1910s presented an undeniable public health hazard. But reformers also saw in motion pictures a moral menace. As historians have shown, pioneers in this new and unregulated form of entertainment pushed the bounds of decency. Beginning with the earliest peep shows furtively glimpsed through kinetoscopes, filmmakers used motion pictures as a medium for exposing the female body. Burlesque images, themes, and performers—titillating scenes already visible in the urban entertainment world—provided ready material. The new technology's novelty inhered in its ability to record movement, but the bulky, primitive film equipment immobilized the cameraman, sending early filmmakers in search of subjects that moved in a restricted space. Dancers and other burlesque performers accustomed to performing within the confines of a stage made ideal subjects. One of the earliest peep shows featured "Fatima," a burlesque performer who in 1893 performed the much-heralded and widely banned "cooch dance" in front of a motion picture camera. Clothed in the diaphanous scarves and pantaloons of a Middle Eastern belly dancer, Fatima and other coochers gyrated wantonly, tantalizing the viewer as they gradually disrobed.[22]

Early filmmakers did not merely borrow risqué themes from burlesque. They filmed racy images that burlesque managers had refused to stage, including completely nude women. The more sophisticated productions forestalled condemnation by exhibiting female nudity in carefully selected contexts. An untitled 1910 film, for example, showed a young woman scramble onto a boulder, unabashedly and hurriedly peel off her clothes, and dive, nude, into a sparkling lake. Such early "sex films," as they were known, usually included either nudity in the purifying context of nature or art, or relative modesty combined with a sexually suggestive scenario. Many created the latter situation using the theme of a bride's first night. Knowing that most viewers would associate the wedding night with coition, filmmakers could create a scintillating scene without disrobing a female body. Nudity and sexual activity rarely appeared together except in stag films. These circulated around urban centers as early as 1904, occasionally appearing in commercial theaters where exhibitors "sneaked erotic 'teasers' into the action." Such films contained graphic depictions of sexual acts, including intercourse and fellatio.[23] Thus, like other media pioneers before and after them—book publishers at the dawn of the printing press, webmasters in the age of the Internet—motion picture entrepreneurs exploited sexuality.

Unsurprisingly, theater reformers added concerns about morality to their worries about safety, decrying the inspiration for immoral behavior offered by suggestive films as well as the potential for misconduct provided by darkened auditoriums. Alarmists warned that pimps and white slavers stalked young female movie patrons.[24] More somber citizens expressed outrage that women and children encountered immoral shows daily. *Minneapolis Tribune* reporters insisted that unlit theaters compromised patrons' physical and moral well-being, arousing sexual feelings among members of a mixed audience who could engage in forbidden fondling under cover of darkness. Reform-minded aldermen in Minneapolis responded in 1911 by drafting a theater ordinance to prohibit "suggestive language and acts." Joining other municipal officials around the country, they also discussed creating a motion picture censorship board. Meanwhile, local police arrested the proprietor of a penny arcade for exhibiting movies with the evocative titles *The Lady of the Lake, Too Hot to Sleep, The Frisky Boarding School Girls,* and *Scenes through a Key Hole.* Aldermen, journalists, and police officers enthusiastically conducted mass safety inspections, passed new obscenity ordinances, and detained violators, all in an effort to align the city's motion picture theaters with middle-class standards of safety and decency.[25]

As elsewhere, women in Minneapolis had little voice in these early public debates, but men's diagnosis of theater problems pivoted on women's and children's vulnerability. City fathers echoed nineteenth-century forebears when they voiced concerns about women's and children's moral and physical safety, fretting over the possibility that the lack of fire escapes and presence of lewd performances would endanger tender female and juvenile patrons. During city council hearings regarding theater regulations, one alderman dramatically queried: "Must the women and children of Minneapolis risk their lives to swell the pocketbooks of moving picture show proprietors?" He was joined by another alderman who insisted on rigid standards for "theaters which cater to women and children." Similarly, a private citizen concerned about theater safety and morals entreated public officials to "protect the innocent—it may be your own wife and child!" Journalists also invoked the fragility of women and youth when they questioned the ability of inexperienced movie projectionists to "quiet a crowd of frightened women and children." Echoing these sentiments, a censor in another midwestern city passed only films "which I consider proper for women and children to witness."[26] By invoking the welfare of women and children to justify their crusade against unsafe and immoral motion picture theaters, twentieth-century male reformers extended the paternalism of their nineteenth-century predecessors, reasoning that their work protected womanhood, allowing women to remain chaste, devout, deferential, and domestic in an increasingly urban, commercial, and sexual environment.

The Woman's Club of Minneapolis, 1907–1911

Increasing numbers of women, meanwhile, concluded that their troubled cities wanted housekeeping. Among these was Alice Ames Winter, a Minneapolis woman groomed for civic engagement in the reform hotbed of late-nineteenth-century Boston, Massachusetts. Born in 1865 to Julia Frances and Charles Gordon Ames, young Alice grew up the daughter of a Unitarian minister whose advocacy of abolition, temperance, and woman suffrage attracted to his congregation Boston's most elite progressive citizens. Julia Ward Howe, for instance, attended Ames's services regularly, counted him a dear friend, and exerted a profound and lasting influence upon his daughter. Other visitors in the Ames household included such notable activists as William Lloyd Garrison, Booker T. Washington, Frances Willard, Susan B. Anthony, and Lucy Stone. This environment cultivated the young woman's political interests, leadership skills, and aspirations for community service while providing her with valuable social connections. Marriage to Thomas G. Winter extended those connections into the Midwest and the realm of business. British by birth, Winter emigrated to Minneapolis from Canada in 1890 and soon developed prosperous businesses in railroads and grain, two of the region's major growth industries. He probably met Alice Ames through her older half-brother, Charles Wilberforce Ames, also a Minneapolis resident, who worked in railroads, banking, and publishing. Thomas Winter and Alice Ames married in 1892, and within seven years the brothers-in-law formed what would become a very successful partnership, Winter & Ames Company, operating grain elevators in Minnesota and North Dakota. The Winters built an elegant home in the fashionable Loring neighborhood and proudly added their names to the *Dual City Blue Book,* a directory of "the best families" in the Twin Cities.[27]

Alice Ames Winter spent her first fourteen years in Minneapolis sustaining her ambitious husband, writing two novels, participating in a study club on infant welfare, and bearing and rearing two children. Gilbert arrived within a year of her wedding and Edith two years later. Gilbert turned fourteen and Edith twelve in 1907, the year that disrupted Winter's happy domestic world, bringing her profound sorrow but also a new source of hope. A mysterious accident killed her first-born son, devastating the forty-two-year-old Winter. But in April of that year, a grieving Winter joined several influential women to found the Woman's Club of Minneapolis, one of the first local women's clubs, its members noted, whose mission went beyond "the culture of its members" to embrace "public service." The affluent, educated, and gracious Winter presented a natural choice for the club's first president, and she dutifully accepted the nomination. Under Winter's leadership, the club drafted a plan to recruit members, charted a course for the following year, and established departments to address the problems of school cleaning, railroad smoke suppression, billboard regulation, wildflower preservation, and medical examinations of school children.[28]

The Woman's Club may have broken new ground in Minneapolis and emerged on the cutting edge of midwestern clubwomen's civic improvement work, but it joined a long line of women's clubs dating back to the antebellum era. Initially, these literary clubs focused on collective self-improvement, providing members with educational opportunities and a public community otherwise unavailable to them. As institutions of higher education began to welcome women, the need for self-improvement clubs diminished and many refocused on civic betterment. By the 1910s, few cities in the United States remained untouched by clubwomen, who endeavored, among other things, to "care for cemeteries, remove garbage, plant trees and shrubs and flowers, clean and sprinkle streets, distribute seeds, improve vacant lots, abate public nuisances, establish and maintain parks and playgrounds, induce railroad officials to beautify station grounds, and found hospitals."[29]

In spite of its upstanding leadership and modest civic improvement agenda, the Woman's Club of Minneapolis sparked controversy from the outset. Many local women opposed the new club, fearing that its public service programs would supplant their study clubs. Some men feared that club work would lead women to become involved in politics, while others worried that the time women devoted to club work would reduce domestic output. One went so far as to "blame women's clubs for the decrease in America's output of homemade pies." The husband of a prominent member of the Woman's Club expressed great annoyance about the amount of time his wife invested in it. "Mother's extensive club work," he complained, making pointed reference to his wife's maternal role, caused him great "irritation."[30]

Discomfited by these criticisms, Woman's Club leaders attempted to allay their detractors' fears. To pacify female critics, they apportioned a significant amount of club time and resources to the traditional self-improvement activities of reading classics, presenting papers, enjoying and producing dramatic and musical performances, procuring and listening to guest speakers, and nurturing each others' intellectual and cultural interests. Linking club activities to domestic roles helped to deflect men's criticism while tapping women's historical traditions. So, like women of the revolutionary era who defended education for women as training for republican motherhood and nineteenth-century temperance activists who waged war against alcohol on behalf of families, clubwomen insisted that their activities enhanced wifely and maternal roles. One Woman's Club member self-consciously scribbled these sentiments in her journal, admonishing herself to "make yourself intelligent for the sake of your children." In a similar vein, but one that captured the collective and civic aspects of club work, Winter explained that "the Woman's Club is to the community what the individual is to her home . . .

It represents maternal and housekeeping instinct made community-wide."[31] Thus, the Woman's Club simultaneously subverted and reinforced the status quo, elevating the importance of female intellectual and moral pursuits even as it aligned those pursuits with domestic and maternal responsibilities.

Under Winter's eight-year presidency, the Woman's Club of Minneapolis cast its net further and further beyond the immediate interests of its membership to include the wider community. Leaders vowed, however, to keep their civic improvement program noncontroversial, apolitical, and "respectable" as they added new projects, raising funds for a monument one month and lobbying city officials for additional lighting in public parks the next. These early projects carefully avoided acrimonious municipal politics and the seamier side of city life. In Winter's words, they allowed the club "to cooperate, positively, with good" rather than to "fight, negatively, with the shadows of evil."[32]

To the extent that early clubwomen used private domestic experiences as models for their more public club work, they infused the club with family ideals, shaping it around the values of the Victorian middle-class home. Ideally, in this sphere, selflessness, love, and mutuality reigned. Unlike men's clubs, then, which celebrated rugged individualism and economic profit, women's clubs emphasized the spiritual and emotional health of the club community. This represented no small task for Winter, since the Woman's Club membership reached 340 in its first year and increased to 540 by its fifth. In one of her many paeans to the women's club movement, Winter warned against allowing civic improvement work to undermine sisterhood. "The zeal for betterment needs to be tempered by a thousand agreeable things," she wrote. "Our music and our art and our reading together and our listening to interesting speakers, above all our delight in our relations with each other, are not the froth on the top of an otherwise excellent organization. They are of its very essence—the yeast that sets pulses to throbbing and happiness harnessing itself to good." Other clubwomen echoed Winter's sentiments. "We hear so much of the *brotherhood* of man. It is refreshing to know of the *sisterhood* of women," another club president exclaimed.[33] When club activities caused conflict between members, clubwomen maintained unity and harmony by prioritizing their sisterly relationships with each other over other club goals. In order to avoid unpleasant and divisive exchanges, many clubs banned discussions of religion and politics. Indeed, the rules of women's clubs bear a striking likeness to feminine calling etiquette of the day. A local 1911 "Ladies' Calling Guide," for example, instructed female callers to omit "discussion of religion, politics or scandals," topics likely to provoke and expose disagreements among women.[34] For most clubwomen, then, as for middle- and upper-class society women generally, homogeneity and harmony delimited sisterhood.

Woman suffrage posed a special challenge for clubwomen. It became a pressing issue in the early 1910s as a number of western and midwestern states adopted woman suffrage and Congress voted on the Susan B. Anthony amendment for the first time in over two decades. Few clubwomen lacked an opinion on the issue and many campaigned on one side or the other. Pro-suffrage members of the Woman's Club held joint memberships in the Woman's Suffrage Club of Minneapolis, the Minnesota Woman Suffrage Association, the Hennepin County Suffrage Association, and the Minnesota branch of the National Woman's Party. Other club members fervently opposed suffrage. Lavinia Coppock Gilfillan, a charter member of the Woman's Club, even presided over the Minnesota Anti-Suffrage Association and worked in the Minneapolis Association Opposed to the Further Extension of Suffrage to Women. Acutely aware of clubwomen's differences on this issue, Woman's Club leaders monitored activities carefully in an effort to prevent dissension. In 1912, when local suffragist Josephine Simpson presented herself as a Woman's Club presidential hopeful, the nominating committee refused to consider her, fearing that her candidacy would offend anti-suffrage club members. Winter, who easily won reelection, also approved of woman suffrage, but maintained an impartial image by refusing to take a strong public stand on the issue. She and other Woman's Club leaders arranged lectures on suffrage but carefully balanced pro-suffrage with anti-suffrage speakers and stipulated that the meetings "be devoted to the lecture alone and shall not be discussional."[35]

In 1914, the balancing act became more difficult. That year, when the General Federation of Women's Clubs—to which the Woman's Club of Minneapolis belonged—endorsed woman suffrage, local Woman's Club leaders struggled to maintain internal harmony by reaffirming their ongoing neutrality on the issue. In a public statement issued to "clear the air," leaders announced that the Woman's Club embraced "women of every shade of opinion," had never "taken a stand either for or against suffrage," and would not do so. The Woman's Club is a meeting place, leaders explained, "where we can all work for civic good, with mutual respect and good understanding, in spite of our differences." As late as 1918, after the state of New York granted women full voting rights and Woodrow Wilson endorsed woman suffrage, Minneapolis Woman's Club leaders still deemed the suffrage question too delicate for club discussions. That year, the Hennepin County Suffrage Association asked Woman's Club leaders to consider a resolution supporting the federal suffrage amendment. Most Woman's Club leaders supported suffrage but not at the expense of internal harmony. At Winter's suggestion, they endeavored to gauge individual suffrage sentiment without provoking divisive debate by mailing cards to members asking them to indicate their position on woman suffrage. Divided returns convinced leaders not to introduce the suffrage resolution for discussion or a vote.[36]

Women's clubs around the country made similar choices, refraining from endorsing or even discussing suffrage in order to preserve private feelings of sisterhood and a public image of female unity. Local press coverage suggests that Minneapolis clubwomen succeeded on these counts. As a rather sentimental editorial on the Woman's Club declared, "There is something in the title that suggests not merely the women members of the organization, but the collective womanhood of the community." The very existence of the Woman's Club, the author continued, prompted "more thinking in terms of womanhood than in terms of women as individuals."[37] Cautious leadership preserved this image of unity by preventing divisiveness among club members.

A relatively homogeneous membership eased their task. All members of the Woman's Club of Minneapolis were white, and most were Anglo-Saxon, Protestant, married, middle-aged mothers supported wholly by a male income. Many of the founding members lived near each other in the elite Loring neighborhood where opulent mansions graced the parklike landscape.[38] Several, including three of the original fourteen founders, boasted family connections that tied them closely to the Citizens Alliance. Carolyn McKnight Christian and Kate Koon Bovey (daughter of Judge Martin B. Koon), each had a father and a husband active in the alliance, while Beatrice Goodrich Lowry had a husband and a brother in the organization. (Not until 1917 would Alice Ames Winter's husband and brother join the Citizens Alliance.) The Woman's Club of Minneapolis did not explicitly withhold membership from working-class women, but it probably alienated them, and a number of factors, including lack of leisure time, money, and social connections, effectively excluded them. Club membership required payment of an initiation fee and annual dues of ten dollars—not an inconsequential sum in the 1910s. In 1913, for example, when another local association requested half that amount in annual dues, even affluent women considered the fee exorbitant. Woman's Club members met several times each month, usually during the day when most employed women worked. Moreover, the Woman's Club controlled the composition of its membership by limiting it to women nominated by other members. Unsurprisingly, nominees and members usually occupied like social and economic positions. Finally, club leaders' commitment to a policy of volunteer service meant that, unlike many women's reform organizations, women's clubs did not provide income-earning opportunities for their members.[39] As a result, women responsible for their own or their family's financial support could not afford club membership even if invited to join.

Homogeneous though the Woman's Club may have been, it provided opportunities for middle- and upper-class women to develop an appreciation for a wider range of women than a modern observer might immediately appreciate. Outside the club, most of these women's social circles revolved around kinship, religion, and male relatives' political affiliation. As members of the Woman's Club, however, Republicans, Democrats, Methodists, Lutherans, Unitarians, and even a Jewish woman or two all joined together in sisterhood, unbounded by familial ties. Not surprisingly, clubwomen thought of themselves as remarkably heterogeneous and took great pride in their "unity in diversity." As one local clubwoman noted, women's clubs helped members to attain "a new understanding of one another" and "a new loyalty to womankind."[40] Thus, if clubwomen celebrated and cultivated a sisterhood largely circumscribed by racial, class, and ethnic identities, they also developed a consciousness of women as a group. This notion of sisterhood, this collective female identity, eventually inspired a reform impulse in many clubwomen.

Representing Womanhood and Protecting Girlhood

When, in the early 1910s, members of the Woman's Club turned their attention to a type of work they and others called municipal housekeeping, they joined a wave of Progressive reform engulfing Minneapolis, one that had already transformed other American cities. Like male theater reformers, clubwomen expressed particular concern about the sexual vulnerability of young urban women, "new women," whose numbers had, since the turn of the century, increased dramatically. Young, independent, and uninhibited, new women mingled publicly with men as counter clerks at department stores, "co-ed" students on college and university campuses, clerical workers in mixed-sex offices, and pleasure seekers in dance halls, penny arcades, and motion picture houses. In this heterosocial urban context, clubwomen feared that risqué movies and burlesque shows would whet the sexual appetites of unscrupulous men. The prospect of unattached, financially distressed young women who might, in desperation, exchange sexual favors for economic assistance troubled clubwomen even more.[41]

Minneapolis and its sister city of St. Paul presented special cause for concern. The Twin Cities' abundant employment opportunities in textile manufacturing and clerical and sales work attracted female migrants. In the early twentieth century, women constituted a majority of rural-to-urban migrant workers, a phenomenon proceeding from earlier immigration patterns distinctive to the upper Midwest. Most immigrants to the United States gravitated to cities, but those bound for Minnesota sought farmland and settled in rural areas, where differential treatment of boys and girls shaped the next generation's migration patterns. While sons inherited and remained on the family farm, daughters found few rural opportunities. Hence young women dominated the early-twentieth-century migrant stream to the Twin Cities. Many clubwomen feared that young women living apart from families and working for low wages in a city with myriad inducements to immorality could be easily lured into prostitution. Indeed, the Minnesota Bureau of Labor Statistics indicated that most working women in Minneapolis did not earn enough money to support themselves independently. Moreover, while low wages rendered many women destitute, the quasi-legal status of prostitution made it a viable alternative. As one local prostitute reported, "I tried for three years to support life on the wages I was paid as a cashier in a big store . . . I gave up the struggle at last . . . They call me unworthy of any decent person's notice now, but I don't starve and freeze since I quit being respectable."[42] The urban conditions that pulled this woman into prostitution gave local clubwomen cause for concern.

Members of the Woman's Club gathered on an afternoon in 1912 to hear a talk sponsored by their Department on Social Economics, "The Problem of the Working Girl, the Problem of the Woman's Club." Their interest piqued and anxieties raised, clubwomen created a full-blown class on "The Problem of the Unprotected Girl" and found themselves discussing topics that would have embarrassed and silenced their mothers. Willingness on the part of proper clubwomen to discuss such topics bespoke a growing openness about sexuality and an ability to identify with working women. But their objectives also reflected older values, suggesting that clubwomen conflated working women's interests with their own; their concerns usually focused on department store clerks and retail shop girls—working women whose independent lifestyles were the envy of most domestic workers—and their solutions were usually to recruit these women into domestic service. Woman's Club members joined their peers throughout the Midwest in bemoaning the shortage of domestic servants. Mary Belle Sherman, a clubwoman and close observer of midwestern women's clubs, lamented, "We have no servant class, because working women are generally un-willing to accept domestic service as a means of gaining a living."[43] Believing, like other clubwomen, that women avoided domestic service because they con-sidered the work degrading, Sherman praised efforts to correct the problem by elevating the status of housework, cloaking it in the scholarly garb of the sciences and professions through the establishment of independent schools of domestic arts and science and university departments of home economics.

The Minneapolis Woman's Club tried to solve "the domestic servant prob-lem" in its twenty class sessions on household economics. After hearing a series of talks and papers by club members, attending lectures by the supervisor of do-mestic sciences in the Minneapolis public schools, and even engaging in "the unique experience of listening to the servants' side of the question from two maids," participants resolved to establish "a bureau of expert helpers, such as seamstresses, cooks, nurse girls, etc.," survey employers of domestic servants with the aim of creating uniform standards regarding pay and working hours, and equip their kitchens with labor-saving devices.[44] Significantly, all of the coping strategies adopted by Woman's Club members as a result of their year-long course promised to address their own needs and desires more than those of work-ing women. This clearly self-centered response to "the servant problem" raises questions about the sources of clubwomen's concern for working women. Per-haps, as another historian has suggested, middle- and upper-class clubwomen linked working women with prostitution at least partly as an expression of their resentment toward women employed outside of domestic service. Nevertheless, clubwomen who attended the class on "The Problem of the Unprotected Girl," concluded that immoral amusements posed serious dangers for young girls by stimulating the lust of unprincipled men, breaking down the sexual modesty and reserve of innocent young women, and generally eroding the community's moral foundation. Many clubwomen wanted to follow up their study with policy rec-ommendations to city officials, but others envisioned a more sweeping and in-terventionist approach to the problems of working girls, fashioning a reform agenda that challenged the club's founding mission.[45]

In the 1910s, women at all levels of the women's club movement struggled to chart their course amid changes in themselves and their environment. Many clubwomen adamantly opposed involving their clubs in reform or political causes. Having already experienced derision for their self-indulgent intellectual efforts, indecorous distractions from domesticity, and potential political med-dling, many clubwomen resisted further arming their critics. Others worried that reform work would erode the loving, sisterly relations that bolstered women's clubs, undermining female solidarity in the process. Voicing some of these concerns in a 1910 speech to a meeting of the General Federation, Mrs. J. L. Washburn of Minnesota cautioned clubs against reform work, warning that "enthusiasm for reform waxes and wanes, causes are won and lost. In the face of repeated failure it is sometimes difficult to hold an organization together." Urging the General Federation and its member clubs to remain focused on self-improvement, she concluded that "the strong basis of self-interest supporting our constituent clubs is a rock upon which we may rest."[46] To some clubwomen, reform veered too far into the realm of the political, violating the private, womanly purposes of women's clubs and threatening sisterhood by increasing the likelihood of dissension and disappointment among members. Many members and observers of women's clubs equated reform with fighting "the shadows of evil"— a distinctly distasteful activity to those who treasured the original club goals of promoting sisterhood and pursuing literary and cultural improvement.[47]

Traditional clubwomen confronted sisters determined to construct a more political role for their clubs. The same General Federation convention that heard Washburn inveigh against the deleterious impact of reform on women's clubs listened to Sarah Platt Decker extol reform activity as necessary for clubs to remain meaningful participants in society. Lamenting that most clubs avoided reform and political work because they "were founded as a culture club, pure and simple," Decker declared sardonically that such a passive agenda "will go far to prevent grand achievements" by clubwomen.[48] Several Minneapolis clubwomen agreed, inspired more by the vision of Decker than by that of their own Washburn. Grounded in the sentiments and work of the Woman's Club, they, like Decker, appreciated the self-confidence and sense of sisterly responsibility inspired by club work but grew increasingly alienated from the club's singular focus on self- and civic improvement. They would be among the first women to assume leadership in the realm of anti-obscenity reform.

Many women supported, some women participated in, but no women led the major anti-obscenity movements of the nineteenth century. Nor did they exercise significant influence over the implementation and adjudication of obscenity laws before 1915. During these years, essentialist notions of true womanhood limited women's involvement in anti-obscenity reform. When Anthony Comstock and his fellow anti-vice reformers barred women from their work, they relied on arguments rooted in gender norms already popularized by anti-suffragists: female delicacy and purity ill suited women for the dirty worlds of politics and vice crusades. The legislature and the risqué show, in other words, were no places for true women. Essentialist notions of womanhood also influenced what material men targeted as obscene, moving them far beyond items likely to fall into children's hands in their efforts to eradicate material that might corrupt women, like contraception and sex education as well as salacious novels and tabloid newspapers. The same logic that excluded women from the anti-obscenity movement pulled them into the women's club movement. Here, women could nurture each other socially and intellectually, work to improve the aesthetics and hygiene of their community, all while cultivating and expressing womanly ideals, enhancing female solidarity, and reassuring critics of the propriety of their work. Individual and collective aspirations to true womanhood initially impeded women's involvement in anti-obscenity reform. The issue of obscenity did not seem relevant to the tightly circumscribed lives of clubwomen, who rarely, if ever, encountered disturbing material or attended motion picture theaters before 1911. Others feared that reform of any sort would introduce divisive elements into their carefully selected sisterhood, and most would have recoiled at the idea of involving their precious club in such vile work.

The WCTU displayed more interest in the anti-obscenity cause, but by 1915 it narrowed its agenda, throwing itself into the constitutional fights for prohibition and woman suffrage.[49] Thus the twentieth century's woman-led anti-obscenity movement would not spring from the WCTU but from two less likely sources: men's anti-obscenity reform and the women's club movement. Little did early clubwomen know that a few of their number would develop a reform urge to build working girls' clubhouses, draft censorship legislation, and negotiate with theater managers. Still less did aldermen suspect that, in their crusades to protect defenseless women and children against unsafe and immoral theaters, they were beginning a wave of theater reform that would not crest until enfranchised local women pushed it to the national stage in the 1920s. And none of them could have predicted how women would reframe the issue.

CHAPTER TWO

Dressing Elsie

Women's Theater Reform, 1912–1919

In 1915 William Koenig, award-winning manager of the Gayety Theater in Minneapolis, received a letter describing a burlesque show soon to appear on his stage. "It is a very beautiful act and one that I am sure will cause considerable comment," wrote the main burlesque booking agent for the Midwest. "If you can get away with it," he explained, Elsie's act "is done in the nude, she being painted white to look like marble." Realizing that not all theaters could stage such a racy performance, he suggested an alternate plan: "In case you cannot do it in the nude, she, of course, will wear a union suit, giving you practically the same effect."[1] Local newspapers advertised the show with sensational references to Elsie's body, which they said resembled "the form of a Venus."[2] Despite the hype and the $225 price tag that accompanied Elsie's act, Koenig knew better than to send Elsie onto the Gayety stage *au naturel*. His customary discretion was a considered response to the work of a women's organization that had only recently appeared on the local scene, the Woman's Welfare League of Minneapolis.

Members of the Woman's Club of Minneapolis founded the Welfare League in 1912. That year, Gratia Countryman and several other clubwomen, all of whom attended classes on "The Problem of the Unprotected Girl," became distressed after learning about "the bad influences surrounding young girlhood." Low wages, homelessness, loneliness, and naiveté could, they discovered, combine with immoral urban amusements to heighten young women's vulnerability to seduction, prostitution, and rape. With horror, they learned that countless midwestern women endured forced sexual servitude as "white slaves," or victims of organized pimps, with more unfortunate girls added to their numbers every day. The women made repeated efforts to get the Woman's Club to deal with these problems, but each of their proposals for action collapsed under the weight of bureaucratic delays, lack of enthusiasm, and outright opposition.[3]

Countryman realized that she would need a new organization if she hoped to help young women and, with more than twenty like-minded clubwomen, she founded the Woman's Welfare League.[4] From the outset, the Welfare League aimed not so much to advance the interests of its own members as to serve an expansive sisterhood by reforming the city. Whereas conventional clubwomen avoided direct engagement with issues likely to taint their unsullied image or incite dissension, moral reformers like those who founded the Welfare League targeted problems involving sexuality and female poverty. Conventional clubwomen treasured their status as exemplary and true women, but those who founded the Welfare League demonstrated more concern about the *new* womanhood than their own *true* womanhood, and they stood ready to put a bit of their own purity at risk to protect their vulnerable sisters. Embarking on an activist reform agenda, they set out "to awaken among all women a strong protective sentiment toward the young women of the city, to modify or change the conditions under which young women and girls live, as regard[s] their living places and their recreations."[5] Members of the Welfare League approached this work with savvy, resolve, and a willingness to sacrifice. But why would Koenig, an accomplished motion picture exhibitor and one of the most successful burlesque theater managers in the 1910s, modify his shows to please them?

Working Girls' Clubs and Legislative Reform

Born in Dakota County, in 1866, to Levi and Alta Chamberlain Countryman, Gratia grew up among the first generation of white Minnesota settlers. Her father farmed, fought in the Civil War, earned a master's degree, and taught school before entering the agricultural machinery business and moving his family to Minneapolis to enroll his two daughters at the University of Minnesota. Gratia Countryman graduated with a bachelor of arts degree in 1889, promptly accepted employment at the Minneapolis Public Library, and worked her way up to chief librarian by 1904. She also established a national reputation among librarians, winning election in 1902 to a five-year term on the council of the American Library Association. In 1907, she joined Alice Ames Winter and others to found the Woman's Club of Minneapolis and, a mere five years later, became a founder and the first president of the Woman's Welfare League.

During the new organization's initial year of operation, Countryman led studies of the living conditions of "our 19,000 working girls." She and other members found their apartments woefully inadequate—too few, too expensive, unsupervised, unsanitary, poorly located—and concluded that Minneapolis needed a series of nice boarding homes equipped with recreational facilities that would distract young women from dance halls and motion picture theaters. Unlike conventional clubwomen, who built clubhouses for their own comfort and entertainment, Welfare League members produced a vacation lodge, a convalescent home, and a clubhouse for working girls. The clubhouse, called Linden Club, provided living quarters for 120 young women, offering "many of the comforts, much of the liberty, and always the sympathy and inspiration of homelife"—all within walking distance of several factories and many large stores. Through operating these facilities, Welfare League members learned more about the economic problems faced by young working women, provided "women adrift" with much needed material assistance, and made the domestic dimensions of their work concrete.[6]

Like clubwomen, women of the Welfare League assumed that they represented womanhood and failed to consult meaningfully with the young women they strove to protect. They failed to realize that some young women migrated to the city for the express purpose of escaping family constraints, enjoying commercial amusements, and experimenting with their sexuality. More resourceful than their elders could bear to imagine, many young women participated in a system of "treating," trading men promises of sexual favors for an extravagant meal, a coveted dress, or an evening's entertainment. These women risked sexual coercion, but because they received their pleasure up front, they could later deny their date his pleasure by claiming a misunderstanding or simply slipping away at an opportune moment.[7] Of course, even if Welfare League women had understood how young women could exploit the treating system, they would not have approved of this exercise of female agency. Their domestic model of womanhood could not accommodate such a highly sexualized and individualized mode of heterosocial interaction.

Even as leaders of the Welfare League described themselves as "homemakers and housekeepers" for the city of Minneapolis, they fought for a variety of legal and legislative measures to rid the city of "vicious influences," including commercial amusements they considered obscene and likely to lure young women into illicit sexual activity with men. They secured endorsements from the Woman's Club, anticipating that such support would enhance the Welfare League's claim to represent Minneapolis womanhood. They enjoyed clubwomen's support when they lobbied public officials for anti-prostitution legislation, pressured the chief of police to enforce the juvenile curfew ordinance, and petitioned the mayor to appoint more female police officers and apply child labor laws to juvenile stage performers.[8]

The mission of protecting young women from risqué city amusements turned

Welfare League attention to local theaters. Men's 1911 theater reform campaign had improved safety features but failed to eliminate the sexual suggestiveness and seminudity prevalent in modern burlesque performances and motion pictures. Especially disturbed by motion pictures, a new and unfamiliar medium that carried special appeal to children and increasingly solicited middle-class patronage, the Welfare League formed a twenty-five-member Motion Picture Committee in 1912 and invited several carefully chosen men to join. The men, including an attorney and a school administrator, consulted with state and city officials, enlisted the support of local religious leaders, and drafted a sweeping motion picture bill that imposed safety standards and inspections, prohibited "immoral" and "suggestive" films, licensed movie barkers, required that movie houses be built more than five hundred feet from public schools, obstructed alcohol consumption by forbidding the sale of any liquid other than water, and provided for an official board of censorship to monitor every film entering the state. The Welfare League, meanwhile, mobilized a petition and letter-writing campaign "to reach the legislator through the club women and teachers."[9]

The Welfare League's early legislative and legal reform efforts met with mixed success. Its anti-prostitution bill passed in 1913.[10] Meanwhile, persistent problems with curfew enforcement led the league to post curfew placards in public places, report violations to police headquarters, and propose a city ordinance holding parents responsible for their children's offenses. Appeals for a second female police officer garnered assurances that, while limited finances prevented immediate action, another woman would eventually be hired. Unsatisfied, the women promptly drafted legislation to create a women's police department. Welfare League pleas for a crackdown on theaters that violated child labor laws produced a mayor-appointed, twelve-woman commission charged with investigating conditions and prosecuting violators. Notably less successful was the league's motion picture bill. The *Minneapolis Tribune*, the same newspaper that rallied readers around men's anti-obscenity work one year earlier, published a flippant article entitled "Pink Lemonade Not Liked at Motion Picture Shows," misrepresenting the bill and mocking its least significant provision—the one that forbade the selling of colored drinks in an effort to prevent alcohol sales. The bill experienced no more success in the legislature, where, in 1913, lawmakers swiftly defeated it. Welfare League leaders attributed the bill's failure to its breadth and promptly drew up a narrower one to include "merely the establishment of a State Board of Recreation" with minimal censorship power. But even this watered-down version failed. Finally, at the end of the year, the league lowered its expectations and drafted an ordinance establishing a municipal motion picture censorship board—to no avail.[11]

Women of the Welfare League bemoaned the defeat of their motion picture legislation, speculating about the cause of their failure. Likely, they knew little and worried less about the cluster of free speech activists in New York City who—in protest against the repression of anarchists following President McKinley's assassination—founded the Free Speech League in 1902 and, since then, claimed First Amendment protection for a wide range of expression, including "obscenity" and motion pictures. However significant they appear to historians today, these radical libertarians exercised almost no influence outside of their immediate locale until much later in the century; they experienced serious setbacks in the 1910s when Congress considered the first bill for federal regulation of the motion picture industry, and reformers secured state motion picture censorship boards in Pennsylvania (1911), Ohio (1913), Kansas (1913), and Maryland (1916), and municipal boards in Chicago (1907) and Portland, Oregon (1915). The Supreme Court of Minnesota ignored free speech issues when it allowed the mayor of Minneapolis to prevent the showing of *The Birth of a Nation* on the grounds that it demeaned black people, falsified history, and incited racial hostility. Meanwhile, the United States Supreme Court affirmed their work in 1915 when it upheld the Ohio censorship law, declaring motion pictures beyond the purview of the First Amendment.[12]

Evidence of growing support for motion picture legislation across the nation raises questions about the failure of the Welfare League's bill. One might surmise that legislators rejected the bill in anticipation of a different Supreme Court ruling, but the case did not even reach the Court until well after it could have influenced deliberations in Minnesota. Another possible answer lies in the state's prevailing political climate, which prevented passage of most progressive laws in the first half of the 1910s. More immediate impediments to the Welfare League's motion picture bill included diminished support from clubwomen, who rejected continued motion picture reform on the grounds that male reformers had the matter in hand. In 1913, the Woman's Club even quietly voted to discontinue its financial contributions to the Welfare League.[13] Perhaps legislators and the newspaper editors who belittled the Welfare League's bill agreed with clubwomen that men had already solved the motion picture problem. Whatever the reason for the bill's failure, women of the Welfare League remained dissatisfied with motion pictures and determined to reform them, with or without legislators' help.

Cooperative and Consumerist Strategies

If the Welfare League lacked the political clout to budge Minnesota's dead-locked legislature, its public image placed it in a strong position to employ moral suasion and consumer pressure on behalf of womanhood. Welfare League lead-ers assessed their strengths, noting that their forte lay not in power but in per-suasion, not in enforcement but in exhortation. Rather than continuing to en-treat government institutions to supervise or censor theaters, they began to capitalize on their assets by exerting pressure through their own regulatory ap-paratus—a voluntary censorship board.

The Welfare League began to experiment with this approach on a small scale during its first year of operation. It commended the Lyric Theater for its whole-some performances and motion pictures in 1912 and promptly received a packet of complimentary tickets and a request from the theater's manager. Would the women, he wondered, endorse a series of white slave films for exhibition at his theater? White slave films at their best instructed young women about the dan-gers of urban streets, the ploys of would-be pimps, and the tribulations of pros-titutes, but at their worst, such films titillated rather than educated. The Lyric manager knew that a Welfare League endorsement would help to attract a re-spectable audience and avert criticism, but his request also conveyed to league leaders that their endorsement carried political and commercial value. Bending this discovery to their own ends, the women cautiously offered the Lyric a let-ter of endorsement provided that *each* of its films first obtain the approval of the league's new voluntary censorship board.[14]

Welfare League members decided to pursue this strategy with new vigor after the defeat of their motion picture bill, investigating the possibility of coordi-nating the work of their voluntary censorship board with the National Board of Censorship in New York—the same board touted by local motion picture ex-hibitors, in 1911, as evidence that films were clean. In 1915, a National Board representative, Robbins Gilman, addressed the Minneapolis Welfare League, de-livering an inspiring account of National Board successes in New York City. Not only had motion pictures improved during the past six years, he declared, so had advertisements. Urging the women to hitch their work to this successful reform program, he suggested that they enlarge the scope of their voluntary censorship board and coordinate it with the National Board by using it to investigate indi-vidual films' adherence to National Board standards. The Welfare League could thereby help the National Board police producers by encouraging local ex-

hibitors to show National-Board-approved films, indirectly pressuring producers to create such films. The National Board possessed no real enforcement
power, Gilman admitted. But local theaters would cooperate with the Welfare
League's voluntary censorship board, he explained, because in exchange, they
would enjoy endorsements, patronage, and freedom from legal threats.[15] The
genius of the National Board lay in its ability to address the interrelated concerns
of reformers and exhibitors and, at a time of mounting pressure for official censorship, threaten to cut off or blacklist uncooperative producers. Impressed with
Gilman's report, the Welfare League rapidly transformed its fledgling voluntary
censorship board into a citywide apparatus closely linked to the National Board
of Censorship. To staff the expanded board, it recruited women from the
Woman's Club and other organizations, enlisted the mayor's support, and persuaded Gilman—who had recently relocated to Minneapolis—to serve as the
league's liaison to the National Board.[16] Like women in other cities, who founded
the Cleveland Cinema Club, the Women's Civic Club of Duquesne, and the Indiana Indorsers of Photoplays, the Welfare League invited local exhibitors to
submit all of their films for approval in exchange for women's public endorsement, patronage, and commitment to oppose official censorship.

Motion picture industry representatives affiliated with the National Board
recognized in women's clubs a vast network of energy and organization that
threatened to push for official censorship if not converted to the idea of voluntary censorship. Robbins Gilman's presentation to the Welfare League represented part of a larger National Board campaign to cultivate women's groups. In
1916, the National Board advanced this agenda by creating the National Committee for Better Films to coordinate the work of local women's groups with the
National Board of Censorship. The Committee for Better Films quickly attracted dozens of local women's organizations and began to place prominent articles in the magazine of the General Federation of Woman's Clubs. Men
founded and led the National Board of Censorship, but women—primarily midwestern women—operated most of the local organizations that made the increasingly elaborate system work. The Welfare League, with its use of a voluntary censorship board to regulate the Lyric Theater in 1912, counted as one of
the earliest of these. But by 1917, so many women's organizations had joined the
better films movement that one critic accused it of being "the biggest woman's
club machine in the country."[17]

Local cooperative and consumerist tactics made sense for female motion picture reformers in the 1910s. A national organization already existed to coordi-

nate them. The movie industry remained disorganized, competitive, responsive to its patrons, and, especially after the high court's decision, intimidated by the proliferation of state censorship boards. Equally important, most vaudeville and burlesque theaters *also* exhibited motion pictures, making influence over motion picture exhibitors tantamount to influence over burlesque and vaudeville managers. Finally, whereas Welfare League women could not vote, they could purchase theater tickets; legislators stood to gain little by supporting their bills, but theater managers recognized in them a source of revenue as well as a potential threat to their profits.

Women of the Welfare League found theater managers much more attentive than legislators and law enforcement officials had been. Theater managers actually heeded their complaints and cultivated their approval. Owners of the local Bijou Opera House, for example, one of the many theaters that staged live performances as well as motion pictures, organized a ladies benefit, offering free passes to league members who sold the most tickets.[18] The Woman's Club, too, received solicitations from theater managers; clubwomen had discontinued their financial support of the Welfare League but several served on the voluntary censorship board, and the two organizations remained publicly affiliated. It came as no surprise when, in 1914, the Bainbridge Theater offered to contribute 25 percent of the proceeds from its stage play *The Bluebird*, to help the Woman's Club establish a children's aid society. Not to be outdone, the Lyric Theater pledged more than one hundred dollars of its motion picture receipts to clubwomen's work. William Koenig, manager of several local theaters—including strictly motion picture houses and the burlesque theater that featured Elsie La Bergère— proved even more creative, fashioning several gimmicks especially for "increasing the woman patronage at night." He suggested that his business partner hold a weekly "free ladies matinee" at the Star Theater "to let the women know that your shows are clean." Koenig later concocted what he called "the best stunt you can get to advertise your ladies performances." This involved developing a two-part theater ticket and imprinting the stub with an advertisement for "ladies" shows. Whether women kept or dropped their ticket stubs, they would promote the theater's programs. Managers of burlesque, vaudeville, and exclusively motion picture theaters all vied for women's patronage. As they did so, the Welfare League noted a marked decline in morally objectionable movies. One year after forming their voluntary censorship board, members happily reported a decrease in "objectionable" and "sex problem" shows.[19]

Fig. 2.1. Gayety Theater advertisement with William Koenig's prized illustration, as it appeared in the *Minneapolis Tribune*, August 26, 1917. Courtesy of the Minnesota Historical Society

Whereas the National Board focused on motion pictures, the Welfare League demonstrated as much concern about the stage, and in this arena, with the co-operation of William Koenig, the women experienced their best-documented success. Extant sources do not reveal conversations between Koenig and league members, and we cannot know whether he visited with them personally or merely read about them in the newspaper. We do know, though, that Koenig understood and respected the Welfare League's demands. Manager of several motion picture theaters as well as one of the most successful burlesque houses in the nation, the Minneapolis Gayety Theater, Koenig won the American Burlesque Association's top prize for gross annual receipts in 1916. Sexually daring performances usually distinguished burlesque from other types of theater, but Koenig attributed his success to "giving a good lively burlesque show, but not smut." "Unclean or suggestive" performances would, he insisted, deplete his audience and profits.[20] "I do not believe in a smutty show for this theatre and I will not run one," Koenig informed his booking agent, adding that the Welfare League would not tolerate smut.[21] The Minneapolis press applauded Koenig, reporting that people "who have come to the Gayety for a sort of adventure in naughtiness have found nothing naughty here." Newspapers rewarded him with liberal advertising privileges, allowing him to promote his shows with illustrations. Admittedly "tickled to death" to receive such favored treatment, Koenig wrote, "I think it is pretty nice nowadays for a burlesque house to get a [picture] in the papers." And an entire decade after his tenure as manager of the Gayety, Minneapolis residents still commented on Koenig's "clean" burlesque theater.[22]

Koenig's reputation for demanding inoffensive shows also spread throughout the burlesque circuit of the 1910s. A Chicago manager wired Koenig to warn him about an act soon to arrive in Minneapolis: "Mae Clark was fined $25 for cooching." The Welfare League objected to cooch dancing, Koenig acknowledged, gratefully assuring his Chicago informant that he would double Clark's fine if she dared to cooch in Minneapolis. Repeatedly, Koenig exhorted his booking agent to send him cleaner shows, personally removing acts he thought likely to offend women, including those containing cooching, profanity, or nudity.[23]

World War and Woman Suffrage

Burlesque and movie houses suffered a lean year in 1917. The European military theater diminished attendance at the local entertainment theater, as thousands of male patrons left to become soldiers. At the same time, military mobilization relocated many men at nearby Fort Snelling, in Minneapolis's twin city of St. Paul. Local residents expressed concern about the potential moral consequences of housing so many young men in the vicinity of cities teeming with single young women.[24] Their fears escalated when military medical examinations revealed a shocking rate of venereal disease among new recruits. Public health officials responded with drastic measures, including showing enlisted men graphic educational films on venereal disease—such as *Fit to Fight*—and, under the Chamberlain-Kahn Act, detaining and forcibly examining women thought likely to be disease carriers.[25]

When the Minnesota legislature joined other states in creating a Public Safety Commission to address these and other hindrances to the war effort, including labor unrest and antiwar protest, it brought Alice Ames Winter, founder of the Woman's Club of Minneapolis, and her family into the heart of city government. Winter's brother, Charles Ames, chaired the Safety Commission; her husband, Thomas G. Winter, supervised intelligence operations, and Winter herself chaired the woman's committee. Referring to the Safety Commission as "a private snap for the family of C. W. Ames," a radical trade union paper protested against the commission's close ties to the Citizens Alliance.[26]

Alice Ames Winter, now an officer in the General Federation of Women's Clubs, used her new position on the Safety Commission to encourage women in Minnesota and around the country to buy liberty bonds, conserve food and fabric, write cheery letters to the boys abroad, join the Red Cross, applaud the war effort, speak English, and hate Germans. To her great satisfaction, the Woman's Club of Minneapolis exchanged its usual programs for war work, sharing tips for coping with wheat-free days, raising nearly $2,000 for a soldiers' library fund, sharing dress patterns for less elaborate gowns, making tens of thousands of surgical dressings and bandages, and entertaining servicemen. Only occasionally did clubwomen have to remind each other to heed wartime labor shortages and order no more than one delivery a day from their grocers and butchers. So completely did clubwomen convert to war work that Winter felt moved to reassure them, through an article in the *General Federation Magazine*, that the war had not eliminated women's conventional club work but elevated it by channeling it into patriotic service.[27] Much of Winter's work involved "speechifying," as she put it. In two years, she delivered over 250 speeches and organized Americanization committees in 58 of Minnesota's 86 counties—a task that seemed especially important given the heavily immigrant population in Minnesota's rural areas. "You better believe I am giving them straight patriotism," she wrote her husband, "saying just what I think about slackers, pro-Germans, Pacifists, teaching in foreign languages and all the rest." While she worked hard to get people "stirred up against the Germans," she also worried about outbreaks of "mob vengeance," applauding sedition laws as tools for replacing vigilantism with justice.[28]

Winter understood and probably shared most of her husband's and brother's anti-labor politics. For instance, she kept her husband informed about the local political progress of the Non-Partisan League, the Socialists, and the American Federation of Labor while he served the Red Cross in France in 1918. And she clearly agreed with her male relatives that wartime patriotism required the rejection of anything not purely "American" and revulsion for anything German. But she also acted on a sense of cross-class sisterhood, using her husband's absence as an opportunity to assist union organizers of working women. In April of 1918, for example, she hosted a gathering of thirty people to welcome Miss Henry, an Australian Women's Trade Union League (WTUL) organizer. Henry stayed with Winter for a week, allowing Winter to introduce her to social workers and shuttle her around the city for speaking engagements among "unionizing girls." It seemed a revelation to Winter that Henry, "though radical," could be "kindly in her attitude toward every one." On more than one occasion, Winter informed her husband that Henry, "a white haired woman," "is a most interesting person," confessing finally, "I am giving free reign for all my radicalism" with you away. Ironically, given her husband's fiercely anti-labor activities,

Winter may have played an instrumental role in bringing the WTUL to Minneapolis; shortly after Henry's visit, woman unionists established the first WTUL committee in the city.[29]

Meanwhile, as labor leaders feared, under the leadership of Charles Ames and Thomas Winter, the Safety Commission waged a campaign of oppression against radicals and unions, using Pinkerton detectives to raid, infiltrate, and intimidate local branches of the Non-Partisan League and the International Workers of the World (IWW). During 1917, Winter and Ames persuaded federal authorities to ransack local IWW headquarters around the country, prosecute the editor of the local IWW newspaper, and finally deport him to Sweden. Under cover of the Espionage Act, Winter suppressed the *New Times*, a Socialist newspaper. Ames tried to obtain federal support for a crackdown on the Non-Partisan League (NPL) on the grounds that, in "war time we cannot look tolerantly on any movement which seeks to crystallize discontent and to establish class distinctions," but because the NPL supported the U.S. war effort, federal authorities ignored Ames's requests. The motivations behind other Safety Commission activities are more difficult to ascertain. One historian claims that the commission forced many places of public amusement to close in an effort to wipe out the IWW. But the commission also shut down saloons and theaters in response to the inspector general of the U.S. Army, who threatened to remove five thousand soldiers from Fort Snelling because of its "vicious conditions"—code for prostitution. Whatever the reason, as theater manager William Koenig wrote in 1917, "this Safety Commission's power is unlimited."[30]

Koenig worried that the Safety Commission might close his theaters as well in its drive against "women of the streets." Wartime financial losses caused him equal stress. One of his motion picture theaters showed a deficit of over $800. Many theaters simply closed their doors, a strategy Koenig himself contemplated if he could not soon turn a profit. Like numerous other managers in the burlesque circuit, Koenig kept his doors open by appealing to a broader audience. Notwithstanding recent Safety Commission restrictions on women, he redoubled his efforts to attract them.[31] Alerting other managers in the burlesque circuit to his plans, Koenig announced that, because Minneapolis would lose to the military at least seven thousand young men, 80 percent of whom patronized burlesque, he was "making a special effort this year to increase the lady patronage at the Gayety." Linking this strategy directly to profit concerns, he declared, "We should go after the ladies to get them interested in burlesque to try to keep up our business." Koenig suspected that attracting ladies required shows of a high moral character, so he fortified his ban on cooching and expanded his prohibitions to cover "smut of any kind." Regarding language, Koenig specified that he would "permit one 'hell' or 'damn,' providing it is not said to a woman." All gestures and jokes "must be used in a way that will not offend any of our lady patrons," he directed.[32] A *Minneapolis Journal* editor sustained Koenig's analysis, advising momentarily pinched theaters to play for the "ladies" by cutting out risqué shows. Meanwhile, Koenig's success in attracting female patrons reinforced his belief that women, as a group, desired shows free of profanity and sexual display. In August 1918 he virtually crowed, "My lady attendance at night is wonderful nearly as many women every night as men."[33]

By the end of 1918, a new plague visited theaters: influenza. Twenty million Americans contracted the deadly illness and over half a million succumbed to it despite drastic measures taken by public health officials around the nation. Most cities closed public facilities for a time in an effort to prevent the scourge from spreading. When officials forced Twin Cities' theaters to shut down between October and December, managers spent five weeks speculating about when they would be able to reopen, how much money they had lost, and whether the quarantine, coming so near an election, served the Safety Commission's political purposes. But Alice Ames Winter reported that even her speeches on behalf of patriotism had to be canceled on account of the flu epidemic. After the nationwide flu epidemic subsided, Koenig proceeded to capitalize on his wartime business acumen, buying up struggling theaters and running shows modified for a female audience.[34]

In 1919, theater managers confronted another development destined, they thought, to change their business dramatically. All performers must "refrain from making any fun of the suffraget [sic.] question," Koenig urgently notified his booking agent in March 1919, shortly after Minnesota legislators passed a suffrage bill. "Already the women are voting and in another year they will be elected to all offices in the City," Koenig fretted, predicting that, unless we eliminate suffrage jokes, dirty skits, and scantily clad dancers, "the Women's League will do it for us and make it very disagreeable for burlesque."[35]

Members of the Woman's Welfare League never saw Koenig's correspondence, but it would have delighted them. Koenig treated the league as representative of the city's women, and league women strove to project just that image, pursuing a mission couched in assumptions about womanhood and the universal female roles of mother and homemaker. Indeed, Countryman characterized the organization's constituency in sweeping terms limited only by sex. Calling

Fig. 2.2. Minneapolis women lined up to vote for the first time at a downtown Minneapolis precinct, 1920. Courtesy of the Minnesota Historical Society

the Woman's Welfare League "a very democratic organization," she described it as a place where "all women, rich or poor, young or old, might take counsel together for the benefit of womankind in this city."[36] League women vested their claim to moral authority in their identities as exemplars of womanhood. With Koenig, they clearly succeeded. When Koenig tried to attract female customers, or avert female criticism, or appease female voters, he offered shows that would appeal to women of the league. He did not just treat league women as if he believed they represented Minneapolis womanhood. He staked his business on it.

The Minneapolis Woman's Welfare League broke new ground, assuming leadership in a crusade—combating obscene amusements—that men had cordoned off as their own. With great finesse they navigated their way into position, deferentially seeking male assistance and framing their mission in terms of protecting young women from urban vice. The league agenda diverged from men's when it linked female vulnerability with youth, positing older women as young women's proper protectors. But the two movements also converged; just as vice societies excluded women, adducing female weakness as well as children's innocence as a justification for their efforts, so the league effectively excluded from membership the same working women whose vulnerability justified its work. To the extent that the league succeeded in its attempts to represent womanhood, it silenced other women, implicitly denying their existence. At the same time, the league undermined paternalism by claiming for women roles as arbiters of obscenity.[37]

Initially, the Woman's Welfare League failed; neither aldermen, legislators, nor newspaper reporters welcomed its anti-obscenity proposals. But outside the realm of formal politics, the league succeeded beyond its wildest dreams, inducing William Koenig to adapt his shows to league women's tastes by forbidding Gayety performers to cooch, appear unclothed, curse at women, or deride woman suffrage on stage. In retrospect, founders of the league could not have chosen a more auspicious decade to pursue anti-obscenity reform. Female reformers around the country experienced similar triumphs in the 1910s. Some theater managers, eager to legitimize their business by attracting the ennobling patronage of middle-class women, enticed them with gimmicks and clean shows. But they also cleaned up in response to local women's organizations like the Minneapolis Woman's Welfare League. Much more than passive cultural symbols, organized women brokered dramatic if temporary changes in local theaters as discriminating consumers, resolute reformers, and future voters who claimed to represent womanhood.

Women of the Welfare League parlayed their unified and exemplary image—in part a legacy of their Woman's Club roots—into consumer and political power, exercising measurable influence over theater owners who exhibited motion pictures and staged burlesque performances, often in the same space. But the Woman's Welfare League accomplished all of this in a unique cultural, political, and economic milieu, one that integrated an emergent sexual revolution, a modernizing theater industry, and the incipient woman suffrage amendment with the exigencies of war. It was a milieu that would not be seen again. And a mere decade later, even the nude version of Elsie La Bergère's 1915 burlesque act would look tame to Minneapolis audiences.

CHAPTER THREE

"Censorship Does Not Protect"

Women's Motion Picture Reform, 1919–1922

Just as the Woman's Welfare League tasted its first success in theater reform, a local sex crime shook the Minneapolis reform community, once again altering the landscape of women's local politics. The crime, committed by Joseph W. Bragdon, involved seven young girls between the ages of nine and fourteen, all of whom knew Bragdon only as "Uncle Ned," the name he assumed when he took them for rides in his "big green automobile." We do not know how Bragdon became acquainted with the girls. Perhaps he came upon them emerging from a motion picture theater, giggly, carefree, and eager for adventure. Or maybe he met them at church, where, after the service, he persuaded their parents to let him treat their daughters to ice cream cones. However he encountered them and wherever he took them, Bragdon found a way to use these girls for his own sexual pleasure. Authorities arrested him after several girls reported that he took them "back of some bushes for unnatural practices," and a grand jury indicted him on three counts of statutory rape. He may have thought that his standing in the community as a generous contributor to the Humane Society and a member of the Minneapolis Club and the Citizens Alliance network would protect him. Fearing that very thing, members of the Minneapolis Woman's Club, the Woman's Welfare League, the League of Catholic Women, the Council of Jewish Women, and others convened a special women's committee to monitor court proceedings and press for conviction.[1]

As Bragdon's three trials unfolded, he seemed increasingly likely to escape punishment. Two of his personal friends served on the jury and his team of attorneys included a former justice of the state supreme court. The first indictment resulted in an acquittal, and the second a hung jury, but members of the women's court committee resolved that the third would end differently. After consulting with prosecutors and offering advice and support, they rallied organized women to turn out for the trial en masse. When the final trial culminated in a guilty verdict and a stiff prison sentence for Bragdon, the women found ample cause for celebration and pride; they believed that the support of the women's court committee—"representing as it did the majority of the organized women of the city"—had turned the tide against Bragdon. But the trial also left them with the knowledge that even respected men among the city's elite engaged in predatory sexual behavior that endangered young people of all classes.[2] Children were unsafe everywhere, it seemed.

With the conviction and sentencing of Bragdon, members of the women's court committee had "felt their power," and they now aimed to expand the influence of their "cosmopolitan" winning coalition. They promptly created the Women's Cooperative Alliance, an organization designed to oversee court proceedings in sex crime cases, "seek the causes of the increasing sex delinquency," and find ways to prevent it.[3] Many of the women who fashioned this agenda had cut their reform teeth on work in the Minneapolis Woman's Club or the Woman's Welfare League, organizations that instilled a faith in womanhood, concern about obscene amusements, and commitment to cooperative and consumer-oriented reform strategies. Unlike women in earlier years, however, alliance women possessed the right to vote. What difference that would make remained to be seen.

Motion Pictures and Juvenile Delinquency

Catheryne Cooke Gilman, a thirty-seven-year-old suffragist, settlement house worker, and newlywed who had only recently moved to Minneapolis from New York, helped to found the Women's Cooperative Alliance, bringing to her work a deep familiarity with the rural Midwest. Born in 1880 to Jeremiah and Aditha Cook, Catheryne grew up in small Missouri and Iowa towns where her father, a railroad worker, struggled to support a family of seven. Unlike her parents, who received only the most rudimentary education, Catheryne graduated from Iowa State Normal School and completed a year of postbaccalaureate work at the University of Chicago. Here she met Sophonisba Breckinridge and Jane Addams, social work pioneers who transformed Catheryne's life, introducing her to urban problems and progressive solutions and inspiring her to take up settlement house work in New York. At University Settlement House, she fell in love with the director, Robbins Gilman, an upper-middle-class banker's son whose politics and proclivities drove him first from Wall Street, then, ironically, out of his University Settlement job. In 1914, Gilman's public support for strikers affiliated with the IWW damaged his fundraising ability and forced his resignation, after which

Fig. 3.1. Catheryne Cooke Gilman, c. 1920s. Courtesy of
the Minnesota Historical Society

he accepted the directorship of Northeast Neighborhood House in Minneapolis and proposed to Catheryne Cooke.[4] Her assent came quickly, but the wedding proved more difficult since the Cooke family could not afford a ceremony
befitting the Gilman family's status. Catheryne's sister offered to sell a braid made
from her own hair to help cover expenses, while their mother encouraged Catheryne to explain her financial situation to the Gilmans. "If I was in Robbins
place," she offered, "I would say we will be married just as we are. I would not
care for so much waist [*sic*] of good money." The wedding took place December 31, 1914; Gilman became pregnant shortly thereafter, and the couple moved
to Minneapolis to settle into their new home—a sitting room, bathroom, and
bedroom on the second floor of the settlement house. The birth of Catheryne
Cooke Gilman Jr. did not delay the Gilmans' plunge into the Minneapolis reform scene. Already deeply concerned about the threat of unwholesome motion

pictures, Robbins Gilman continued his affiliation with the New York–based National Board of Censorship as liaison for the Woman's Welfare League.[5] Indeed, he helped to shape the league's anti-obscenity efforts, most notably its successful campaign to establish a voluntary censorship board to monitor the pictures local theaters screened. Catheryne Cooke Gilman extended her new maternal concerns into work on the board of Maternity Hospital, the Minnesota Child Welfare Commission, the Bragdon child molestation case, and the Women's Cooperative Alliance, an organization she would lead for more than a decade.[6]

Although prosecution of one of the city's leading businessmen gave rise to the Women's Cooperative Alliance, still, in its early years, the organization secured considerable support from leaders in the business community. Whether motivated to distance themselves from the Bragdon scandal, obtain influence over one of the city's newest reform organizations, or please their wives, several men involved with the Citizens Alliance, for example, generously contributed seed money, office space, and secretarial staff to the fledgling organization.[7] The Women's Cooperative Alliance also enjoyed access to the Community Fund, a public purse devoted to social welfare work at the end of World War I and controlled largely by the Citizens Alliance network. In addition, Gilman and several other women answered a call to join Mayor Edward Meyers and members of the Citizens Alliance to form the Committee of Thirteen, a citizen law enforcement association—much like Chicago's Committee of Fifteen and New York City's Committee of Fourteen—ostensibly designed to eliminate prostitution and associated crime. Gilman hoped to use the Committee of Thirteen to check the sort of corruption and sexual predation revealed in the Bragdon case.[8]

Within a year of founding the Women's Cooperative Alliance, leaders had forged strong relationships with businessmen, recruited several wealthy and generous women, attracted representatives of a range of women's organizations—including the Council of Jewish Women, the Woman's Club of Minneapolis, and the League of Catholic Women—and built an active membership of more than three thousand female volunteers. By 1920, their mailing list comprised more than ten thousand names; nineteen local women's organizations enlisted as cooperative members, and alliance coffers supported twenty-four paid workers, including Gilman, its salaried leader, who had, in the meantime, borne two more children. Unlike settlement house activity, which provided services primarily to immigrants and the poor, Gilman conceived of her alliance work in broader terms designed to cross class lines and unify all women through their roles as mothers. "Motherhood is common to all women," Gilman asserted. "It is our

Fig. 3.2. This cartoon depicts the Women's Cooperative Alliance as a confident woman handing a broom to a feckless man (representing the grand jury or local government) with instructions to clean up vice conditions. *Minneapolis Daily News*, October 12, 1922. Courtesy of the Robbins Gilman and Family Papers, Minnesota Historical Society

one common bond." Like women of the Woman's Club and Welfare League before them, alliance leaders used motherhood and wifehood as metaphors for their public activity, effectively linking their organizational work with domesticity. Appropriating this imagery, the local press incorporated it into a one-frame cartoon that depicted the alliance as a woman furnishing a broom to a man (representing the grand jury), instructing him to sweep up the debris of urban problems and municipal corruption. Under this rubric, alliance women pursued a wide range of activities, many of which emerged directly from their Welfare League roots. Concerned about the large population of young, solitary, and self-supporting girls migrating from rural areas or immigrating from abroad, alliance workers styled themselves "Big Sisters," providing employment and housing assistance, offering advice on educational or health matters, and even supplying suitcases full of clothing—all in hopes of lessening the vulnerability of young migrant women to urban vices and lecherous men. The need for their services appeared great; in one year alone, the alliance worked with 2,773 different young women.[9]

Like many Progressive reformers, Women's Cooperative Alliance leaders based their work upon painstakingly gathered "scientific" data. Their ongoing observations at sex crime trials, for example, not only provided female and juvenile victims with support and male officials with female oversight, but also facilitated data collection on the judicial system's treatment of women and children. In addition, the alliance's Research and Investigation Department conducted studies of moral conditions in urban neighborhoods. This information bolstered the reformers' efforts to pressure city officials to monitor dance halls, install lighting in public parks, and enforce the juvenile curfew law.[10] Alliance social workers spent a great deal of time in the community, canvassing neighborhoods, surveying moral conditions, and distributing educational literature in door-to-door visits. Meanwhile, local officials and concerned citizens visited the organization's downtown offices to report problems or propose solutions. Alliance women responded by devoting much of their time and energy to investigating complaints filed by local residents regarding prostitution, juvenile delinquency, and obscene shows.

Adult sexual misconduct inspired the formation of the alliance. But because alliance leaders linked adult behavior to childhood experiences and conceived of their work as an extension of maternal roles, they focused increasingly on juvenile sexuality. Innocence and malleability, they believed, rendered children highly trainable in rational, humane, and moral behavior. Ready receptacles for adult ideas, children also served as connective tissue to the next generation.[11] Thus, alliance women and like-minded reformers pinned their brightest hopes and their darkest fears on the nation's youth.

New forms of public amusement—especially the movies—topped alliance women's list of concerns. By 1920, they surveyed a burgeoning metropolis boasting sixty-three motion picture theaters. To many members, this scene threatened the city's moral fiber. Dark motion picture auditoriums admitted a mixed-sex audience of all ages and exhibited suggestive and even salacious films that escaped the fledgling municipal regulatory apparatus. Many alliance women brought extensive motion picture reform resumés to their new affiliation, having successfully employed cooperative and consumerist reform strategies in the late 1910s as members of the Welfare League. Working with the National Board of Censorship while in New York had acquainted the Gilmans with these tactics. In addition, Gilman and other alliance members belonged to the National Consumers' League, an organization that used consumer power to pressure employers to improve wages and working conditions.[12] Unsurprisingly, given this wealth of experience, alliance leaders began their motion picture work committed to cooperative and consumer-based reform strategies.

Optimistic, but far from naïve, alliance women anticipated that cooperating with businessmen would be difficult. So many of their interests seemed to conflict with the profit-making goals of commerce—from their desire to improve the lives of working women and families to their determination to eradicate risqué commercial amusements. But pragmatism prevailed; the Women's Cooperative Alliance needed support from those with money and power. Harbingers of conflict emerged almost immediately. In 1919, at the height of the first Red Scare, directors of the Community Fund requested that Gilman disavow the "socialistic tendencies" many people attributed to her and permit a men's committee to work with the Women's Cooperative Alliance. Gilman compromised, crafting a narrow statement that made no mention of her support for the IWW but denied membership in the Socialist Party. She ignored the suggestion regarding a men's committee and managed, for the next couple of years, to prevent her differences with the Citizens Alliance from destroying her connections to the Community Fund and the Committee of Thirteen.[13]

Initial disagreements with motion picture men surfaced over the issue of culpability for juvenile delinquency. Noting an increase in childhood criminal and sexual activity late in the 1910s, many civic leaders blamed juvenile delinquency on the influence of movies. Among the first to voice these concerns, Jane Addams, renowned director of Chicago's Hull House and personal friend of the Gilmans, lamented the lack of wholesome recreation for city children and the pervasive influence of motion pictures that promoted sexual license, crime, and other antisocial behavior.[14] Many reformers claimed that the motion picture exercised mimetic power over children. "Our children are rapidly becoming what they see in the movies," asserted a 1921 pamphlet by motion picture reformer Minnie Kennedy. Substantiating these sentiments with shocking anecdotes of child suicide, murder, and sexual exploits—all presumably provoked by movie portrayals of these activities—Kennedy insisted that children who witness "terrible or horrible scenes" risked becoming "callous or brutalized . . . because of the instability of their nervous systems." The Women's Christian Temperance Union went further, holding movies responsible for the failures of prohibition enforcement as well as children's misbehavior. Alliance women agreed, calling motion pictures "one of the greatest contributing factors to juvenile delinquency."[15]

In the late 1910s and early 1920s, most people agreed that juvenile delinquency had increased alarmingly. But the question of what and whom to blame proved more controversial. A local woman writing to the *Minneapolis Tribune* concurred with the alliance that movies contributed to the problem but asserted that "mothers are to blame for all this. The women can stop all this if they will." Alliance women objected strenuously, exonerating parents, especially mothers, and entreating the community to shoulder responsibility for unwholesome public entertainments. Gilman asserted that "the 'movie' picture thru its subtle suggestions has given rise to the largest number of incipient criminals." The fault lay not with parents, she insisted, but with "the voting public who permit conditions to exist in the city that are known to demoralize boys and girls."[16]

Motion picture industry representatives, including those on the National Board of Censorship, resisted efforts to hold movies accountable for juvenile delinquency and Prohibition violations. In an elaborate defense of the movie industry, they assembled and published expert testimony attributing children's delinquent behavior to bad parenting, and, in 1920, the National Board issued a pamphlet entitled "Motion Pictures Not Guilty" to argue that "improper homes," rather than movies, caused juvenile misconduct. Another board pamphlet insisted that movies actually served as "a fine preventive of delinquency" because "they cause leisure time to disappear on winged feet."[17] Aware that the movie industry denied a causal relationship between movies and juvenile delinquency, Women's Cooperative Alliance leaders sought cooperation not agreement with industry representatives, suspecting that their new status as voters would render this strategy even more effective than it had been previously.

In 1920, alliance representatives asked a National Board officer, Orrin G. Cocks, for advice regarding the alliance's motion picture reform program. Cocks first suggested that reformers find ways to utilize motion pictures for their own purposes. The new medium, he pointed out, offered extraordinary fundraising and educational possibilities. His enclosed pamphlet, "Make the Movies Pay for . . . Various Kinds of Social Work," advised reformers to establish theaters and use the profits for their own projects. Regarding commercial theaters, Cocks maintained that "the whole problem for the exhibitor is one of a paying house. This throws much of the responsibility back on social and civic groups to build up sentiment." Thus Cocks urged the women to support exhibitors who arranged children's matinees and family nights and to endorse and even advertise films that met with their approval. This would encourage exhibitors to show "good" films and pressure producers to create more of them. Consumer pressure applied at the grassroots level would percolate up, Cocks insisted, ultimately persuading the industry to produce better films.[18]

"Selection—Not Censorship; Cooperation—Not Antagonism"

The Gilmans wasted no time implementing Cocks's recommendations. In the summer of 1920, under Robbins Gilman's direction, Northeast Neighborhood House established its own community theater, prompting Catheryne Cooke Gilman to quip that "the Gilmans have suddenly gone into the movie business." In the fall, under the auspices of the alliance and in cooperation with the National Board, Gilman organized a mass meeting to begin a citywide campaign for better movies. Community response overwhelmed her when more than three hundred people attended, including thirty-five theater managers. A mere two months after the kick-off meeting, the movement boasted several hundred members and thirty-eight committees, fast approaching Gilman's goal of sixty-three better film committees, one for each motion picture theater in the city. For the next three years it continued to grow, with 150 new members added in 1921, and another 200 in 1922.[19]

The film committees of the Minneapolis better movie movement revolved like a series of pinwheels around the city's neighborhood theaters. Within each, recruits from "constructive agencies" (such as churches, schools, and clubs) appointed volunteers to view and report on each movie, as well as the theater's physical condition, audience conduct, and the announcement and enforcement of the juvenile curfew law. In particular, committee members scrutinized films bearing the National Board's seal of approval in order to verify that they did not contain scenes of drunkenness; cruel treatment of women or children; robbery; suggestive, sensuous, or lewd acts; indecent or suggestive clothing; or material likely to incite racial prejudice.[20] The local theater manager and alliance representative forwarded copies of the reports to the National Board in New York, which sent them on to motion picture distributors and producers. In addition, committee members cultivated relationships with local theater managers, apprising them of neighborhoods demands for wholesome movies and enlisting their support. In Gilman's estimation, this system promised to avoid the worst excesses while preserving the greatest strengths of centralized organizations by allowing community groups to function independently but still enjoy the support and coordination of a sizable association.[21] Gilman and her colleagues had not expected "spectacular results," but they marveled at the movement's immediate, even "miraculous" accomplishments.[22] "We do find splendid co-operation among both men and women who are eager to serve on committees and a willingness on the part of managers to please these community committees," one alliance secretary wrote.[23] Indeed, by the spring of 1921, alliance leaders announced that most theater managers agreed to cooperate with the better film committees. "Several theatres reduced or took off entirely the objectionable serial," they reported, while "in some places special programs planned for children were put on."[24]

Even as the alliance pursued motion picture reform, it took an aggressive stand against censorship, eagerly adopting the slogan of the National Board of Censorship, recently renamed the National Board of Review: "Selection—Not Censorship, Cooperation—Not Antagonism." Opposition to censorship and commitment to cooperation with motion picture exhibitors and producers derived from two convictions: first, that the vast majority of people wanted—and, moreover, agreed on what constituted—moral, wholesome movies, and second, that producers would create such movies if they realized that the public wanted them. As Gilman explained, "The great majority of people have never been satisfied with the type of film produced but they have never had their forces organized to convey this idea definitely and unmistakably to the film management and the producer." Thus the alliance set out to provide a medium for the expression of public opinion to motion picture exhibitors and producers.[25] Better film committees advanced this effort by mobilizing concerned citizens and applying consumer pressure.

Coupling this consumer-based strategy with strong anti-censorship rhetoric, Gilman insisted that "censorship does not protect. It only invites graft and abuse with little if any remedial results to the public." Her sincere and adamant opposition to censorship did not mean that Gilman interpreted the First Amendment broadly. Rather, like most of her contemporaries, she defined censorship idiosyncratically. In the years after World War I and before the ascendance of the American Civil Liberties Union, ideas about and understandings of speech and censorship varied widely. Some people insisted that only prior restraint by the state constituted censorship, exempting from the definition punishment for speech already uttered and speech constraints imposed by private entities. Even civil libertarians allowed limits on speech that they would consider unconscionable restrictions within a few decades. Leaders of the Civil Liberties Bureau, for instance, did not think it censorship for the state to punish one for speech ruled obscene by a jury. In marked contrast, Gilman classified various forms of prior restraint as regulation but defined censorship as alterations or prohibitions imposed upon a work after production—the activity, essentially, of official censorship boards.[26]

Most people agreed that the job of censorship boards qualified as censorship, but in 1915 even that unequivocal form of censorship received sanction by the Supreme Court. Still, Gilman opposed censorship boards, believing that, constitutional or not, they violated the most basic precepts of democracy as understood by most Americans. Revealing a keen sense of cultural relativism, she wrote, "In America, censorship has failed, and the principle of censorship under our form of government and with our psychology, is futile." Though perhaps a little annoyed by this legacy, in the early 1920s Gilman accepted it, allowing that "we each have to conform to the conditions under which we reside." The better movie movement represented the alliance's effort to reform motion pictures while honoring American values. Censorship boards also impressed Gilman as corrupt and inefficient. Editing the end product, she argued, could never elevate the moral quality of an intrinsically immoral film. Rather, such censorship resulted merely in "spasmodic attempts to cut or remove certain scenes," with little impact on the subtle, unwholesome messages that threaded through many movies. In addition, knowledge of official censors who accepted bribes from the motion picture industry in exchange for overlooking offensive scenes heightened Gilman's concern about the susceptibility of local censorship boards to extortion. Just as important, Gilman argued that the current system of scattered state and municipal censorship boards could not manage a national industry involved in interstate commerce. This system also frustrated filmmakers, because it meant that they created for a national market but endured the vagaries of myriad local censorship boards. Finally, Gilman worried that official boards of censorship promoted apathy among citizens who presumed, wrongly, that censorship rendered movies harmless. Although Gilman exonerated parents in general and mothers in particular, she held the community as a whole accountable for providing a wholesome environment for young people. An official censorship apparatus would, she feared, discourage individuals from assuming this community responsibility. Thus Gilman maintained that existing systems of censorship led not to cleaner movies but to corruption, harassment of filmmakers, and the unfortunate pacification of rightfully concerned citizens.[27]

In the early 1920s, the better movie movement earned Gilman and the Women's Cooperative Alliance acclaim among motion picture exhibitors, producers, and free speech activists—many of whom had little patience for other reformers. Henrietta Starkey, an exhibitor in Le Seuer, Minnesota, commended Gilman for her "broad minded and educated views." Heralding the potential for cooperation between exhibitors and reformers even as she highlighted nascent divisions among organized women, Starkey observed, "You have made a study of this problem, whereas the women of the Le Sueur County Republican Club who are advocating censorship are those who never attend a theatre, or when they do, it is an event to be recorded."[28] Twin Cities exhibitors joined Starkey in praise of the alliance's work. One in particular, Theodore Hayes, not only cheered alliance women but sought a collaborative affiliation with them. Alliance leaders instantly recognized in Hayes a valuable potential ally. Known as the "father of show business in the Northwest," he helped introduce motion pictures to Minneapolis audiences in the 1890s and, by the early 1920s, controlled twelve theaters, headed a local organization of exhibitors, the Theatrical Protective League, and earned respect as a major player on the national motion picture scene as well.[29] With the careful diplomacy of seasoned negotiators, alliance leaders responded to Hayes's overtures with a mild and mutually beneficial request. Hoping to curb children's late-night movie attendance, they asked him to project juvenile curfew laws onto the screen each evening. He not only agreed, but urged members of the Theatrical Protective League to adopt the policy. Many exhibitors found curfew violators annoying and welcomed the suggestion. They knew that poor working women sometimes used motion picture theaters as cheap child-care centers, allowing their children to attend movies well past the legal curfew as a way of providing some sort of supervision and distraction from mischief. Several exhibitors reported that unaccompanied children often fell asleep in the theater and, after awakening, could not recall their names or addresses, causing managers no small amount of trouble finding their homes.[30]

The agreeable interchange over juvenile curfew laws encouraged Gilman and Hayes to consult on other matters. On one occasion, alliance leaders asked Hayes to recommend a speaker involved with movie production to address their group. He complied and in return asked the alliance to propose a woman to help monitor the moral conditions associated with a new entertainment venture. Later that same year, alliance workers met with Hayes and other local theater managers to learn about the system of theater exchanges and the workings of a movie theater.[31] In these early days, alliance reformers and theater managers strove to educate and learn from each other. They not only cooperated but found common cause.

Alliance leaders also communicated to Hayes their approval and disapproval of individual films, sometimes relying on reports from better film committees but at other times viewing the films themselves.[32] Hayes agreed to forward complaints to producers and frequently simply shortened the run of a particularly "offensive" picture. But he also took advantage of these communications to demonstrate to the women that even reformers disagreed on films. For example, in response to an enthusiastic message from Gilman applauding the showing of *Hail the Woman*—a movie reported to contain "'freedom of women' propaganda"—Hayes thanked her for the ringing endorsement but enclosed a letter from a local clergyman who strenuously objected to the movie.[33] Like Starkey's complaint about women's clubs, the minister's letter reminded Gilman that even reform-minded citizens disagreed on which motion pictures were morally objectionable.

Disagreements among local reformers erupted in 1921 when the Minnesota state legislature considered two motion picture censorship bills. The bills' sponsors—"men who had helped with other social legislation"—confidently solicited a Women's Cooperative Alliance endorsement. Apologetically but firmly, Gilman refused, explaining that the alliance did not support official censorship.[34] Theodore Hayes, who also opposed the bills, knowing that state censorship would burden exhibitors, realized that cooperation with locally and nationally respected motion picture reformers would enhance the credibility of a campaign to block state censorship. He promptly appealed to the alliance for help.

Recognizing in Hayes's request for help several rare opportunities, Women's Cooperative Alliance leaders assented even though they knew that working with him would pit them against erstwhile partners in reform. Joining forces with Hayes not only offered them a chance to help avert what they perceived as the counterproductive and undemocratic establishment of state censorship; it also promised to strengthen the alliance's cooperative relationship with exhibitors and provide occasion for asking reciprocal favors. Above all, the alliance needed money. For the past year, it had failed to raise funds to publish its better movie movement reform plan—a plan that, as Gilman explained to Hayes, strengthened the alliance's anti-censorship stance by advocating cooperation with exhibitors as the most effective means of influencing filmmakers. Hayes agreed to cover the costs of publication. In exchange, alliance leaders testified against the censorship bills, urging reformers to be patient and "to give the movement which we had started among women only the year before, another two years' chance."[35]

Hollywood Scandals, Scandalous Pictures, and Self-Censorship

Exhibitors and reformers together subdued censorship forces in Minnesota. But around the country, state censorship achieved stunning victories in 1921 and 1922. Behind many of these censorship successes stood the General Federation of Women's Clubs. Throughout the first half of the 1910s, the General Federation managed to avoid the issue of motion picture reform, focusing instead on conventional club activities: literary pursuits, city beautification projects, clubhouse building, and, later, work for the war effort. Motion pictures appeared in the *General Federation Magazine* as opportunities for club entertainment and fundraising, subjects for review, and as advertisements—but not as reform causes. Many women's clubs enjoyed motion pictures and ignored the censorship issue, while others fought for state or federal censorship.

Individual clubs might have agreed to differ on motion picture reform. But in 1916, that possibility vanished when proliferating state and municipal censorship boards provoked a National Board of Review campaign to secure the cooperation of women's clubs. National Board representatives, following Robbins Gilman's example with the Woman's Welfare League of Minneapolis, appealed to individual clubs for their cooperation. Proponents from each side tried to win over the General Federation at its biennial convention. Chicago clubwomen presented a mildly pro-censorship resolution while a National Board of Review spokesman denounced official censorship, encouraging the General Federation to join forces with the National Board. Resulting arguments settled into a tense truce only after members agreed to postpone any policy decisions until a nationwide motion picture survey could be completed. Tensions erupted again at a 1917 meeting when the General Federation's Special Motion Picture Committee presented the results of its survey. After the committee's chair—Helen Varick Boswell, also an affiliate of the National Board—recommended that the General Federation oppose official censorship and cooperate with the National Board's better films movement, pandemonium ensued, leading to the swift dissolution of the motion picture committee. The National Board, meanwhile, continued to place regular articles in the *General Federation Magazine*, praising cooperating women's clubs and touting "the value of the motion picture." One filmmaker, Vitagraph, crafted an advertising campaign—if not a whole motion picture—specifically for clubwomen, billing *Womanhood, the Glory of the Nation* as a film that "every one of the 2,500,000 members of the General Federation of Women's Clubs should see," and offering a cash award for the best essay on the film's topic.[36] Clubwomen courageously revisited the motion picture question at their 1918 convention in Hot Springs, Arkansas. Once again, National Board supporters faced off against clubwomen bearing a pro-censorship resolution. In a scathing rebuke of both motion pictures and the National Board's better films movement, the resolution declared more than 25 percent of all motion pictures unfit for children and condemned the voluntary censorship methods of the National Board as ineffective and inappropriate uses of women's time. It is neither "the province, the duty, nor the desire of women to review films each day," the resolution declared, calling on clubwomen to work for state censorship. To the National Board's dismay, the resolution passed.[37]

The General Federation sustained immediate and unfair external assaults on its new pro-censorship agenda. *Moving Picture World,* a national magazine, launched a singularly pernicious attack by announcing that the General Federation had, in fact, *rejected* state censorship! Because the resolution's power derived from its ability to influence public opinion, inaccurate publicity threatened to neutralize clubwomen's work. Other publications reported the resolution accurately but criticized the General Federation for not giving the National Board a fair hearing, a charge belying the fact that National Board supporters had, if anything, dominated the convention's motion picture session. Stung or swayed by anti-censorship clubwomen, the *General Federation Magazine* responded to its critics by publishing in September of 1918 a series of anti-censorship articles by producers, exhibitors, National Board representatives, and even an editor of the cunning *Moving Picture World.* After pro-censorship clubwomen complained, articles representing their perspective appeared in the January 1919 issue.[38] And so it went, back and forth; the Pandora's box of motion picture reform refused to close.

In 1921, the National Board of Review confronted a major setback in its ongoing efforts to persuade the General Federation to reverse its 1918 state censorship resolution. That year, several scandals involving motion picture stars confirmed many women's suspicions of Hollywood immorality. In 1921, Roscoe "Fatty" Arbuckle, a film comedy star whose popularity rivaled Charlie Chaplin's, participated in a "wild drinking party" that linked him to the rape and death of a young and little-known actress, Virginia Rappe. Rappe became violently ill at the party and died a few days later, diagnosed with peritonitis caused by a ruptured bladder. Several testimonials and most newspaper accounts of her death implied that Arbuckle—a man of legendary proportions—crushed the young woman in the process of raping her. The courts concluded otherwise. After two hung juries, a third absolved Arbuckle of any wrongdoing. The law exonerated Arbuckle, but his employers—the public and the movie industry—proved less forgiving. At issue was not the content of Arbuckle's films but the character of the star himself.[39] The Women's Cooperative Alliance, clubwomen, and other organized women around the country demanded that Arbuckle be banned from the motion picture screen, invoking their roles as moral guardians of the nation's children in letter campaigns and press releases. As one branch of the General Federation asserted in a letter to the *New York Times*, despite Arbuckle's acquittal, "the testimony at his trial was of such a character as to bar him forever from appearing before a decent self-respecting public." The letter claimed to represent a vast and formidable group—"our membership of more than two million, the majority of whom are mothers," and all of whom, the letter might have pointed out, were potential voters.[40] Arbuckle's acquittal alleviated but did not eliminate the impact of the scandal on the General Federation and other women's organizations. That one of motion pictures' most famous stars had become entangled in such a gruesome incident called the morals of the entire industry into question.

Motion picture releases between 1919 and 1922 only deepened these fears. Treatments of rape and adultery in suggestively titled films such as *Male and Female*, *Why Change Your Wife?*, *Foolish Wives*, and *The Truth about Husbands* provoked protests around the nation. The latter drew particular ire from Minneapolis better film committee members, who condemned "the captions, the nude figures, the suggestive dancing, the banquet scene with all its sex appeal, the bedroom and bathroom scenes." Even more offensive than these individual elements was the overall message of the film, which "seemed to be to teach the double standard of morals and that the inevitable results should be cheerfully accepted by wives." Such movies signaled a shift toward racier rather than reformed motion picture fare. Hollywood scandals, coupled with scandalous motion pictures, energized censorship efforts around the country.[41] In 1921—the same year that Minnesota rebuffed state censorship—the New York legislature, prodded by local clubwomen and religious leaders, embraced it, becoming the sixth state to do so. Within a year, thirty-seven other state legislatures considered over one hundred different censorship bills, raising for the motion picture industry the specter of myriad capricious state censorship boards threatening to make distribution of films for a national market a nightmare.[42]

Motion picture industry leaders acted quickly to stem the tide of pro-censorship activism. In 1921, seventeen producers—among them, William Fox, David W. Griffith, Lewis J. Selznick, Carl Laemmle, Samuel Goldwyn, and Adolph Zukor—formed the Motion Picture Producers and Distributors of America (MPPDA), an organ of self-regulation that differed from the National Board of Censorship (Review) in several key respects. Unlike the National Board, which presented itself as a private reform organization, MPPDA founders candidly acknowledged that their organization served industry interests; they claimed, however, that the industry's interests were the public's interests and that the MPPDA would advance the cause of reform, by allowing producers to censor themselves and each other. To make their new organization effective, producers needed a skilled public relations representative. Suffering a tarnished public image, they sought someone with impeccable moral credentials, and, given their legislative difficulties, they also wanted someone politically well connected. Because the most prominent MPPDA producers were Jewish immigrants, and their most vocal detractors often employed anti-Semitic arguments, they also sought a native-born gentile. Will H. Hays suited their needs perfectly. Born in Indiana, an elder in the Presbyterian Church, postmaster general under President Warren G. Harding, and chair of the Republican National Committee, "Hays brought the respectability of mainstream middle America," an already legendary charisma, close personal relationships with General Federation leaders, and the savvy of a Washington politician to the film industry.[43]

The Hays Office, as the MPPDA's public relations bureau became known, quickly addressed a variety of pressing problems confronting the industry. After World War I, the movie production metropolis of Hollywood emerged and with it employee unionization, strikes, and boycotts. Studio heads, determined to maintain an open shop, responded like the Minneapolis Citizens Alliance and other employer groups around the country; they banded together, imposed lockouts, secured replacement workers, and refused to negotiate with union representatives or federal mediators. Even as they united against workers, the major studios forged a system to reduce competition among producers and gain control of film distribution and exhibition, integrating the motion picture industry horizontally and vertically. Such blatantly monopolistic practices did not escape federal notice, and in 1921 the Federal Trade Commission filed the first of many

Fig. 3.3 Will Hays (*center*), signing his initial contract with the Motion Picture Producers and Distributors of America, March 1922. Courtesy of the Indiana State Library

complaints against Adolph Zukor's combination, Famous Players-Lasky (Paramount). As attested by Will Hays's voluminous correspondence regarding labor and trade practice issues, the Hays Office addressed these concerns in tandem with censorship. Indeed, Hays considered censorship not only an evil in itself but an opening wedge to unwanted government intervention in the motion picture industry's labor relations.[44]

The Arbuckle scandal claimed Will Hays's immediate attention, dominating his initial strategy planning sessions. He first heeded clubwomen's demands and persuaded producers and distributors to cancel all showings of Arbuckle films, an act that amounted to the loss of tens of thousands of contracts, millions of dollars, and Arbuckle's motion picture career. In another frank overture to the nation's reform communities, Hays recruited representatives from more than sixty educational, religious, and reform organizations to staff his Committee on Public Relations. Will Hays required each member to renounce official censorship in return for influence over and knowledge about the inner workings of the MPPDA as well as generous funding for communications (mailings, travel, etc.) related to motion pictures. Realizing that, however desirable his New York location as an entrée to financial and political power, its remoteness from Hollywood severely limited his ability to supervise motion picture production, Hays appointed an MPPDA representative to monitor and report on industry conditions on the West Coast.[45]

Will Hays acted quickly on his concern about the pro-censorship work of organized women, the General Federation in particular. Organized women had achieved major reform goals through their voluntary associations, and now they approached politics, singly and in massive groups, with ballots in hand. Experienced political analysts voiced uncertainty as to how female voters would affect the political game. Would they form a women's political party? Would they promote a women's voting bloc? Would they disband women's organizations and join the political parties instead? The myriad possibilities concerned many observers, including Hays, who linked recent censorship victories to female enfranchisement and legislators' efforts to appeal to female constituents. With great interest, then, Hays scrutinized the new president of the General Federation, none other than Alice Ames Winter, founder of the Woman's Club of Minneapolis.[46]

Soon after assuming the highest office of the largest women's organization in the nation, Winter began to field questions about the General Federation's plans for its newly enfranchised membership. No, she assured her audience, the General Federation did not support a women's party. Nor did it condone "sex antagonism" in government. It would remain "non-political," but continue to promote female solidarity on what Winter called questions of justice. "No matter what our party affiliations," she counseled clubwomen, "we women should stand together for social welfare legislation."[47] Winter's statements received overwhelmingly positive responses from clubwomen and from journalists. One reporter expressed approval of Winter in a parody of feminists:

> [Alice Ames Winter seems] to have no respect for the idea that the sexes must declare war upon each other . . . We [feminists] . . . cannot understand such a cast of mind—in a woman. We know that the natural antagonist of woman is man . . . We want the war of the sexes . . . Our program is simple. We are against anything the men are for . . . If the women will but unite, we can make a clean sweep of the elections . . . We will then have an all-woman government, and nothing else will sat-

Fig. 3.4 Alice Ames Winter, 1923. Courtesy of the Minnesota Historical Society

isfy us . . . We deny vigorously the imputation that we intend to abolish men. The most we intend to do is to subjugate and enslave them as they have subjugated and enslaved women in the past . . . Our movement is now underway . . . But how can we keep our gallant fight when such women as Mrs. Winter strike us blows like these? No hostility to the brutes, indeed! No use for the sex war, indeed! Well, we [feminists] know where we stand. Henceforth, Mrs. Winter is on our blacklist.[48]

Voicing contemporary apprehensions about woman suffrage, this satirist recognized in Winter one women's leader who could help prevent those fears from becoming a reality.

Hays, too, had reason to feel optimistic about Winter's presidency, even though her position on the motion picture issue remained something of a mys-

tery at the time of her election. Winter took no part in Minneapolis theater reform and managed to escape the motion picture debates at the General Federation's recent biennial conventions. But Winter and Hays had met before, in the
course of campaigning for Warren G. Harding, and Hays suspected that Winter's deep commitment to the Republican Party would work in his favor. If Winter had not taken a side on the motion picture issue before becoming president,
her position began to develop soon after. Not only did she commend motion pictures in the national press, but she exhibited little enthusiasm for the General
Federation's 1918 state censorship resolution. She also maintained close ties with
General Federation women who were close friends of Hays: Frances Diehl and
Anna Pennybacker.[49]

These very friends helped Hays secure an invitation to address the 1922 biennial convention of the General Federation—an engagement he approached
with trepidation, knowing that he desperately needed to persuade clubwomen to
denounce censorship and cooperate with his organization.[50] His odds of winning
over a group still seething over the Arbuckle scandal and so recently receptive to
censorship must have seemed long. Sparing no flattery, he assured his audience
that American womanhood had already done a tremendous amount of good for
the nation. "There is no organized movement of people," he continued, "which
can accomplish more for the general welfare than the organized womanhood of
the country as represented by you." The balance of the speech argued against
censorship and for consumer-driven reform. Public opinion expressed through
box office receipts, Will Hays contended, would impose adequate pressure on
motion picture producers. General Federation members need not be passive;
they could assist the process of motion picture reform by endorsing good films
publicly and attending them regularly. To help clubwomen relate personally to
his message that they could simultaneously support morality in movies *and* oppose censorship, Hays offered the audience an analogy between film and fash-
ion. You "are for modesty in dress," he pointed out. "Yet you are against political censorship of fashions . . . You do not want any public official to have the right
to walk up to you at the post-office and take out a yard stick and proceed to determine whether you are within or without the law." Closing, he exhorted the
women to be patient, registering their opinions at the box office while avoiding
seductive yet destructive appeals for official censorship.[51]

Hays rejoiced over the immediate fruits of his labor. On the last day of the
convention, the General Federation replaced its earlier pro-censorship resolution with one condemning censorship and pledging to cooperate with the

MPPDA and Hays. Hays's speech must have been compelling, but his success cannot be attributed to eloquence alone. Just as his personal connections paved the way for his speaking engagement, they also played an important role in his ability to obtain the General Federation's ratification of an anti-censorship resolution. Admitting this in a private letter to Pennybacker—a General Federation chairwoman whose approval sealed the resolution—Hays expressed gratitude for her "help in all of the matters in which we are interested. The things you are doing are not only the greatest help of all, but a great comfort."[52]

Will Hays scored a momentous victory with the General Federation of Women's Clubs. But, as he soon learned, leading the MPPDA required superior juggling skills. And in 1922, the balls just kept coming at him as legislature after legislature considered bills for state censorship.

The Massachusetts Referendum, 1922

Massachusetts was unique. Its clubwomen and other reformers pushed a state censorship bill through to a popular vote, producing the only motion picture referendum in the nation's history. "It would be very serious if it passed," an MPPDA agent wrote to Will Hays, "as it would establish precedent for the first time in this country that the people by their own vote were in favor of political censorship of a method of expression." Hired to ward off just such threats, Hays organized a campaign to defeat the referendum, dispatching MPPDA agents to Boston to join forces with a budding indigenous group, the Committee of Massachusetts Citizens against Censorship. Together, these anti-censorship activists blanketed the state with propaganda and campaign workers, using the motion picture screen to publicize their cause and the ward and precinct system to organize their efforts.[53] Anticipating the appeal of military heroes to citizens still raw from "the Great War," Hays capitalized on the popularity of Brigadier General Charles H. Cole, chairman of the Massachusetts anti-censorship committee, and even showcased "one-armed and one-legged veterans" who supported his cause.[54] Hays personally secured—and sometimes purchased—"the good will and editorial support of newspapers and influential public men," ranging from Joseph Kennedy, ministers, and leaders of the Anti-Saloon League to justices of the state supreme court, paying special attention to the Catholic clergy in this heavily Catholic state.[55] Ingeniously, Hays united these disparate groups by combining themes of patriotism with suspicion of state power, insisting that, if passed, the referendum would violate American values by imposing "political censorship." Playing fast and loose with history, his agents pointed out that "political censorship drove the Pilgrims to Plymouth Rock; political censorship faced the Minute men at Concord; political censorship caused the Boston Tea Party."[56]

Newly enfranchised women voters would play an important role in the outcome of the contest. Home to more charter clubs of the General Federation than any other state, Massachusetts tested Hays's ability to sway female voters, and he carefully crafted his campaign strategy with them in mind. "See that women are featured in this campaign," his agents directed. "The moral effect of their being publicly known as being with us is important . . . Name them on committees. President [*sic*] of branches—interviews—Have them phoning and phoned to." Suspecting that Massachusetts clubwomen would respond more positively to a sister reformer than to an MPPDA employee, Hays scoured the country for women who both opposed censorship and possessed impeccable reform credentials. Unsurprisingly, his eyes fell on Gilman.[57]

By 1922 the Minneapolis better movie movement had gained nationwide attention. Leaders in motion picture reform and the motion picture industry commended Gilman and the Women's Cooperative Alliance. National magazines and newspapers praised the organization's "very liberal and intelligent attitude toward motion pictures." Thanks to funds recently provided by Theodore Hayes, the alliance enhanced its own national reputation by printing and disseminating literature on its motion picture reform plan. A National Board of Review representative who received a copy of the alliance's plan declared it "more effective than any other" and, with Gilman's permission, printed and distributed yet more copies of it. In addition, Will Hays's Minneapolis contacts informed him of Gilman's triumphant collaboration with Theodore Hayes to defeat state censorship in Minnesota.[58] By 1922, few Americans interested in motion picture reform and industry issues had failed to hear about Gilman and the Minneapolis better movie movement.

Gilman possessed all of the qualities Will Hays needed—a national reputation among reformers, dedication to cooperative reform strategies, and a record of effective anti-censorship activity. Two months before the Massachusetts referendum, Hays invited Gilman to New York to present her anti-censorship motion picture reform plan to the MPPDA strategy board.[59] Impressed, the MPPDA offered to finance the implementation of Gilman's plan in Massachusetts, providing Gilman herself with $150 for each week she spent there. Gilman agreed and a couple of weeks later she and five other alliance women began to reproduce their better movie movement in Massachusetts, recruiting small groups of educational, religious, and social leaders to monitor local theaters, communicate with the National Board, and "cooperate with Mr. Hays in shaping public opinion for the production of better films." As in Minnesota, Gilman endeavored to develop a motion picture evaluation system and a procedure for citizens to communicate their concerns to exhibitors and filmmakers—a plan that promised to relieve pressure for censorship by diverting reformers' energies toward cooperative reform activities. For several weeks, Gilman and her MPPDA-financed entourage of trained organizers and educators toured the state, interviewing community leaders, delivering speeches against censorship, circulating MPPDA literature, disseminating MPPDA-funded copies of the Women's Cooperative Alliance's better movie movement plan, and advocating cooperation with the motion picture industry.[60]

Not for the first time, Gilman found herself torn between loyalty to reformers and opposition to their censorship agenda. In the sponsors of the Massachusetts referendum, Gilman once again confronted erstwhile allies—clubwomen, suffragists, and others whose cause Gilman shared but whose methods she opposed. Even as she prevailed upon them to reject censorship, she understood their reluctance "to repudiate their own bill." By the end of her stint in Massachusetts, though, Gilman's empathy ebbed. In communications with the MPPDA, she described pro-censorship groups as "unreasonable and disagreeable," explaining that pro-censorship activity "was more aggressive in the women's organizations, especially in the Woman's Club and the League of Women Voters." Other MPPDA agents agreed, citing "the hostile attitude of women, particularly those of mature age, including mothers" as "the greatest difficulty of the campaign."[61]

While Gilman and her coworkers complained about their female opponents in Massachusetts, some male MPPDA officials complained about their female *allies*, including Gilman. No documents lay out the precise nature of the complaint, but MPPDA efforts to reassure Gilman indicate that two of Hays's men resented women's involvement in politics. Entreating Gilman not to take the men too seriously, Hays's right-hand man, Courtland Smith, explained that her detractors "were old time politicians and could not understand the place women were taking in politics today." Hays, however, the architect of the Massachusetts anti-censorship campaign, heartily approved of Gilman's work, finding it more than worth the nearly $5,000 it cost. He appreciated the political potential of women's combined moral status and electoral power and, through Gilman and her coworkers, attempted to harness both for his own ends.[62]

Armed with a hefty purse earmarked for anti-censorship work, Hays spent upwards of $300,000 to hire assistants, buy advertisements, and collaborate with the local press to convince Massachusetts voters that censorship violated American ideals. Doing so in the middle of a Red Scare produced a striking paradox. Journalists allied with Hays inveighed against Red Scare–inspired censorship, calling the Massachusetts referendum "the first step toward the death of free speech in this country" and directly linking the Red Scare with motion picture censorship. At the same time that reporters denounced the censorship tactics of Red-baiters, they capitalized on fears of Soviet Communism by comparing the Massachusetts referendum to Soviet censorship. "In Russia," noted one article suggestively, "they can suppress a picture . . . a photograph or a drawing just because the Government does not like it." Still another insisted that censorship such as that contained in the Massachusetts referendum mirrored government repression in Russia.[63] Thus, in a complicated but effective media ploy, Will Hays and his allies denounced the excesses of the Red Scare even as they aggravated and appropriated fears of Communism for their own purposes.

With election day on the horizon, Hays and his associates exchanged compliments and expressions of confidence. At the end of a creative, energetic, and costly campaign, advance surveys and political analysts predicted a victory for anti-censorship forces. But knowing the devastation a defeat would inflict upon the motion picture industry provoked great anxiety among them. "TODAY IS THE DAY," announced a telegram from Henry Hogan, a Massachusetts-based MPPDA agent, to Hays on the morning of November 7, 1922. Hogan kept Western Union busy all day, wiring frequent updates on the weather, electoral turnout, and vote returns. Finally, at 4:51 P.M., he sent the message for which Hays had been waiting: "CONGRATULATIONS THE VICTORY IN A LARGE MEASURE A PERSONAL TRIBUTE TO YOU."[64]

Will Hays's clever tactics had brought a resounding defeat to state censorship in Massachusetts. During the campaign itself, he lay low, directing his partisans—political allies, female reformers, and journalists among them—from behind the lines. At the time, Gilman commended him "for thinking that the State people and women's groups have the right to decide this issue." Although hindsight would lead many women to reinterpret as Machiavellian his strategy of recruiting women outside of Massachusetts to campaign among women within the state, in 1922 Gilman saw it as an effort to empower women in general and Massachusetts voters in particular.[65] Soon after learning that two-thirds of the state's voters rejected the censorship measure, Courtland Smith cabled Gilman the news, thanking her for her "valuable support." Gilman wired back, "Rejoice with you on Mass. situation. It was a glorious victory. Hope it will be followed wisely with effective action for the future. Many are waiting eagerly for the next move." Having fought against censorship in order to facilitate cooperation between consumers, reformers, exhibitors, and producers for the improvement of motion pictures, Gilman eagerly anticipated phase two of the project. Meanwhile, Will Hays fully exploited the defeated referendum, invoking it as proof that Americans opposed motion picture censorship.[66]

As the Massachusetts campaign suggests, in the early 1920s shifts in the local context as well as transformations on the national political scene generated dramatic changes in women's anti-obscenity politics. Free speech and censorship emerged as major political issues in response to wartime and postwar speech restrictions, such that, by 1920, planks supporting free speech began to appear in the major party platforms. These developments encouraged the Women's Cooperative Alliance to align its anti-obscenity campaign with opposition to censorship even as other segments of society exploited government censorship to further their own agendas. Many clubwomen, for example, believing that military mobilization and wartime dislocations had loosened moral standards but that a public accustomed to wartime speech restrictions might quietly accept extending those to motion pictures, seized upon censorship as a means of returning the motion picture, at least, to prewar values.[67] Armed with the ballot, clubwomen attracted the attention of major players in the motion picture industry. Women's grassroots activism posed serious threats to the motion picture industry in the early 1920s. While the motion picture industry's reputation suffered as a result of sex scandals and racy pictures, and producers had just begun to organize, middle-class women not only symbolized morality—they transformed it into authority through their long-established organizations. In 1922 they also represented a potential female voting bloc that inspired Will Hays—like theater managers William Koenig and Theodore Hayes, before him—to associate his industry more closely with organized women, both to capitalize on their moral authority and to deter them from organizing against him.

Women's Cooperative Alliance leaders glimpsed success on the horizon as they negotiated with producers, exhibitors, and even the celebrated Will Hays from what seemed an unprecedented position of power—as moral authorities, heirs to the triumphant Woman's Welfare League, representatives and leaders of an incipient female voting bloc, and as women willing to play politics in order to gain access to men with power and money. They had helped motion picture men defeat censorship in two states and looked forward to their new allies' assistance with their anti-obscenity campaign. In 1922, the young decade still seemed to promise a golden age that was theirs to make.

CHAPTER FOUR

"Woman vs. Woman"

The Leading Ladies of Motion Picture Reform, 1923–1930

Motion pictures needed the influence of womanhood. On that, Catheryne Cooke Gilman and Alice Ames Winter agreed, as suggested by their eagerness to cooperate with Will Hays on motion picture reform. They also agreed that maternity and domesticity defined and unified womanhood, drawing women, in Winter's words, into a union "greater than their diversity." Echoing her, Gilman declared that women's shared experiences transcended religion, party, race, and class.[1] Ironically, these pronouncements of female unity presaged open warfare within the ranks of organized American women and between Gilman and Winter. Between 1923 and 1930, motion pictures and obscenity issues provided their battleground. Most female reformers and clubwomen agreed that indecent modern movies imperiled the morals of youth, but they disagreed passionately over which movies qualified as indecent and what should be done about them. Although Winter and Gilman shared a common approach to motion picture reform in the early 1920s, they soon found themselves leaders of bitterly opposed factions, battling each other in an effort to earn organized women's loyalty and advance their respective motion picture reform agendas. But why would these two women, both committed to womanhood and to motion picture reform, wage a war against each other, dividing their beloved sisterhood and making a mockery of the golden-age visions that tantalized so many organized women in the wake of their suffrage and anti-censorship victories?

Realignments in Reform

Relations between the Women's Cooperative Alliance and Minneapolis business leaders soured between 1922 and 1924. Recall that businessmen who directed the Community Fund—mostly members of the Citizens Alliance network—conveyed their suspicions of the Women's Cooperative Alliance leadership at the outset, demanding that Gilman disclaim "socialistic tendencies" and establish a men's committee. By 1921, having received only a halfhearted response from Gilman, they cut the women's budget, declaring publicly that they could not fund the women's court committee or budding sex education program, because such activities did not fit the social welfare rubric of the Community Fund.[2] Privately, they called the women's sex education work "repulsive," and complained that "women in the court rooms were intimidating the judges and coercing the jury." But Gilman and her colleagues clung to control over their work even as men tightened the purse strings. Unwilling to compromise the alliance's agenda or its integrity by submitting to Community Fund requirements, Gilman and her coworkers voted, in 1922, to withdraw from the fund and raise their budget independently.[3]

That same year, they abandoned the Committee of Thirteen, yet another local organization controlled by the Citizens Alliance network. Gilman had joined the group anticipating that it would supplement police efforts to eliminate rape, prostitution, bootlegging, and obscene amusements. In 1920, she applauded the committee for breaking up a prostitution ring headed by Mike Weisman and uncovering Prohibition violations that implicated several municipal officials, but she became disenchanted when the committee suppressed radicals and labor organizers while bungling or neglecting prostitution and obscenity cases referred by the women. When Gilman finally severed ties with the Committee of Thirteen, she cited "fundamental" conscience problems.[4] The Women's Cooperative Alliance's efforts to work with the Community Fund and the Committee of Thirteen ultimately collapsed over the fundamental incompatibility of their agendas. As Gilman wrote later, each group pursued an agenda set by members of the Citizens Alliance network—"those whose business practices are at the root of the cause of social maladjustments which social workers attempt to remedy." These men, she concluded, cared more about their own property and power than "protective work for women and children."[5]

Gilman's inability to work with business groups developed largely out of basic conflicts between the interests of social workers and businessmen. However, because Gilman also held gender differences responsible for the fallout, she failed to anticipate the negative response of other women's organizations to the alliance's new policies. Even though members of the Woman's Club of Minneapolis had helped to establish the Women's Cooperative Alliance and had maintained an official affiliation with it, clubwomen ended their support after the alliance withdrew from the Community Fund. "Sympathy with the Community Fund," they decided, required them to cut all connections with the Women's Cooperative Alliance and demand that the alliance discard all letterhead listing the Woman's Club as an affiliate.[6] The secession of the Woman's Club from its board would be the Women's Cooperative Alliance's first serious indication of trouble within the ranks of organized women.

Still reeling from these local setbacks, Gilman began to question the intentions of Will Hays—her recent businessman-ally in the Massachusetts anticensorship campaign—when the interminable Arbuckle scandal once again reared its ugly head. Despite organized women's virtually unanimous and steadfast opposition to Arbuckle's screen return, Hays announced in 1922 that he would no longer stand in Arbuckle's way, a decision that came at the end of several months of pressure from Arbuckle, Arbuckle's wife, motion picture producers, and "15,000" disgruntled motion picture industry employees on the West Coast. Public censure of Hays's reversal came more quickly. Newspapers published more than five hundred critical editorials within a week of his announcement, and one senator introduced a new federal censorship bill. Hays's own Committee on Public Relations issued a resolution urging him to prevent Arbuckle from reappearing on screen. Women's groups canceled addresses by motion picture industry speakers, and the Women's Cooperative Alliance of Minneapolis at once mailed Hays a protest letter, as did the General Federation of Women's Clubs. Anxious to escape the overwhelmingly negative reaction to his policy shift, Hays worked furiously to quiet the criticism by procuring for Arbuckle a position behind the scenes, literally. A flurry of coded telegrams between Hays and his Hollywood representatives resulted in a directing contract that would keep Arbuckle out of the public eye—a brilliant recovery for Hays, albeit one that failed to mollify Gilman, the Women's Cooperative Alliance, and the General Federation.[7]

Will Hays became especially concerned about his relations with Alice Ames Winter, the General Federation's new president. Her popularity had soared by 1922, as she streamlined the federation's archaic organizational structure, nearly doubled its membership, and purchased its first headquarters in Washington, D.C. Clubwomen admired her writing and acting talent as well. In January of 1923, one of her articles, "What's Your Market Value, Madame?"—an argument for remunerating women's housework—became *This Wife Business*, a motion picture with Winter in the leading role. Knowing that he could not afford to lose the much-loved Winter's support, Hays privately assured Winter that film companies would not release movies starring Arbuckle. He and Winter then planned a series of motion picture conferences for clubwomen to discuss how they could cooperate with producers. Later in 1923, Winter accepted an invitation from Hays to tour the major studios in Hollywood. Identified by him as an important ally of the motion picture industry, Winter received the royal treatment, meeting female executives and dining with movie stars. As Hays and his agents hoped, she concluded her visit with a statement for the Associated Press, endorsing producers' efforts to improve motion pictures while exclaiming, "Women are doing wonderful work in the motion picture industry."[8]

Even as Winter's relations with the motion picture industry warmed, Gilman's chilled. From Gilman's perspective, Will Hays, Theodore Hayes, and the National Board of Review had reneged on their promises to hold motion pictures to high moral standards. Not only had Will Hays retracted his ban on Arbuckle, but Gilman saw no evidence that the motion picture industry had begun to clean itself up.[9] Writing in 1924 to Theodore Hayes—the exhibitor with whom she had worked to defeat Minnesota censorship—Gilman stated flatly, "The motion picture situation has not improved." On the contrary, recent releases indicated an alarming increase in "salacious" and "suggestive" motion pictures. Titillating titles matched content in *Manhandled, Changing Husbands,* and *Worldly Goods*; Paramount's new film, *Enemy Sex,* featured "wild parties," "highly sexual" situations, and a heroine who seduced a succession of men, at least one of them married. *Three Weeks,* a less sensationally titled but even more risqué motion picture, featured a heroine who draped herself seductively across a tiger skin, inflaming a young man's passions until "the inevitable" happened. When Theodore Hayes suggested that perhaps movie fans desired such entertainment, Gilman retorted that, by pandering to unhealthy "interest or curiosity" in sex, filmmakers actually produced it. Exhibitors should show "only those films which could be passed by a sincere but broad-minded group of women," she declared.[10] Disenchantment with the National Board of Review heightened Gilman's conviction that, with regard to motion pictures, only women could exercise sound judgment, untainted by commercial pressures. The National Board had begun to pass movies that Gilman and other reformers found "questionable" or "detrimental," its priorities inclining ever more sharply toward the interests of filmmakers. A series of investigative articles published in the *Brooklyn Daily Eagle* revealed what Robbins Gilman, a participant in several National Board meetings, had also discovered. Motion picture producers attended National Board meetings and intervened to rescue films threatened with condemnation. The board's credibility slipped so low that, when the Gilmans finally canceled their memberships in 1924, they joined an impressive list of national women's organizations including the Women's Christian Temperance Union and the National Congress of Parents and Teachers.[11] Severing their connection with the National Board of Review, the information clearinghouse of the alliance's better movie movement in Minneapolis, brought an end to the Gilmans' support for cooperative motion picture reform.

The Women's Cooperative Alliance's optimistic efforts to reform motion pictures through consumer pressure and cooperation with the industry faltered on a number of unanticipated developments. Most basic of all, the agendas of reformers and businessmen diverged sharply. After alliance women discovered that local businessmen never intended to advance reform efforts but instead to co-opt and control their work, they approached motion picture industry representatives with suspicion and impatience. Equally important, corporate consolidation undermined consumer power and the efficacy of locally based cooperative reform. Like their forebears in the railroad, steel, and meatpacking industries, motion picture producers pursued a course of corporate consolidation that undermined local influence and autonomy while maximizing Hollywood producers' control and profits. Most egregious from the exhibitor's perspective was the ingenious practice of block booking. In order to obtain a popular Mary Pickford film, for example, exhibitors had to rent several other films of lesser quality and questionable moral content. Under this system, pioneered by Adolph Zukor in the late 1910s, exhibitors bore nearly the entire financial burden of box office failures while producers profited on each film made, regardless of box office appeal. By combining production and distribution within one corporate structure, producers strengthened themselves at great cost to local exhibitors and, by extension, reformers. Block booking rendered better film committees impotent. Exhibitors in Minnesota complained loudly against producers' "unfair trade practices," insisting that they could not be held responsible for the quality of their motion pictures while these practices remained in place. Gilman and many other reformers agreed, believing that, in the absence of block booking, most exhibitors would cater to the wishes of the community—or at least the vocal elements within it.[12] Paradoxically, then, centralizing industry maneuvers ultimately disabled the consumerist and cooperative reform strategies promoted by the National Board of Review and the Hays Office, two of centralization's pioneers.

Gilman accepted differences of opinion and priorities when she entered into cooperative endeavors with motion picture people. She realized, for example, that, whereas she blamed movies for juvenile delinquency, producers and exhibitors blamed parents. And she understood that she would have to help defeat impending state censorship before producers and exhibitors would help her improve motion pictures. But she expected a two-way street of cooperation and resented it when Theodore Hayes and Will Hays neglected to hold up their end of the bargain. Feeling misled and manipulated by 1924, Gilman publicly apologized for helping Theodore Hayes defeat state censorship in Minnesota. She still opposed censorship, but regretted fighting against it without offering a more realistic reform strategy. In a dramatic reassessment of Will Hays, she told a friend that his goal in bringing her into the Massachusetts anti-censorship campaign was to "secure my services to exploit women's organizations." Henceforth, she resolved to have nothing "further to do with his plan for organizing the women of the United States to secure better motion pictures."[13] Thus growing alienation from cooperation with business, in general, and the motion picture industry, in particular, led Gilman to abandon her better movie movement and to question the utility of local motion picture reform efforts.

At the same time, Will Hays, already persuaded by Gilman that local better film committees deterred censorship, began actively to encourage such work. After the Massachusetts anti-censorship victory, two of Hays's closest advisers strongly encouraged him to continue the "better picture" work of "Mrs. Gilman" and her entourage of women. "The greatest difficulty of the campaign arose from the hostile attitude of women," they explained, and better film activities calmed and diverted that hostility by giving women something to do, calling their attention to their own disagreements over particular movies, and distracting them from legislative remedies.[14] Between 1922 and 1924, Hays invested heavily in women's better film committees, and, when he convinced President Alice Ames Winter to incorporate better film committee work into the General Federation agenda, he handily replaced Gilman as leader of women cooperating with the movie industry.[15]

In Winter, Hays found a more prominent and loyal ally, though one who had nearly completed her two-term limit as General Federation president. Indeed, when Winter stepped down in June of 1924, Hays's problems with the General Federation began all over again. Winter's successor, Mary King Sherman, instigated an immediate reconsideration of the organization's motion picture policy. Noting that the National Congress of Parents and Teachers (National PTA) had recently declared the Hays Office ineffective at improving movies and had discontinued its affiliation, Sherman's executive council voted in closed session to authorize her to do likewise. Hays got wind of this highly confidential discussion shortly afterward, informed by two of his many General Federation friends. Temporarily headquartered in Hollywood, he plotted strategy with his most trusted New York associates via telegram and telephone, directing them to arrange a meeting with Sherman.[16] The meeting, of February 20, 1925, in Washington, D.C., did not go well from Hays's perspective. At the outset, Sherman announced her opposition to maintaining a relationship with the Hays Office. Motion pictures had not improved, she declared. Nor would they as long as block booking negated the influence of local better film committees. Like Gilman, she concluded that Hays simply used affiliated women's groups as a "smoke screen." Hays's associates, discouraged by what they called Sherman's "cold and cynical" demeanor, reported that they had made no headway. Two months later, Sherman issued a press release stating that the General Federation would no longer cooperate with the Hays Office.[17]

With delight, Gilman joined forces with the new General Federation president as she and a host of leaders among women and Protestants created the Federal Motion Picture Council, an organization committed to federal motion picture regulation. "Only a centralized authority," Federal Council members agreed, "can effectively regulate the centralized Motion Picture Industry."[18] Their plan relied heavily on the Federal Trade Commission, an independent regulatory body created in 1914 to enforce antitrust laws. As a tool, the FTC could eliminate unfair business practices like block booking, practices that corrupted politics as well as commerce, by empowering motion picture monopolists who defeated troublesome reform bills by bribing public officials and controlling filmed political advertisements. In the absence of such regulation, Federal Council literature declared, "our democratic form of government of the people, for the people, by the people, has been changed into a government of the Trust, for the Trust, by the Trust." Federal Council members also saw the FTC as a prototype for a motion picture commission—a body that would join the system of federal regulation already widely accepted by Americans. Instead of monitoring food and drug production or railroad operations, for example, this new agency would supervise the motion picture industry, inspecting and modifying, if necessary, films containing "sex, white slavery, illicit love, nudity, crime, gambling, or excessive drinking." Like the FTC, a federal motion picture commission would have a legislatively mandated membership ratio, but one that took gender into account as well as political affiliation; women would occupy at least four of the commission's nine seats.[19]

Differing understandings of democracy, definitions of censorship, and concepts of moral authority brought Federal Council members into conflict with

Will Hays and leaders of the fledgling American Civil Liberties Union (ACLU). All agreed that obscenity existed, could be defined, and should be suppressed, but they disagreed over proper procedures for determining and eliminating obscenity. Federal Council leaders insisted that without federal regulation motion picture producers like Adolph Zukor and William Fox, both Eastern European Jews, would "be the real censors of what films the children of America shall see." Neither had been born in the United States or elected by popular vote. Neither answered to the mothers and fathers of America. Nor was either a public servant motivated by concern for the commonweal. Zukor and Fox, corporate giants motivated by profits, answered to their stockholders. The federal government, by contrast, consisted of elected representatives motivated by the public good and accountable to the people. A distinct strain of xenophobia accompanied the Federal Council's anti-business bias. Even Gilman, who, like her mentor Jane Addams, usually emphasized immigrant contributions to American culture, occasionally resorted to xenophobic rhetoric. "Those who do not respect our institutions, do not even understand them," she wrote in 1925, "should not be permitted to remain in a position to teach through the eye, the most effective medium." Thus Federal Council leaders argued that a federal motion picture commission would not undermine America's democratic traditions but preserve them by replacing profit-seeking, foreign-born businessmen as the arbiters of motion picture decency with officials chosen for their public spiritedness and high moral values.[20] Hays concurred that moral leaders should shape motion picture content, but insisted that producers rather than politicians appoint and empower them, as in his cooperation with women's better film committees. Only such a system of self-regulation would preserve free speech and free enterprise, Hays argued. Leaders of the ACLU disagreed, calling both of these systems despotic. Obscenity, they maintained, should be determined democratically, by a jury. Inasmuch as juries in most states in the 1920s and 1930s barred women from serving, the ACLU threatened to expel women as arbiters of obscenity even as Hays and the Federal Council invited them in.[21]

Women quickly assumed leadership of the Federal Motion Picture Council. Within one year of its formation, Gilman delivered the keynote speech at the organization's annual conference. Meanwhile, Maude Aldrich, another charter member, became the Federal Council's field secretary and major spokesperson, delivering "some 300 addresses" on motion pictures in 1926. Along with several men on the Federal Council, Aldrich and Gilman testified before Congress on behalf of federal motion picture legislation. After the death of the organization's first president, Dr. Charles Scanlon, in 1927, the board of directors agreed that motion picture reform was " ultimately a woman's responsibility," and suggested that a woman succeed Scanlon. Gilman's election to the presidency brought a subtle shift in the organization's regulation rhetoric, from analogies with meat-packing and railroads to child labor laws and children's courts.[22] The new child-focused agenda and female leadership appealed to thousands of women and their organizations. Seventy-seven organizations endorsed federal motion picture regulation and several major national women's groups affiliated formally with the Federal Motion Picture Council. These included, at various times, the Women's Christian Temperance Union, the National Council of Women, the General Federation of Women's Clubs, and eventually the National Congress of Parents and Teachers.[23]

Many organized women, realizing that Will Hays sustained a major blow when Gilman and Sherman turned against him to launch the Federal Motion Picture Council, worried that Hays would locate and groom a new leader from within their ranks. "The Hays group immediately cultivates members of any committee appointed by the General Federation, puts them on the Hays committees and otherwise destroys their value for the Federation," one leading club-woman lamented. "The industry leaves no strategic person untempted," Gilman agreed, thinking back to her own experience, no doubt.[24] As she suspected, Hays worked diligently to recruit women's organizations, addressing their assemblies, commending better film committees, promoting programs for children's mati-nees, cultivating relations with well-placed women, and even sponsoring the pro-duction of a movie, *Rising Woman*, that featured leaders among organized women.[25] Hays experienced some success, especially with clubwomen, but they required constant attention. Charles Pettijohn, Hays's general counsel, scored a real victory when he gained a foothold within the Chicago Board of Censor-ship and the Chicago Women's City Club through Mary Langworthy, the board's civil service examiner and the club's president. Langworthy quieted several women who opposed Hays, persuaded others to support him, and procured a particularly important exhibition permit from the city's censors. Another Hays agent capitalized on friendly relations with Rita McGoldrick, a leader in the In-ternational Federation of Catholic Alumnae, to obtain inside information on a New Jersey censorship resolution. Meanwhile, Augusta L. Fraser, an influential clubwoman in San Diego, kept southern California women's censorship senti-ment in check.[26] Most important, in 1928 Bettie Monroe Sippel, an acquaintance of Will Hays, replaced Sherman as General Federation president; Sippel removed the current motion picture chair, a member of Gilman's Federal Motion Picture Council, and appointed Frances Diehl, a close personal friend of Hays.[27] Cheered by Sippel's election and Diehl's appointment, Hays nevertheless tired of watching his public relations fortunes career up and down with the comings and goings of General Federation presidents.

By the end of the decade, Hays's legal problems multiplied when Federal Motion Picture Council complaints and exhibitor protests about the industry's trade practices began to bear fruit in the form of government investigations and legislative proposals. In 1927, the Federal Trade Commission ordered Paramount Pictures to discontinue its block-booking practices, and two years later Senator Smith Brookhart (R-Iowa) introduced a bill to prohibit block booking and other restrictive trade measures. These charges prompted a governmental investigation, which was a "very serious matter" to Hays—indeed, one serious enough to attract the attention of his friend, President Herbert Hoover.[28]

In August 1929, Hoover informed Hays, "Your industry is causing me a lot of worry." Hays admitted that the motion picture industry might be guilty of "overreaching," and he apologized, assuring Hoover that he "would go to the limit to relieve you and the Administration" of any negative repercussions from the industry's dealings. Still, Hays needed Hoover's help, first, with the Justice Department, where Hoover agreed to put in a good word for Hays, and second, with the General Federation of Women's Clubs. Hays enjoyed the support of the current General Federation president, Bettie Sippel. But, Hays informed Hoover, Sippel felt unwelcome at the White House, because she thought another clubwoman had slandered her in Hoover's presence. If Hoover would develop "an intimate personal relation with Mrs. Sippel," he could help Hays strengthen his alliance with the General Federation. Sippel "is much abler and is going to have a much greater influence in affairs of that group than Mrs. Sherman," Hays declared. Then, as if unaware of his own disruptive influence on the General Federation, Hays closed with a curious observation: "There is more monkey business politically in that Federation outfit than in both the political Parties combined."[29]

"The Woman's Ambassador": Representing and Dividing Organized Women

Although pleased with Bettie Sippel, after four years of flattering and pacifying a bevy of unruly clubwomen, Hays cast about for a new plan, one that would stabilize his support and boost his public relations by streamlining his work with clubwomen and distracting attention from the troublesome Federal Motion Picture Council. First, he created the Studio Relations Committee, headed by Colonel Jason Joy, to provide representatives from major women's organizations—like the General Federation of Women's Clubs and the International Federation of Catholic Alumnae—the opportunity to "preview" and evaluate motion pictures in a special Hollywood projection room, develop lists of recommended films by category, and air-mail them to local branches and communities around the nation—all on Hays's budget. Second, growing more and more disconcerted by the Federal Council's annual conferences, Hays staged his own "National Conference on Motion Pictures" in 1929, with motion picture activists, producers, and exhibitors in attendance.[30] This meeting launched Hays's most ingenious scheme for dealing with organized women.

At Hays's invitation and expense, several women's leaders attended the conference, among them Sippel and Winter. During one of the panel discussions, Sippel rose to suggest that Hays appoint to the Studio Relations Committee a woman charged with enhancing community understanding of the motion picture industry and conveying to producers the views of organized women. Hays immediately agreed, asking Sippel to head a committee of nine women to choose their representative. None of the women had received her organization's authorization to choose such a representative, but those in attendance hailed from several major national organizations, among them the General Federation of Women's Clubs, the Daughters of the American Revolution, and the International Federation of Catholic Alumnae. Sippel spoke first, eagerly nominating Alice Ames Winter. A unanimous vote sealed the appointment, positioning Winter, once again, to lead women cooperating with the motion picture industry.[31] Newspapers announced that organized women had appointed an ambassador to relate "the feeling and wishes of womanhood" to the motion picture industry. Behind the scenes, Will Hays had orchestrated the whole thing.[32]

Winter proved an inspired choice. Since serving as General Federation president, her work had, if anything, bolstered her credentials for becoming woman's ambassador to the motion picture industry. After receiving accolades as "America's first wonder woman" from the women she led for four years, Winter retained her public presence by contributing monthly articles to the *Ladies Home Journal* and publishing two celebrated books—*The Business of Being a Club Woman* (1925), a handbook for clubwomen the profits from which she donated to the General Federation, and *The Heritage of Women* (1927), a prize-winning women's history. Establishing herself as an expert on home economics, Winter supervised the creation of the Alice Ames Winter Demonstration Home in Minneapolis in 1926; two years later, as director of the homemakers' group in the women's division of the Republican National Committee, she forged a national Homemakers-for-Hoover campaign. Still, she remained active in the General Federation and in 1928 addressed the nineteenth biennial convention in San Antonio, Texas. That year, she and her husband moved to Pasadena, California. Winter's unquestioned commitment to women's clubs and issues, ongoing support for Hays's motion picture work, and California residence all made her appointment ideal from Hays's perspective as well.[33]

In a gracious acceptance speech, Winter pondered the question of what drew women, at this particular historical moment, into motion picture work. "The job of women is a cherishing of the social relationships," she pointed out, while men focused on the defining achievements of civilization, mechanics and industry. "The reason we women are coming into power now," she reasoned, is "to introduce this feminine element which is our particularly cherished province." Of all industries, the motion picture industry most needed female influence, because movies exercised a strong pull on human emotions, women's specialty. Promising to stick "feminine hatpins" into the Studio Relations Committee, making it work harder and more productively than ever, Winter assured women that she would make herself "a sensitive wire which will carry your message and your purpose."[34]

Soon after her appointment, Winter contacted leaders of women's organizations, explaining the mechanisms of her office and her goal to incorporate organized women into the process of motion picture self-regulation. In accord with the Studio Relations Committee motto, "patronize the best, and ignore the rest," Winter urged organized women to frequent good movies and avoid bad ones, promising to disseminate movie reviews to help them distinguish between the two. Winter also offered women's organizations various perquisites in return for their official endorsement of her work. For example, she encouraged the president of the National PTA to recognize the ad hoc previewing committee set up by three of its California members as its official previewing committee. In return, Winter offered to instate the National PTA previewing committee as a permanent Studio Relations Committee, a privilege that included full funding for printing and mailing its film reviews. Organizations that accepted Winter's offer included the Daughters of the American Revolution, the Young Men's Christian Association, the International Federation of Catholic Alumnae, and the General Federation, whose leaders responded most enthusiastically, promising Winter full support and expressing confidence in her ability to represent "the women's point of view."[35]

Maude Aldrich and the Women's Christian Temperance Union

Winter did not represent all women. Maude Aldrich, for example, field secretary for the Federal Motion Picture Council and director of the motion picture department for the Women's Christian Temperance Union (WCTU), felt more betrayed than represented. A single, self-supporting native of Indiana—Hays's home state—she had recently rejected an invitation to serve on Hays's public relations council, working instead to turn the WCTU against the Hays Office. A multipurpose organization rooted in nineteenth-century temperance activism, the twentieth-century WCTU grew increasingly concerned about the impact of movies on "prohibition, purity, and peace" and endorsed the first federal motion picture regulation bill heard by Congress in 1914. But the organization had no motion picture department to formulate and synchronize policy until 1925, when Aldrich took over. With persistence and patience, Aldrich prodded the state chapters into line against Hays and for federal motion picture legislation.[36]

Aldrich worked hard, updating members on motion picture reform developments through articles in the WCTU newsletter, the *Union Signal*, and traveling around the country, delivering an average of five speeches per week as she rallied supporters and raised funds for the shared motion picture agendas of the WCTU and the Federal Motion Picture Council. Aldrich expressed greatest concern, not about thoroughly offensive movies—discerning patrons could easily avoid such shows—but about the "otherwise good picture" that contained one "objectionable scene." That scene, Aldrich maintained, served "to educate those who attend only good pictures to accept, or overlook, the thing that is off color." Aldrich herself had fallen for this trick when watching *Ben Hur*, a movie she genuinely liked. In one scene, "half clad women" marched among a crowd of hundreds in a street parade. "They are so small a part of the entire scene," Aldrich explained, "that I did not consider it objectionable." Only later, when she saw a life-sized still of these women on an advertisement for the movie, did she realize that she had been manipulated to accept female nudity in a movie. Such producer ploys dulled moral sensibilities and caused motion picture audiences to tolerate escalating levels of indecency, Aldrich argued.[37]

Most state WCTU chapters responded positively to Aldrich's message.

Whereas in 1927 only seven state organizations actively worked for state or federal motion picture regulation, one year later that number had grown to eighteen, and the national convention adopted a strong resolution condemning the motion picture industry for producing unwholesome movies and pledging the organization to fight for federal regulation. Aldrich exulted in her accomplishments among the rank and file, but her work soon encountered challenges from other national WCTU officers. In 1928, editors of the *Union Signal* printed a full-page propaganda spread for the Hays Office; in "How Women Can Help for Better Films," Jason Joy exhorted women to recognize their "personal responsibility" to advertise and patronize wholesome movies, declaring women's job to "look for the good and support it."[38] Despite Joy's brazen challenge to her motion picture agenda, Aldrich reported that ten more state chapters joined the fight for federal regulation in 1929, bringing the total to twenty-eight. Interference from the Hays Office only increased. Hays's executive assistant, Carl Milliken, complained to WCTU president Ella Boole about Aldrich's speaking and fundraising work, and two months later a national officer rejected Aldrich's motion picture plan for 1930, instructing her to rewrite it. "The object of the department is not to secure federal regulation of motion pictures," the officer maintained, "even though we have given our approval to such a plan." Nor was it to condemn the Hays Office or any other entity. Rather, she argued, Aldrich's department should focus on promoting "good" and educational films, pursuing, in effect, the cooperative "better films" strategy promoted by Hays and Winter. "Give us something that will help the women to judge pictures which they want the public to see," she insisted, "and make the department of Motion Pictures a positive factor in our work." Although fearful of losing her job, Aldrich assured her friend Gilman that she would not align her motion picture department with the Hays Office or abandon her efforts on behalf of a federal motion picture law. Gilman, meanwhile, urged WCTU President Boole to support Aldrich and oppose Winter, explaining that, for women's organizations to cooperate with motion picture interests made as much sense as for temperance and peace activists to cooperate with brewers and munitions producers.[39]

Tensions within the WCTU only deepened as Aldrich and editors of the *Union Signal* battled over whether to accept Winter as their ambassador to the motion picture industry. Aldrich criticized the chief editor, Julia Deane, for discarding material supporting federal regulation and using "the *Signal* to bolster up the faith of W.C.T.U. women in Mrs. Winters [*sic*]." In an angry letter to Deane, Aldrich objected to "giving publicity to or arousing confidence in the paid representatives of the motion picture industry." She complained that, as director of the motion picture department for the past four years, WCTU policies that disallowed criticism of individuals or organizations prevented her from telling "the truth about the industry or the workings of the Hays machine of which Mrs. Winter is now a part." Publishing propaganda by Winter, "a paid tool of the motion picture industry," without allowing a rebuttal, implicated the *Signal* in Hays's efforts to deceive the public and disarm effective motion picture reform, Aldrich argued. She closed ominously with the hope that "the W.C.T.U. has no special cause to fear the Hays Office."[40]

Gilman, as unwilling as Aldrich to cede to Winter the role of representing organized women in motion picture reform, declared Winter's appointment "the motion picture industry's latest attempt to betray the women and children in this country."[41] She had feared, at one time, that censorship boards would make parents complacent about movies; now she worried that Winter's appointment would do the same thing, mollifying organized women by persuading them that their ambassador would single-handedly clean up movies. Most of all, Gilman worried that women's organizations would accept the relatively passive roles of movie reviewer and ticket purchaser reserved for them by Hays and Winter, advertising and attending "good" pictures while mutely tolerating "bad" ones. Accordingly, the motion picture industry would benefit from women's patronage and promotion, while heading off their troublesome protests. To prevent this, Gilman worked to turn women's organizations against Winter, using her new position as motion picture chair for the National Council of Women to advance her agenda.

Catheryne Cooke Gilman and the National Council of Women

The United States' National Council of Women, founded in 1888 during suffragists' anniversary celebration of the Seneca Falls Woman's Rights Convention, boasted a long history of activism on behalf of women, ranging from dress reform to suffrage to world peace. An umbrella organization for other American women's groups, the National Council rooted its work in an expansive vision of unified womanhood—one designed, from the start, to extend around the world, bringing women together over such issues as their universal potential for motherhood, political and economic disadvantages relative to men, and vulnerability to sexual abuse. By 1927, the International Council of Women that emerged from this vision included national councils of women in thirty-four countries.

That year, an overcommitted Gilman—head of the Women's Cooperative Alliance and the Federal Motion Picture Council—reluctantly accepted the invitation from the National Council president, Dr. Valeria Parker, to chair the organization's new motion picture committee. Gilman could not risk allowing such an important post to fall into the hands of a woman "susceptible to the influences" of the motion picture industry. Unlike her position with the Women's Cooperative Alliance, National Council of Women chairmanships paid no stipend and required substantial out-of-pocket expenses, including an annual transatlantic voyage to the meeting of the International Council of Women, travel to the yearly National Council of Women Convention, postage and stationery costs, and time to perform unremunerated tasks.[42]

Soon after assuming this costly if prestigious position, Gilman rushed to prepare her motion picture committee report for the International Council of Women meeting in Geneva, Switzerland, in June 1927. She solicited information about the motion picture activity of member organizations, discovering only eight with motion picture committees, six of which pursued the "endorsing and ignoring policy" advocated by the Hays Office. Still, Gilman predicted that inattention to motion pictures among the vast majority of member groups would free her to position the National Council of Women firmly behind federal motion picture regulation. Thus her motion picture report made a strong case for motion picture bills pending in Congress, severely criticizing Will Hays for deceiving the public and failing to reform motion pictures. Fearful that tight family finances might prevent her attendance at the Geneva conference, Gilman soon learned that Kate Koon Bovey, a generous benefactor of the Women's Cooperative Alliance, would support her journey, and she set about making contacts with social hygiene activists and motion picture reformers in London, Copenhagen, and Paris, arranging to make the most of her precious time abroad.[43]

But Gilman had gravely overestimated the level of National Council support she could expect for federal motion picture regulation. Three weeks before the international convention, the National Council vice president, Anna Garlin Spencer, rejected Gilman's report, instructing her to revise it to eliminate support for specific legislation and negative references to Will Hays or anyone else connected with the motion picture industry. At the same time, Spencer criticized Gilman's association, through the Federal Motion Picture Council, with William Chase, a nationally known New York clergyman who also headed the conservative International Reform Federation. "He is of the Anthony Comstock type," she asserted. "If the people who are behind the attempt to get a Federal Motion Pic-

ture Commission have such persons in leadership as Canon Chase," she continued, "they will not get anywhere and I should not myself appear in support of any
Bill such people advocated." Thanking Gilman in advance for "toning down" her
report, she emphasized the "difficulty of securing united opinion" on legislative proposals and the importance of avoiding discussions that could prove disruptive.[44]

Spencer endeavored to minimize discord among organized women partly in
response to the divisive impact of recent Red-baiting on women's organizations.
In 1924, for example, the War Department's now-infamous "Spider Web Chart"
traced a tangled web of relationships among women's organizations and Communist groups, suggesting that the resulting network represented a vast international Communist conspiracy. Subsequent versions of the chart implicated the
National Council of Women, whose internationalism heightened its vulnerability to charges of Communism. Spurred by internal protests from several member organizations and worried lest the taint of Communism jeopardize the National Council's political viability, leaders conducted a polite purge, asking the
Women's International League for Peace and Freedom—an organization
damned by its inclusion on the original chart—to withdraw its membership. The
National Council president, Dr. Valeria Parker, denounced "spider-web charts"
and "black lists," declaring, "All attempts to weaken the mutual confidence and
united efforts of women must be valiantly resisted." She and Spencer looked forward to the 1927 meetings as an opportunity to heal and reunite.[45]

If Spencer feared Gilman's report would spark unwanted controversy, Gilman
began to suspect that her National Council position might clash with her commitment to federal motion picture regulation. Still, she removed from her report specific references to legislation and individuals but included a cleverly
crafted history of American motion picture reform, complete with information
about the Federal Motion Picture Council. She also cautioned women who "in
their zeal, and uninformed status . . . are easy preys to the plausible proposals" of
motion picture interests. Gilman returned from her first International Council of
Women meeting enthused about possibilities for creating an international check
on Hollywood and reassured that she could avoid dissension and satisfy Spencer's
demands by couching her opposition to Hays and support for federal regulation in subtle, ladylike suggestions. Gilman's 1928 reports received no criticism.[46]

But all of this changed in 1929, when the National Council of Women and
many of its leaders experienced growing financial difficulties. Unable to pay international dues, which amounted to more than $1,000, the national leadership
turned to Adele Woodard, an affluent member and motion picture activist who

cooperated with the Hays Office. After covering the National Council's bills, Woodard assumed several of Gilman's duties, prompting members to inquire if Woodard had replaced Gilman as motion picture chair. In a telling letter of apology to Gilman, the executive secretary of the National Council assured Gilman that she remained the official motion picture chair but should welcome Woodard's interest in motion pictures, noting that her "generous contributions" had been most helpful. "I am sure you will understand," she concluded suggestively. Gilman recognized that financial problems required the National Council to "accept the services of those who can and will give. I only hope," she confided to a friend, "that Mrs. Woodard is giving her own money and that the Hays organization is not furnishing it for the purpose of securing her a place on the National Council." With or without Hays's help, she realized, Woodard's vast personal means positioned her to exert considerable influence within the organization. Several months later, Gilman's friend and ally Valeria Parker resigned from the presidency, admitting that she could no longer afford to serve. Confessing to similar circumstances, Gilman concluded regretfully that "anyone who acted as President or Chairman should have an independent income if they were to serve properly a national organization."[47]

Events of 1929 convinced Gilman that her carefully edited utterances and cordial silences could no longer underwrite women's unity. Financial resources tilted the balance of power further and further away from Gilman, and Hays had just stolen her most important resource—her claim to represent womanhood—by appointing Winter as "Woman's Ambassador." Throwing caution to the winds, Gilman planned what would prove a memorable motion picture session for the annual meeting of the National Council of Women—a forum featuring a panel of motion picture activists representing a range of views, and a keynote speaker, Don Seitz, known for his aggressive opposition to the Hays Office. Seitz warned Gilman that the scene could get ugly, to which she replied, "I am not only 'prepared to stand for what may happen' but am looking forward to it with real pleasure and considerable glee." Had the session drawn support commensurate with the media attention it attracted, it would have represented a resounding success. The largest newspapers in the country covered Seitz's merciless indictment of the motion picture industry and cooperating clubwomen. After lambasting producers and exhibitors for deliberately luring children "into those infernos on the streets," he declared it "high time that someone should be hanged." Just short of suggesting that the noose be fitted to clubwomen, Seitz accused women's clubs of working for the motion picture industry. "If you women will step aside so that we can get Will Hays from behind your skirts," Seitz concluded with a swagger, "we'll settle him." The national press reported a lively discussion as National Council delegates "lined up behind Mrs. John F. Sippel," General Federation president, "or behind Mrs. Robbins Gilman, chairman of the Motion Picture Committee of the Council."[48]

Officials representing the many women's organizations vilified by Seitz launched a spirited defense of their work. Rita McGoldrick, of the International Federation of Catholic Alumnae, called Seitz an uninformed interloper, and Mrs. Malcolm Parker McCoy, representing the New York State Federation of Women's Clubs, announced, "Mr. Seitz's remarks were an insult to the intelligence of the women's organizations of this country," and she resented his insinuation "that we are either blandly ignorant, easily influenced, or open to the suspicion of connivance." The New York Federation of Women's Clubs would now increase its cooperation with Hays, she announced defiantly. Gilman predicted that lively debate and extensive press coverage would win converts to federal motion picture regulation. The most immediate impact, however, was to rend the National Council—a result that angered Spencer, who had warned Gilman against it two years earlier. General Federation President Sippel announced that clubwomen, angered at the National Council's sponsorship of Seitz's insulting remarks, voted to cancel their organization's membership. Gilman's position on the National Council teetered precariously.[49]

Frances Diehl and the General Federation of Women's Clubs

The General Federation, meanwhile, suffered its own internal turmoil when Bettie Sippel, of Baltimore, appointed a new motion picture chair, Frances Diehl, active clubwoman, personal friend of Will Hays, and wife of Ambrose Diehl, vice president of U.S. Steel Corporation. Diehl immediately returned the General Federation to a program of cooperating with the motion picture industry—and now Winter—by reviewing and listing approved movies.[50] Clubwomen from Sippel's home city protested Diehl's policy shift, calling Winter the woman "high in the councils of the General Federation" whom Hays had for years sought to appoint to his committee. At least one influential clubwoman had already declined Hays's offer, fearing that to accept would jeopardize the integrity of the General Federation. The Baltimore contingent planned a full-scale revolt at the 1930 biennial convention, hoping to use several pointed resolutions to turn the

General Federation rank and file against Sippel, Diehl, and Winter. All of the resolutions referred to the General Federation constitution, Article V, which prohibited exploitation of the organization's name by a member or commercial enterprise.[51] The first resolution would have removed the General Federation name from any corporate advertising. The second expressed General Federation disapproval of "present and past officials of the Federation occupying lucrative positions by motion picture companies." The final resolution, even more pointed, announced that the General Federation opposed Winter's motion picture activities. None of these proposals made it to the floor for discussion; they were waylaid by a combination of "steam roller" tactics by which General Federation leaders tabled the resolutions and refused to recognize Maryland delegates when they attempted to speak.[52]

Clubwomen's arguments over their motion picture policy charted earnest disagreements among them about whether organized women should try to preserve their traditional political roles, raising as many questions about the place of women's clubs in enfranchised politics as about the best method for reforming immoral motion pictures. "If the women's clubs of this country are to remain valuable segments of our national life, they must be kept out of politics," declared Mrs. Malloy on behalf of the Baltimore contingent. Only by remaining above politics—above, in other words, the machinations of politicians and businessmen like Will Hays—could clubwomen preserve their virtue. Ironically, that very virtue, or, more specifically, popular *perceptions* of it, made women especially appealing as public relations symbols for entities suffering a sullied public image. Because corporations and politicians threatened to co-opt and undermine clubwomen's virtue, Malloy contended that clubwomen "must not allow their names to be linked with projects which will make for monetary gain by private individuals, corporations or industries."[53] By intimating that enfranchisement had heightened women's vulnerability to corruption, Baltimore clubwomen echoed the logic of anti-suffragists who premised women's virtue on their disfranchisement. In marked contrast to Sippel and Winter, who endeavored to make the General Federation a player in the modern economic and political system, Baltimore clubwomen exhorted the General Federation to avoid commercial and political entanglements altogether in order to prevent contamination by the electoral process and commercial values. They fought to maintain clubwomen's independence and moral high ground even if it cost them—or perhaps hoping it would preserve a distinctly feminine form of—financial and political power.

The significance and complexity of these issues escaped journalists, who made light of Baltimore clubwomen's protest, attributing it to pettiness, envy—anything but sincere concern for the integrity of the General Federation. "Club Women Jealous of Mrs. Winter's Job," proclaimed one headline. Another newspaper suggested that "this protest might be dismissed as mere internal politics among 'a lot of women'" if not for the fact that male church leaders, "a large and representative, as well as eminently respectable, group," had taken up Baltimore clubwomen's cause.[54] Eager to publicize and sensationalize clubwomen's disagreements, reporters would not dignify their protest with a serious report until they gained the support of male religious leaders.

Winter reportedly "chuckled at the charges being made against her," but she must have regretted the hostility and suspicion her new job aroused. In vigorous self-defense, she announced that her salary as a monthly contributor to the *Ladies' Home Journal* exceeded the $8,000 she earned under Hays. The whole matter, she argued, should not really concern clubwomen, because Hays had appointed her to represent womanhood, not the General Federation. Her statements, all technically true, nonetheless ignored her deep identification with the General Federation. Winter encouraged this association by sprinkling the federation name liberally throughout her Hays-funded correspondence and newsletters, and Frances Diehl reinforced it by conflating the General Federation's motion picture achievements with Winter's. In a 1929 report, for example, she boasted of Winter's appointment as a General Federation accomplishment. Her later reports focused on Winter's work, calling it "the most constructive and outstanding thing that organized women have been able to do to assist in solving the motion picture problem."[55] Thus, even if Winter had scrupulously avoided identifying herself with the federation, observers would have perceived a close relationship because of Diehl's eagerness to associate the organization's motion picture work with Winter.

A sensation-hungry press and public aggravated the schism developing among organized women. As Baltimore clubwomen had already discovered, magazine and newspaper editors considered women's opinions especially newsworthy when they took the form of battles between otherwise decorous ladies. In 1930, Virginia Roderick, editor of the *Woman's Journal*, asked Gilman and Winter to contribute a set of dueling articles about motion pictures. When Gilman suggested that one of her male colleagues in motion picture reform join the debate, Roderick quickly vetoed the idea, saying, "This should be a woman vs. woman discussion." The National Congress of Parents and Teachers newsletter, the *Parent-Teacher Broadcaster*, published a similar set of articles, highlighting Gilman and

Winter's shared womanhood and midwestern roots. "It is interesting to note," the editor's prefatory comments pointed out, "that the two women most active in working out the motion picture problems of the nation are both Minneapolis women." While national women's magazines provided coveted press coverage for Gilman and Winter, they also sensationalized the women's disagreements, using their shared womanhood to heighten the drama.[56]

If Will Hays hoped that Winter's appointment as woman's ambassador to the motion picture industry would divide organized women the way Gilman's anti-censorship work in Massachusetts had, he must have enjoyed watching Gilman and Winter vie for organized women's loyalty. Gilman suspected as much. "Mr. Hays reminds me of the clever ancient who threw a stone into the midst of his enemies and caused them to annihilate each other," she wrote a friend. "He has kept stones coming into the group of women since 1922 and it looks rather hopeless." Major national women's organizations imploded as the Winter-Gilman imbroglio forced them to choose between irreconcilable motion picture agendas. The Women's Christian Temperance Union and the National Council of Women continued to support federal motion picture regulation under Aldrich and Gilman, respectively, but each woman's leadership suffered repeated challenges. Other organizations tentatively entered the fray. The new president of the National PTA, Margaretta Reeve, agreed with Gilman that Winter represented not organized womanhood but "a highly subsidized, highly salaried Committee controlled by the industry." The president of the National Council of Federated Church Women concurred. In March, Gilman proudly, if somewhat prematurely, announced, "One after another of these organizations have repudiated the claim that Mrs. Winter was representing them. Today Mrs. Winter is practically without official support from any of the women's organizations." Only the General Federation leadership's steadfast loyalty, Gilman speculated, kept Winter's so-called ambassadorship from collapsing.[57]

The long-awaited golden era of women's reform did not materialize among motion picture activists in the 1920s. Reformers instead found themselves at war with each other. Early in the decade, Gilman and her allies in the Women's Cooperative Alliance became disillusioned with the cooperative and consumer-based reform strategies that had served them well since 1915, concluding that cooperation with business leaders backfired while corporate consolidation confounded local consumer reform efforts. But even as Gilman, the Women's Cooperative Alliance, Maude Aldrich, Mary King Sherman, and so many of their allies abandoned cooperative reform strategies, other women pursued such strategies with new fervor. Indeed, Alice Ames Winter, Bettie Monroe Sippel, Frances Diehl, and other women whose corporate and political connections stretched from the Minneapolis Citizens Alliance to U.S. Steel and the White House, seemed especially eager to cooperate with businessmen under the pro-business presidential administrations of the 1920s.

While different relations to corporate and political power influenced women's reform strategy choices in the 1920s, other unique features of the twenties made their disparate choices particularly divisive. By aggressively suppressing radicals and organized labor, employer organizations alienated social welfare groups while deepening cleavages between women on opposite sides of labor issues. Red Scare tensions and financial difficulties infused women's organizations with suspicions and resentments rooted in political and class differences. At the same time, unrealistic expectations of female unity, embedded in essentialist notions of womanhood, widened developing rifts. Just as anticipation of a woman's voting bloc empowered organized women by raising their importance to politicians and businessmen, it simultaneously heightened organized women's vulnerability. Those who feared the power of enfranchised womanhood defended themselves by trying to divide or harness the woman's bloc, while women who believed in and tried to represent womanhood treated women who disagreed with them as traitors rather than rivals. In the 1920s, women's hopes for unity around motion picture reform began to splinter on the shoals of class, political ideology, the political machinations of powerful men, and unexamined assumptions about womanhood.

As national women's organizations like the General Federation of Women's Clubs and the National Council of Women towed their battered motion picture reform programs into the 1930s, the Women's Cooperative Alliance gave up on local motion picture work. Gilman and other leaders tried to use the alliance's better film committees to generate grassroots support for federal regulation, but their declaration that local efforts could no longer improve motion pictures provoked a sharp drop in committee memberships, from over six hundred in 1922 to only sixty-four in 1924—the last year that the group's annual reports included such figures.[58] Thus the alliance's new emphasis on federal remedies eroded community involvement in motion picture reform. In the following years, Gilman would escalate her motion picture activism at the national level, assuming leadership within several major organizations while the Women's Cooperative Alliance refocused its anti-obscenity work on issues that seemed more amenable to local efforts—burlesque theater and sex education.

CHAPTER FIVE

"We Don't Want Our Boys and Girls in a Place of That Kind"

Women's Burlesque Reform, 1925–1934

On a cool Minneapolis evening in October 1927 an eager audience awaited the opening of a burlesque show at the Gayety Theater. Most in the crowd were adult men, but a few women and several children could be spotted in the dimly lit auditorium. As they waited, they may have noticed that, while the lavish interior of the eighteen-year-old theater had begun to fade, the plush seats and velvet curtains retained a glimmer of their earlier splendor. A sense of anticipation must have filled the air as they waited in rows facing the proscenium stage wondering whether the new runway would be used that night. A few spectators grabbed seats next to the extended platform, hoping to get a close-up view of some scantily clad burlesque performer. With luck, a stripper would appear. Equally attentive spectators, Gertrude Malin and Grace Paley had a different agenda. As members of the Women's Cooperative Alliance and close associates of Catheryne Cooke Gilman, they attended not for pleasure but for reconnaissance—to investigate reports of obscene performances.[1]

Six years earlier, we probably would have found Malin and Paley viewing a motion picture. But given Gilman's disillusionment with cooperative motion picture reform, the Women's Cooperative Alliance's local motion picture work came to a virtual halt by 1927. Industry consolidation in the 1920s meant that local efforts to reform motion pictures no longer seemed effective. But alliance women expected better results from their efforts to reform burlesque theater, a local enterprise that had yielded to women's influence in the past.

The Gayety Theater and Burlesque in the Twenties

In 1920, soon after the Women's Cooperative Alliance's founding, workers began to log complaints and findings regarding the Gayety Theater. The manager who succeeded William Koenig, Harry E. Yost, modeled his relationship with the alliance on Koenig's relationship with the Woman's Welfare League, extending to alliance members special invitations to attend Gayety shows and urging the women to discuss their concerns with him. Alliance workers accepted Yost's invitation, and, between 1920 and 1924, found no evidence that the Gayety sold liquor or staged obscenity. In the early 1920s, the Gayety continued Koenig's clean burlesque, minimizing sexual innuendo and allowing only fully clothed performers on stage. The Gayety thus attracted a burlesque audience that included such unlikely patrons as social workers from the Child Guidance Clinic and students from the Lutheran Theological Seminary.[2] For more than a decade, the Gayety cast its marketing net widely, drawing an audience considerably more diverse than the working-class male patrons usually associated with burlesque.

All of that changed in 1925, when a new Gayety manager, Harry D. Hirsch, followed the national burlesque circuit by including ever more daring female nudity and sexuality in Gayety programs. Burlesque theaters across the nation used sex to attract an audience when their popularity and profits plummeted, as stage stars and audiences migrated to motion pictures in the 1920s. According to one eye-witness to burlesque's demise, the more liberal sexual trends of the period affected burlesque in contradictory ways, relaxing the constraints that limited its sexual display but ultimately dooming it by allowing on the street what burlesque shows had made tantalizing on the stage—like short skirts and makeup. An anonymous prankster echoed this view in a diatribe against the alliance. "Burlesk was primarily a man's game," wrote "I. M. Modisttee." "Long skirts & high necked dresses made it a success with the poor fools," "Modisttee" continued, but to revive burlesque, it "will be necessary to be more daring than before. No man is going to pay money to see what he can see out of doors for nothing."[3]

Explicitly sexual themes and exposure also crept from burlesque to the stages of vaudeville and "legitimate" theater. One of the first risqué elements to migrate, living pictures—otherwise known as tableaux vivants or tab shows—typically featured women, as in Elsie La Bergère's 1915 "Series of Original Poses," in varying degrees of nudity. By promoting these acts as live artistic renderings of a particular painting or sculpture, the so-called legitimate theaters could stage them. As early as 1919, Koenig worried about losing his burlesque audience to vaudeville tab shows, writing that "tab shows . . . at the vaudeville houses here are being compared with our burlesque shows, and it is surprising to see the amount of men who patronize the cheap vaudeville houses when they have tab shows on." One vaudeville house in particular incorporated weekly tab shows "for the only reason that they know it will bring the men," Koenig complained. "Men will not walk six blocks out of their way to see a poor burlesque show with only sixteen girls and pay seventy-five cents when they can go into a vaudeville house and see a good tab show for fifteen and twenty-five cents."[4] The loss of male patrons to tab shows encouraged burlesque managers in the 1920s to distinguish their programs more clearly from vaudeville by using exaggerated sexual humor and female nudity. The fact that vaudeville could detract from burlesque's profits by stealing its audience illuminates the permeability of boundaries between these entertainment genres. Ticket prices, too, failed to elevate vaudeville above burlesque. As Koenig's letter reveals, vaudeville houses charged considerably less than the Gayety. A decade later, when proponents of the Gayety defended it as "the poor man's theater," others noted that a Gayety ticket cost more than a ticket to several highly regarded legitimate theaters. Even elite theaters began to appropriate aspects of the burlesque sexual motif by the middle of the 1920s when theatrical "revues," such as the Ziegfeld Follies in New York, incorporated female nudity.[5] Thus, by encroaching on burlesque's traditional territory of sexual display, vaudeville and new types of legitimate theatrical presentation joined motion pictures in confronting burlesque with unprecedented competition in the 1920s.

The postwar cultural climate discouraged burlesque managers from repeating their prewar marketing ploy of soliciting middle-class women's patronage with shows designed for a lady's palate. New competition for audiences seeking sexual thrills, postsuffrage failure to create a woman's voting bloc, men's return from war, and loosening moral standards all encouraged burlesque managers to gear their shows even more narrowly to a heterosexual male clientele. They signaled this commitment by focusing more exclusively on female sexual display, introducing the runway and the striptease to enhance the spectacle. So, whereas a racy 1910 show featured a voluptuous woman in a flesh-colored union suit, 1920s performers increasingly dispensed with the suit and showcased their flesh.

The New Daring Burlesque

During the late 1920s, alliance women accumulated a sizable file of complaints about indecency at the Gayety. One woman suspected that manager Harry Hirsch staged more "vile" shows than usual in an effort to attract the hundreds of physicians in town for a hospital convention. Reports of children witnessing female nudity and sexually suggestive acts on stage prompted the alliance to launch an investigation of the Gayety that would continue for the next five years.

Gertrude Malin and Grace Paley approached the first of their many forays into the Gayety in 1927, prepared for a risqué show. Still, they were shocked. One act featured nearly nude women writhing about in "vile and extreme" dances. In another, dancers gyrated up and down the runway while one of the girls yelled, "Shake 'em up girls! Shake all you got for the boys!" A number of children, Malin and Paley noted gravely, observed the entire show. A few months later, the two women attended a performance they found even more offensive. Describing an act involving a man and a woman, they recounted, "They did everything on the stage but have actual physical intercourse. They went thru all the various stages from desire to consummation, commenting freely for the benefit of the audience on the effect produced on each other." Malin and Paley expressed equal disgust at the chorus girls who appeared on stage "entirely nude with the exception of three ribbon rosettes." Describing the strategic placement of the rosettes, their report continued, "Two of these were about the size of a fifty cent piece and were worn one on each breast. The third rosette, slightly larger, was worn over the pelvic region." Once again, the two women spotted unaccompanied children as young as seven years old in the audience.[6]

Alliance leaders agreed with Malin and Paley that such salacious shows would corrupt the morals of Minneapolis youth, and, after a brief meeting, in October of 1927 they decided to approach the city council to seek revocation of the Gayety's license. Anticipating that aldermen might take reports of obscenity from their own members more seriously than from women of the alliance, Paley persuaded two city councilmen, Victor Johnson and John Swanson, both longtime allies of reform, to visit the Gayety. On second thought, Paley decided "that perhaps aldermen of a slightly different type should also see the performance," so she asked Fred Maurer, who patronized morally questionable places of entertainment and opposed moral reform, to attend as well. Paley suspected that if Maurer declared the show obscene, the city council would act.[7]

After attending an evening performance at the Gayety, Swanson and Johnson submitted a formal report corroborating the alliance's account. "The entire show," the men agreed, was "highly immoral and indecent and depraved." One called the performance "the most indecent and obscene exhibition he had ever seen in Minneapolis." Both condemned "the attempted jokes, the dress, the salacious and degrading manner" of the actors. Not only were such shows "degrading to public morals," but they would "corrupt the morals of youth," a number of whom attended that night's show. Both men urged the council to revoke the Gayety's license. When several council members objected "on the basis that they did not wish to make Minneapolis 'a Sunday school town,'" Maurer rose to declare that "he was known not to be a Sunday School kid," but that he had rarely if ever seen a show worse than the Gayety's. As Paley had predicted, Maurer's testimony convinced the council to revoke the theater's license.[8]

At first elated, alliance women soon realized that revoking the Gayety's license concluded only one triumphant battle in a war they must wage throughout the system of municipal government. With great ingenuity Hirsch and his successors endeavored to reopen the theater. In the case of the 1927 license revocation, Gayety attorneys appealed to the judicial system, and within twenty-four hours persuaded Judge Edmund Montgomery to issue a restraining order against the revocation. As in later cases, city council hearings followed judicial action. Sometimes these resulted in a Gayety victory, other times in defeat. Hirsch achieved one Gayety success by promising that "the shows to be given at the Gayety Theater in the future will be of a high grade character from a clean and moral standpoint; that the performances staged will not contain obscene, or suggestive parts either as to dialogue, songs, acts or dancing." In a later contest, the license revocation remained in place, but it barred only the current Gayety manager from reopening the theater—an obstacle Hirsch cleverly circumvented by removing his name as manager and applying for another license under an employee's name.[9]

Alliance women matched Hirsch's cunning with determination. Amassing evidence and organizing opposition to the Gayety, these resourceful women left few strategies untried. At one point, they even convinced the minister of Judge Montgomery's church to urge the judge to cease supporting the Gayety. Along more conventional lines, the alliance collected affidavits from witnesses of objectionable Gayety performances, canvassed the city by telephone, lobbied city officials, appealed to prominent businessmen, and asked all of their allies to petition the city council. The alliance also obtained the support of other local women's organizations, including the Women's Christian Temperance Union, the Women's Christian Association, women's clubs, and local church groups. Several times these coalitions persuaded the city council to rescind the Gayety's license, but aldermen, pressured from within and without, repeatedly reinstated the license within a few weeks or months.[10] The politically volatile municipal regulatory system frustrated alliance efforts to clean up or close the Gayety Theater. In addition, a number of less obvious but even more formidable barriers to the alliance's work surfaced in city council hearings between 1927 and 1932.

Maternalism versus Paternalism

Alliance women rooted their political strategy in their identities as "disinterested" exemplars of morality and representatives of motherhood. Maternal experience and instinct, they argued, as well as female moral sensibilities, afforded women special expertise in protecting young women and children. Their justification of women's political activity mimicked the eighteenth-century language of disinterestedness, with a new twist. Whereas republican mothers' disinterested role in the polity derived from their status as disfranchised, virtuous mothers and mentors of young citizens, enfranchised alliance women invoked a disinterestedness rooted only in maternity and womanhood. Gilman noted that a woman "brings the impersonal selfless service of a mother to the otherwise selfish situation . . . She is working as woman for others." Making the connection between women's domestic and political roles explicit, Gilman explained, "The function of the mother in politics is identical to the function of the mother in the home. Her work is . . . spiritual and moral."[11] The alliance's approach to the Gayety reflected this mission. Supervising a local burlesque theater merely extended into the municipality women's maternal responsibility for protecting the innocent. By relying on female and maternal authority to buttress their reform efforts, alliance women drew upon traditions of nineteenth-century women who deployed this authority behind the scenes. In contrast, though, alliance leaders identified the public spaces of burlesque theater and the city council as proper sites for maternal moral authority.

Men on all sides of the Gayety debate objected to the women's presence. Gayety defenders considered women's moral sensitivity excessive when applied to the public realm, complaining bitterly about efforts to impose female moral values on Minneapolis and turn it into a "Sunday School town." One Gayety supporter taunted city council members. By revoking the Gayety's license "you'll be making yoursel[ves] ridiculous," he declared. "You can't make Minneapolis any better by locking up the town at 9 o'clock and throwing away the key." These men redefined the paternalism characteristic of nineteenth-century male reformers; rather than protecting women from obscenity, their goal—reflecting liberalized attitudes toward sex—became protecting male spaces from women.

With similar effect but for different purposes, male allies suggested that most aldermen would discount women's testimony about obscenity. Neil Cronin, attorney for the city and an alliance ally, recommended that aldermen, rather than alliance women, testify before the city council, because a man's testimony to being offended "should be more telling than the testimony of a woman." Alliance notes remark that "in view of this fact and also considering the nature of the case, Mr. Cronin will not ask G[race] P[aley] to testify."[12] Male allies and opponents of the alliance agreed on one thing: feminine moral sensitivity cast doubt on the validity of women's responses to burlesque performances.

Assumptions about women's special moral sensibilities revived a key aspect of Victorian paternalism, prompting many men to question the propriety of women viewing or even hearing descriptions of burlesque shows. In 1927 Alderman Johnson advised Paley not to attend the city council committee meeting where charges against the Gayety would be aired because hearing the detailed affidavits might embarrass her. The fact that Paley helped to collect the affidavits and knew their contents suggests that Johnson may have been most concerned about Paley listening to the affidavits in the presence of men. Alternatively, he may have anticipated the *men's* discomfort in Paley's presence. Whatever the case, Paley did not consider missing the hearings but helped other alliance members assemble a throng of local organized women to attend. Alliance women limited but could not entirely escape paternalism's impact. Attending the hearings required that they reject the advice of an influential ally on the city council, and, as Paley's decision to send "bad boy" Alderman Maurer to the Gayety suggests, alliance women recognized that assumptions about women's moral sensitivity weakened their ability to convince a roomful of men to condemn a popular theater as obscene. With regard to obscenity, men simply considered other men's testimony more credible than women's. As a result, in 1927 the alliance accepted the city attorney's recommendation that its members refrain from testifying against the Gayety. In preparation for a 1932 hearing, they devised a list of nineteen witnesses to testify, only two of them women. At this hearing a local businessman recommended that aldermen dismiss women in the audience during the presentation of transcribed and photographed evidence incriminating the Gayety. "The license committee should get this report, written and pictorial," he said. "I'd like to have the women excused so it could be done."[13] Like Cronin and Johnson before him, this businessman supported the alliance's case against the Gayety, but sought to safeguard female sensibilities by preventing the women from observing the evidence and hearing men discuss it. Thus accommodating men's notions of credibility and assumptions of women's heightened moral sensitivity induced alliance leaders to surrender an active role in the proceedings as they struggled to retain even a passive role as spectators.

Opponents of the alliance presented the women with harsher, less protective reminders that their anti-obscenity work violated norms for middle-class women's behavior. Two aldermen who opposed the alliance "made salacious remarks concerning the evidence presented and the women present, at which the proponents of the theater laughed." In a proposal made possible by more modern attitudes toward female sexual desire, one alderman suggested that alliance women only *claimed* to disapprove of obscenity. "Some people get a kick by going to the Gayety," he began. "Some get it by listening to what goes on in the Gayety. These women here get their kick by delving into all the dirt." The loquacious "I. M. Modisttee" agreed, ridiculing the alliance as "an organization of women whose spare time [is] taken up in attending Burlesque shows!" In another angry missive, the author exclaimed: "I can't understand for the life of me what any woman can see in looking at their own sex, (your sex) in a state of seminudity"—as if alliance investigators observed burlesque performances out of some lewd, perhaps lesbian-inspired purposes.[14] To Gayety defenders, alliance women who ventured onto the masculine terrain of burlesque theater and city council hearings sacrificed the decorum that normally protected middle-class women from sexual display, insults, and jokes. Such inappropriate female behavior, the men suggested, invited sexually loaded attacks.

In fact, alliance women grew increasingly unnerved as sexual innuendos and material circulated. Preparing to read a stenographic transcript of one of the shows, a local minister apologized to women in the audience for the indecent passages. After the women urged him to proceed, he read several lines, then faltered, "I'm ashamed to read these, gentlemen," he confessed, causing "men spectators sitting behind the women and outside the rail" to laugh. The minister next submitted as evidence several pictures of nude and seminude female models. As these made their way around the room, Gilman sensed discomfort among the women around her and requested that the pictures be presented to the committee only. Several women in the audience agreed, saying, "Submit it to the committee . . . we're convinced."[15]

In order to examine and evaluate obscenity, alliance women endured unpleasant challenges to their dignity and character. Their presence at obscene burlesque performances violated the protective paternalism behind the anti-obscenity work of an earlier generation of men. But unlike Victorian vice crusaders, who banned women from anti-obscenity work for the ostensible purpose of protecting their moral sensibilities, alliance leaders believed that these special sensibilities rendered women especially suited for the task of evaluating and regulating obscenity. The alliance inverted older paternalist notions by accepting their premise of women's greater virtue while redefining the significance, stamina, and proper sphere of that virtue. In doing so, the alliance extended women's time-honored tradition of justifying political activity according to domestic and feminine values and roles. Replacing paternal with maternal control over obscenity, however, created a new paradigm that unsettled men on all sides of the Gayety issue.

Maternalist Conflicts and Masculinity Crises

Alliance women consistently framed complaints against the Gayety in terms of protecting children. Each investigator reported on the ages of youths in the audience, emphasizing the detrimental impact of the shows on young people. In particular, alliance workers objected to children, mostly boys, viewing the likes of Anna Pep, whose "shimmying and hootchy-kootchy dancing was practiced with skirt raised, calling special attention to the sex organs." Children as young as seven years old, they affirmed, gaped at a nude dancer, shielded only by "a square of silk material held in front of her." The dialogue in other acts conveyed material "so frankly obscene that it was nauseating. Two or three one act comedies were built around illicit sex relations and the entire dialogue led up to such relations as the climax." The Gayety not only permitted but encouraged children to attend, as evidenced by the theater program which stated: "Children under 10 admitted free."[16] Alliance women did not balance precision about what they found objectionable in burlesque with specificity regarding burlesque's impact on children. Assuming an obvious connection between the two, they approached the hearings unprepared for challenges from skeptics.

The alliance and its allies employed maternal rhetoric, not as mere political strategy, but as a set of values deriving from their own experiences as mothers. Mrs. O. M. Leland, one of the two alliance women to testify against the Gayety at the 1932 hearing, stated the alliance's motives in practical, maternal terms, declaring that "we're here because we don't want our boys and girls in a place of that kind." Echoing Leland's statement, Mrs. M. D. Webster spoke for the Daughters of the American Revolution. "I shouldn't want my son to go there," she asserted, "and I shouldn't want my daughter to go there, and how do I know

Fig. 5.1 Behind the scenes at the Gayety Theater, a line of women—scantily clothed and prepared to disrobe further—wait to go on stage, c. 1930s. Photo by the *Minneapolis Star Journal*. Courtesy of the Minnesota Historical Society

that if such a place exists that some person may not take them there?" Objecting to the Gayety's interference with their own maternal authority and responsibilities, these women assumed that motherhood would unite the city's women around reforms to protect children. With great consternation, then, they listened to the testimony of Mrs. Mollie Evans. After carefully identifying herself as a mother of "three sons and daughters," Evans recommended that the Gayety be allowed to remain open since it displayed nothing more objectionable than one could see in other public places. "Two weeks ago I went to see the show at the Gayety," Evans admitted, "and I didn't see any more than I have seen on the street cars." Mrs. J. P. Carroll, another Gayety patron, claimed that she had "never heard remarks at the Gayety that would be harmful to children." Besides, she remarked, "I do not know why you want to revoke the Gayety Theatre license any more than any other theatre that does the same thing." Mrs. R. T. Manning concurred. "I have traveled extensively all through the United States, and have attended every show house in these different cities," she told councilmen. "I found nothing in the Gayety Theatre I have not heard and seen in practically every other theatre in the United States."[17] In direct refutation of Leland and Webster, these three women insisted that Gayety performances neither harmed children nor exceeded in salaciousness scenes visible in other public arenas.

Other female Gayety defenders delivered testimony explicitly grounded in their own motherhood. After Emma Smith introduced herself as "a mother and a housewife," she announced pointedly, "and [I] raised my own children." Her credentials established, Smith then stated that she saw nothing immoral in Gayety performances and even allowed her own children to attend them. Smith's statements posed special problems for the Women's Cooperative Alliance, revealing not only disagreements among mothers regarding the morality of Gayety shows but also very different types of mothering practiced by alliance leaders and the Gayety's female supporters. By highlighting the fact that she raised her own children, Smith implicitly but effectively reproached alliance leaders for rooting their reform in motherhood while entrusting the care of their own children to others. To be sure, well-known reformers from Catherine Beecher to Jane Addams instructed other women in motherhood while abdicating it themselves. But unlike Beecher and Addams, Gilman and many of her female allies actually had young children at home in others' care.[18] Moreover, they confronted full-time mothers face to face in a public debate about the proper sphere of mothering.

These conflicts between mothers over motherhood emerged in the context of heated discussions about the role of enfranchised women in municipal politics. One theater manager announced that "if our women voters would stay at home and mind their business the Gayety would get along and we would have a better city." Lydia Leatherman, representing the Concordia Society, politely retorted, "According to what I have heard here today, women should not be heard on this matter, but I have a feeling that mothers should know what is going on in the city and they have a right to express themselves and a right to set things right if they are not right." Like her alliance allies, she premised women's political protest of burlesque on motherhood, advocating that municipal structures assume a maternal role. Nell MacGrath contradicted her. As a former teacher, who claimed to "represent the people as a whole, being the mother of three children and the wife of an ordinary man who likes to go to the Gayety occasionally," MacGrath identified the home as the proper domain for motherhood. Mothers, not the license committee, should prevent children from attending Gayety shows, she argued. Anyway, "everyone who goes to the Gayety is dry behind the ears," MacGrath insisted, "and if anyone who isn't slips in, I wonder where the mother is. If [the Gayety] is patronized by children," MacGrath concluded dramatically, "regulate the children, and not the show."[19] MacGrath and Smith may have disagreed over whether or not Gayety shows harmed children, but they agreed that the burden of protecting children rested with individual mothers, not the city council. Thus, while alliance leaders used motherhood as a metaphor for their public reform work, other women in the community espoused a more privatized motherhood. Not only did they disapprove of using municipal regulatory powers to broaden motherly influence and enforce morality beyond the home, but they opposed closing a burlesque house for the purposes of protecting children; indeed, a few women saw nothing wrong with Gayety performances or children's attendance at them.

One might speculate that those who defended the Gayety represented a lower socioeconomic class than those who opposed it. Nell MacGrath, however, one of the only female Gayety defenders identifiable in other public documents, appeared in the city's *Blue Book*, a calling directory of the area's "best families"— which never listed the Gilmans.[20] Several Gayety partisans identified themselves as "housewives" who stayed home with their children. They may have worked at home, completing piece-work projects to support their families, but it is more likely that their husbands earned a "family-wage" that permitted them to abstain from paid employment. Economic class may not have differentiated women who defended the Gayety from those who opposed it, but organizational affiliation did. All of the women who spoke against the Gayety claimed to speak for a particular women's organization, but supporters of the Gayety revealed no such ties, ostensibly representing no one but themselves and their families. The voices of these women probably would have gone unheard just a few years earlier, because disfranchised women gained access to politics through women's organizations. But Gayety attorneys found individual women's testimony useful in the 1920s, partly because it came from voters, but also because it introduced maternal dissent that exploded the myth of women's unity, dismantling the Women's Cooperative Alliance's efforts to represent a united mother's voting bloc.

Ironically, while defenders of the Gayety challenged female moral authority, their case relied on assumptions of women's elevated moral nature. Just as notions of female moral sensitivity undermined alliance women's credibility regarding obscene shows, these same notions enhanced the credibility of the Gayety's female defenders. If a woman called a show obscene, for example, the show might merely be too racy for a woman's delicate taste. But since men assumed that women applied stricter standards of decency, if a woman pronounced a burlesque show clean, it must be beyond reproach. During the 1928 city council hearings, a new Gayety manager verified the wholesomeness of his theater by noting that it continued "attracting more and more women and is beyond criticism." Another Gayety representative declared, "Our class of entertainment will be for women as well as for men and it will be above reproach at all times."[21] Clearly, notions of female moral authority cannot be considered wholly in decline in the 1920s and 1930s. Rather, organized women lost their monopoly over female moral authority when representatives of commercial enterprises, from Will Hays to Harry Hirsch, employed it to serve their own ends.

Gayety partisans also challenged the alliance's moral authority by arguing that obscenity should be determined democratically, not by self-selected arbiters of morality. During the 1928 hearings, Eugene A. Rerat, attorney for the Gayety, argued that the alliance should not be allowed to determine the theater's fate. "In our opinion, the Women's Cooperative Alliance does not express the true sentiment of the people as a whole," he asserted. "We are not willing that any one organization shall have its views accepted as those of the city as a whole."[22] By suggesting that determinations of obscenity be submitted to the democratic process, Rerat aligned his argument with the Civil Liberties Union and against several decades of obscenity adjudication that had placed authority for determining obscenity in the hands, not of juries and voters, but of postal inspectors, judges, and censorship boards. But just as alliance women claimed positions as arbiters of obscenity, defenders of the Gayety joined the emerging wave of free speech advocates who declared the role itself illegitimate.

Alliance women also suffered a critical setback when their allies on the city council began to retreat in the face of slurs on their masculinity. As anti-obscenity activism became associated with women and motherhood in the 1920s and 1930s, the masculinity of male anti-obscenity activists suffered. One man who recognized that his testimony against the Gayety could undermine his masculinity and credibility closed with a reminder, "I am not in here representing any women's organization. I simply want to say I am here as a man . . . not attached to any group of women. I am here as an individual." Gayety proponents cleverly turned this vulnerability to their advantage by directly questioning the masculinity of the Gayety's male opponents. In a particularly harsh example, Mr. L. F. Melaney, president of the Central Labor Union, stood as if to address Alderman Walter Robb, an alliance ally. "I'll not answer any of your questions, young fellow," Robb declared. "I didn't even consider you," Melaney retorted scornfully. "I was asking this question of a *man*." What the press called a "near riot" broke out when the men shifted from insults to fisticuffs. Such sensational outbursts attracted widespread publicity, leaving many aldermen anxious about political repercussions. When alliance leaders contacted their erstwhile ally Alderman Johnson to report that the Gayety had again begun to stage indecent shows, Johnson expressed reluctance "to take up the Gayety fight again because of the nasty publicity attached to such a move." Alderman Chase, who had also been sympathetic to the alliance's efforts to close the Gayety, refused to continue to help the women by 1932, because "the newspapers had ridiculed him as a result" of his earlier stand.[23] Paradoxically, alliance women's maternalist leadership in the battle against obscene burlesque led the public to identify anti-obscenity activism with women and motherhood, inadvertently jeopardizing the masculine reputations of their male allies.

Entangling and Disentangling Alliances

Class antagonism also complicated the efforts of alliance women to close the Gayety. When the 1929 Minneapolis City Directory announced, "Minneapolis labor conditions are exceptionally good," it really meant that they were good for the Citizens Alliance network, the tightly knit cadre of employers that had turned the "Gateway to the Northwest" into a "one hundred percent open-shop town" or "the worst scab town in the Northwest." By 1934, these organized businessmen had broken every strike attempt since the First World War, leaving laborers underpaid, depriving them of their fair share of the profits accumulated during the prosperous 1920s.[24] The Citizens Alliance network initially supported the Women's Cooperative Alliance, providing practical and financial assistance through the Committee of Thirteen and the Community Fund. But by 1923, Gilman severed all ties to these organizations, concluding that they actually worked at cross-purposes with the women's alliance by suppressing organized labor and tolerating commercial vice. Even so, the Gayety hearings drew the Women's Cooperative Alliance back into the long-standing feud between labor and business.

Alliance women anticipated that their campaign against the Gayety would add yet another chapter to their troubled relationships with local business leaders.

After their first failed attempt to close the Gayety in 1928, Grace Pratt, an alliance worker, characterized the theater's survival as a victory for business: "Business wants to attract more business by the 'open town' policy. Businessmen tell us that traveling salesmen, industries and commercial projects will not come to a town that has no vice. Therefore," she concluded bitterly, "we must have gambling, prostitution, indecent burlesque theaters etc." As if to corroborate Pratt's claim, many local businessmen, including several members of the Citizens Alliance, petitioned the city council to keep the Gayety open. If the Gayety issue divided many businessmen from reformers, it promised to bring these same businessmen together with organized labor. Recognizing this, Pratt observed sarcastically, "A vile theater must not be closed because employees would be thrown out of work and the business of the street on which it is located would be ruined."[25] This rare moment of solidarity between business and labor might have pleased reformers had it not been forged at their expense. Instead, alliance women lamented that labor and business had closed ranks to defend the Gayety.

Labor leaders saw things differently. They accused the Women's Cooperative Alliance of advancing the interests of local business elites, acting on behalf of the Citizens Alliance rather than the mothers and children at the center of their rhetoric. Grist for this accusation lay not in the organization's current affiliations or allegiances but in its early cooperation with the Citizens Alliance network and its dependence on the wealth of individual benefactors with marital ties to the Citizens Alliance. After separating from the Community Fund, the Women's Cooperative Alliance secured more than half of its budget from Kate Koon Bovey and Louisa Koon Velie, daughters and wives of key players in the Citizens Alliance network. Their millionaire father, Judge Martin B. Koon, founded the Citizens Alliance and its social arm, the Minneapolis Club. Kate Koon married Charles C. Bovey, a flour-milling pioneer whose work with the Washburn-Crosby Company made him central to Citizens Alliance activities. Vast financial means allowed Bovey to found, fund, join, and preside over many community organizations, including the Woman's Club of Minneapolis, the Minnesota Birth Control League, the Northeast Neighborhood House, and the Women's Cooperative Alliance. Louisa Koon married Charles Deere Velie, a grandson of John Deere who helped lead his grandfather's conglomerate and found the Citizens Alliance. Louisa Velie participated less actively than her tireless sister in civic organizations, but ranked, nevertheless, as the Women's Cooperative Alliance's second largest contributor. Together, the sisters contributed large sums of money while using their influence and connections to lubricate alliance fundraising efforts. Since 1923, the Women's Cooperative Alliance sacrificed support from organized business for integrity and autonomy, but it relied on the contributions of wealthy women married to local business leaders active in the Citizens Alliance network. Women who financed reform organizations were frequently married to men who led business associations, and often they pursued agendas that directly conflicted with their husbands'.[26] Alice Ames Winter, for example, assisted the Women's Trade Union League even as her husband suppressed organized labor. But while historians might differentiate between a wife's organizational work and her husband's politics, contemporary observers often did not. Understandably, then, the fact that the alliance's chief benefactors were married to members of anti-labor employers' associations led many citizens to associate the Women's Cooperative Alliance with the Citizens Alliance.

In both the 1928 and 1932 hearings, radical local labor leaders denounced the Women's Cooperative Alliance as a capitalist front, identifying it as an agent of the Citizens Alliance, bent on oppressing labor. The Citizens Alliance employed Pinkerton detectives; the Women's Cooperative Alliance hired moral detectives; the result was the same—wealth won and labor lost. "In behalf of all the thousands of labor organizations in the city I wish to enter a protest against the closing of the Gayety," asserted Robley B. Cramer, editor of the *Minneapolis Labor Review*. Closing the Gayety, he insisted, would increase the unemployment rate and thus empower employers citywide by weakening the bargaining position of workers. Attributing the women's alliance's campaign against the Gayety to organized business, Cramer charged, "That labor-hating organization, the Citizens' Alliance, is behind this move." The budget of the Women's Cooperative Alliance, he asserted, came from the same "powerful financial interests that . . . keep men jobless." Alliance women carefully sidestepped allusions to their benefactors, but framed their rebuttal in the economic terms set by Cramer. "If giving work to some people is going to mean a show of the kind we know the Gayety gives," retorted the alliance's Mrs. O. M. Leland, "then I believe it would be better to have charity than employment." Few responses could have better served Cramer's efforts to characterize the alliance as an aloof, elitist organization. Taking full advantage of the opportunity to portray alliance women as cold-hearted capitalists, he argued that only a twisted sense of morality would sentence seventy-five families to breadlines in exchange for a boarded-up Gayety Theater. "If you want to talk about morality," Cramer shouted, "let me tell you there is nothing so immoral as hunger and starvation and unemployment." Morality, he continued, meant providing employment and paying adequate wages.[27] In a futile effort to turn the discussion back to indecency at the Gayety, one man pointed out that "this is not a fight between the unions and the welfare organizations." Nevertheless, the remainder of the hearings focused on relationships between labor, business, and reform organizations.[28]

Relentlessly, Cramer drove his point that alliance women represented wealth and capital, not child welfare. Particularly hostile to women's associations—and perhaps professional, salaried women as well—Cramer called it "disastrous to pay women big salaries in these welfare organizations." He relied, though, on a class-based indictment of reformers, arguing that allowing alliance women control over the Gayety's fate corrupted democracy. "Welfare societies do not speak for us and do not speak for the majority of Minneapolis, and the majority of the contributions to these societies come from those who have always been the enemies of the laborers of this city," Cramer explained. Skillfully working his way to a dramatic climax, Cramer accused the women's alliance and other female reformers of interfering in the homes of the poor while leaving the rich alone. "Can you name me one family on Lake of the Isles Boulevard, or any other boulevard," he asked theatrically, "where a child was taken away from its parents because parents were intoxicated?" When several people dismissed his question as irrelevant, Cramer yelled, "These organizations are always supervising the poor! . . . Well, we don't want them. We can regulate our own morality!"[29]

Cramer dealt a final, fatal blow to the Women's Cooperative Alliance's maternalist agenda by shifting the focus of the hearings from morality and children to economics, workers, and the hegemony of elites. Alliance women, suspecting a business-labor partnership designed to extract profits from vice, attributed their failure to close the Gayety to the economic power and influence of their opponents and to an old boys' network of aldermen and Gayety defenders.[30] Labor leaders, on the other hand, accused alliance women of cooperating with employers to disempower workers. The activity and very existence of the fiercely anti-labor Citizens Alliance, along with financial and marital connections between reform and business, combined with the deepening economic crisis of the Great Depression to provoke such tangled suspicions. While alliance women regretted becoming so alienated from organized labor, finding women and mothers among their most vocal opponents pained them even more. The ideal of female and maternal unity inspired alliance women's work, but the Gayety hearings revealed that women spoke in no single political or moral voice. Some women supported private control over entertainment, while others insisted on public regulation. Many women argued that mothers should take responsibility for protecting their own children from obscene amusements, while others maintained that in an urban, commercial setting only public officials could offer effective protection for youth. Perhaps most disturbing of all, women disagreed on what, exactly, made for an immoral show. Ironically, such disagreements among women accompanied men's sweeping characterizations of female reformers as too morally sensitive to be exposed to obscenity, too morally sensitive to be trusted as arbiters of obscenity in the public realm, or so morally depraved that they must be seeking salacious pleasure under the guise of reform.

When alliance women combined maternalism with electoral power to attack obscene burlesque, they ran up against some of the limits of enfranchised politics. They learned that constituents in a democracy expect to choose their representatives, and that leaders of women's organizations could not claim to represent womanhood without inviting forceful dissent from unaffiliated women. Prior to 1920, the scattered, dissenting voices of such women received little notice and so posed no threat to organized maternalists. But as voters, individual women attracted the attention of aldermen and business and labor leaders; not only did they signal a female constituency beyond organized women, but their testimony revealed the unrepresentative nature of women's organizations, undermining the alliance's efforts to wield political power as envoys of Minneapolis motherhood. Labor leaders assisted this process by exposing class cleavages and making a mockery of alliance attempts to represent a united group of women, bound by shared maternal values. Thus strained relations among reformers, businessmen, and labor leaders in the 1920s and 1930s fueled the forces undermining alliance women's claims to represent morality, womanhood, and childhood. Amid accusations of maternal, moral, and class myopia, alliance women's façade of maternal unity crumbled, taking with it their immediate prospects of domesticating the public realm.

The women of the alliance could not re-create the Woman's Welfare League's success with the Gayety Theater. Rather, their experiences with burlesque mirrored Gilman's with motion pictures when Gayety defenders reproduced Will Hays's tactic of exposing and exploiting divisions among women. Unlike Hays, though, Gayety supporters did not need to appoint a woman's representative to accomplish this. Alliance women did it for them, styling themselves emissaries of womanhood, and hoping, no doubt, to raise the specter of a woman's voting bloc. While this strategy had empowered the Welfare League in the 1910s, it made the alliance more vulnerable in the 1920s when enfranchised women played politics on men's turf, wielding the vote and making demands before the city council. Here, they faced women—none of whom identified with a women's organization—who disagreed with them and whose individual enfranchised voices mattered. Here, too, they confronted aggressive male opponents who sought and aggravated disagreements among women. The local reform scene differed little from the national one. But even as alliance women lost battle after battle to the Gayety, they pursued another local but quieter, more private, and less coercive anti-obscenity reform plan—one that challenged obscenity law at its core.

CHAPTER SIX

"Thinking as a Woman and of Women"

Sex Education, Obscenity's Antidote, 1925–1934

As if to confirm alliance women's worst fears about the effects of burlesque and racy movies, surveys of Minneapolis youth revealed that children engaged in a wide range of sexual behavior, from coerced fondling to attempts at sexual intercourse. Several boys, one as young as five years old, confessed that they had been persuaded "to perform mouth practices" on older boys' penises.[1] After discovering that most of the children frequented local theaters and received no sex education, alliance women concluded that unwholesome adults and amusements, combined with a "conspiracy of silence" on sexual matters, had instilled unhealthy ideas and stirred dormant desires in the children, increasing the likelihood that they would become degenerate adults and victimize the next generation of youth. Once a man's "sex nature has been warped, and his emotions twisted" the women asserted, he could not enjoy a normal sexual life but would prey upon defenseless girls and boys. "Only through the training of attitudes and the building of character in babyhood and childhood," they maintained, "can tragedies like this be averted." Public officials might abdicate their responsibilities to protect children from obscene amusements, but the alliance's early sex education would "protect children against the warped and twisted information that comes to them from outside" and discourage them from engaging in "unwholesome experimentations."[2]

Alliance women endeavored to demystify sex with explicit sex education even as they sought to suppress commercialized sex, challenging and reinforcing contemporary obscenity law by attempting to liberate sexually explicit materials designed to educate while repressing commercial ones created to titillate. This nuanced approach to obscenity confounded other reformers, the vast majority of whom employed an undifferentiated approach to sexually explicit material. William Sheafe Chase, Catheryne Cooke Gilman's anti-obscenity ally on the

Federal Motion Picture Council, condemned graphic sex education pamphlets along with risqué picture postcards. Mary Ware Dennett, Gilman's sex education ally, cast her net as widely, but with the aim of protecting a broad range of material—from contraceptive information to salacious magazines. In contrast, Gilman and her alliance coworkers carefully carved out a middle ground between what they considered Victorian prudery and modern prurience—a risky position that could either inspire collaboration and compromise or intensify the censorship wars by inviting attacks from all sides.

Sex Education as an Antidote to Obscenity

Alliance women did not invent sex education, but they did attempt to revolutionize what in 1920 remained a negative, disease-focused genre. Among the earliest forms of sex education, Victorian advice manuals counseled chastity, instructing their readers—assumed to be male—to banish carnal thoughts and urges or risk blindness, insanity, a defiled marital bed, and eternal damnation. Equally gloomy but more scientific, social hygiene handbooks of the early twentieth century warned against venereal disease and its devastating impact on reproductive abilities. Emerging at a time in which professors, preachers, and even presidents bemoaned declining birthrates among upstanding, native-born, Anglo-Saxon Americans, social hygiene advocates moved beyond calls for celibacy to celebrate marital reproductive sexuality. Elevating science to the level of theology, sex educators from the American Social Hygiene Association and the Young Men's Christian Association published rather explicit material, but deadened its sensational potential by patterning it after the most prosaic medical treatises. In the same decade that women became anti-obscenity leaders, they began to assume leadership in the social hygiene movement, also dominated by men. In 1913, assisted by popular beliefs in women's innate virtue, approval of women as educators and caregivers, advances in higher education for women, and assumptions of women's reproductive and maternal expertise, Superintendent Ella Flagg Young brought a series of physician-delivered social hygiene lectures to the Chicago public schools. Young's "Chicago experiment" began auspiciously, escaping significant protest and attracting parental and student support. But when the U.S. attorney declared promotional materials from the lectures obscene under the Comstock Law, provoking hostility from the board of education, Young reluctantly abandoned her sex education curriculum. The outbreak of war in Europe reinvigorated the social hygiene movement. United

States policymakers, seeking prophylaxes to keep men "fit to fight," created a Venereal Disease Division in the U.S. Public Health Service, staffing it with social hygiene workers, including Dr. Katherine Bement Davis and Dr. Mabel Ulrich, who formed a Women's Section in 1918. The fledgling Women's Cooperative Alliance cooperated with these agencies, endorsing efforts to make syphilis treatment more widely available and distributing social hygiene pamphlets such as "Friend or Enemy" in door-to-door visits with wives and mothers of servicemen. The war brought federal support for social hygiene work and women's involvement in it, but simultaneously focused the movement ever more narrowly on disease, sexual danger, and medical science.[3]

By 1920, alliance women lamented that, while the focus of the social hygiene movement remained virtually unchanged since its wartime heyday, they confronted sex delinquency problems that social hygiene ignored. Leaders set out to create a communitywide sex education program, based, like their concurrent motion picture and burlesque reform, on extensive studies of sex delinquency among local young people. They began by mapping the addresses of children brought before the juvenile court for sexual offenses, identifying areas of concentration, and interviewing their residents. A local teacher helped the women get started, providing them with names of several pupils reported to have engaged in "immoral practices." Alliance women visited a total of fifty-four families, interviewing the six- to seven-year-old children in small, same-sex groups and the older children and mothers individually. Their conversations—which avoided the topic of masturbation but focused on "attempted intercourse between boys and girls"—found girls younger than ten quite forthcoming and unashamed, while boys and older girls, obviously embarrassed, resisted questions relating to sex, all the while proclaiming their innocence. Still, thirteen adults reported witnessing and twenty-seven children confessed to participating in what alliance women called "sexual malpractices." Twelve of the cases involved brothers and sisters, leading to speculation that overcrowding might encourage juvenile sex delinquency. The alliance's overall findings implicated more than 50 percent of the children, the majority girls between the ages of nine and twelve. Alliance women marveled at the prevalence, gender, and youth of promiscuous children, suspecting that—given the reticence of boys and older girls—their study underestimated the pervasiveness of juvenile sexual delinquency and overstated its relative incidence among young girls.[4]

Interviews with mothers indicated that few knew of their children's sexual activity and those who did responded, not with sex education, but with harsh penalties and threats. Alliance women withheld information about particular children when they concluded that the mother could not "take a reasonable point of view" or seemed likely to impose a severe punishment for sexual transgressions. Most of these mothers belonged to what Gilman called the "unaffiliated mother group," meaning that, like the women who defended the Gayety Theater, they had few close connections with "church, school or club." Many knew little or nothing about sex education. Others, however, presented a promising untapped reservoir of knowledge and experience, leading alliance women to develop a plan for collecting and circulating information and ideas. "House to house workers," Gilman noted, could reach "the unattached mother," while social hygiene classes held in alliance offices gathered women into learning and teaching communities. "Scientific research has omitted a large body of facts which mothers know," Gilman observed, but through the alliance "mothers are going to have a real part in pooling their experiences in reference to sex information."[5]

Alliance women began by educating themselves. After seeking the advice of sex education specialists in the American Social Hygiene Association, state boards of health, the Children's Bureau, the U.S. Public Health Service, and various other service agencies, they acquired an array of pamphlets, among them "The Wonderful Story of Life: A Mother's Talks with Her Daughter Regarding Life and Its Reproduction," "The Wonderful Story of Life for Boys: A Father's Talks with His Little Son Regarding Life and Its Reproduction," "Healthy Happy Womanhood," "The Boy Problem," and "The Girl's Part." These made for a good start, but impressed Gilman as too vague, on the one hand, and too sex-specific on the other. Disdain for "birds and bees" analogies to human reproduction and commitment to teaching male and female sexuality together, as complementary aspects of a whole, led her to Mary Ware Dennett's booklet "The Sex Side of Life." Pleased by its precise and accurate explanations of male and female sexuality, Gilman anticipated that it would be most appropriate for teenagers and prepared to write a corresponding set of sex education pamphlets for use with younger children.[6] Before developing their own program, she and other alliance leaders studied and discussed leading texts in the field, including Maurice Bigelow's *Sex Education* and Thomas W. Galloway's *Sex and Social Health.*[7]

The alliance's sex education plan replicated many features of the Sheppard-Towner Infancy and Maternity Protection programs of the 1920s. Like Sheppard-Towner, the alliance targeted mothers and children, addressed public health issues through education, and employed highly trained women to distribute information and offer assistance in house-to-house visits. Rather than nurses, the alliance dispatched college-educated social workers, training them to offer advice on sex education, tailor a set of pamphlets to each mother's needs, run a series of sex education workshops, and gather information for the alliance's ongoing research and writing on sex education. Determined to make their program accessible to Minneapolis's racially and ethnically diverse population, they hired a social worker especially "for the colored group" and several multilingual social workers who spoke Swedish, Polish, or Russian, as well as English.[8] Although the alliance conducted its initial research in a low-income neighborhood, its home visits stretched throughout the city as pairs of social workers canvassed poor and wealthy areas alike.

Received by a primly attired maid at some doors and greeted by a distracted and disheveled homemaker at others, alliance women rarely met rejection. Mothers at home with young children welcomed the opportunity to chat and often joined their visitors in very intimate conversations, ranging from anxiety over cleaning an infant's genitals to memories of a traumatic and frightening first menstrual period. Alliance women transcribed many of the interviews, which, all unique, nevertheless reveal several patterns. Despite alliance policies against focusing on "unwholesome" aspects of sexuality, most mothers brought up the topic of masturbation. A mother of a four-year-old, for example, admitted to being "awfully worried" about her son "because he plays with himself." Certain that "children who do that lose their minds and are idiots," she confessed that "he seems all right so far," but wondered when she would "begin to notice it on him." The social worker, Mrs. C. A. Zuppann, gently explained that physicians no longer considered masturbation injurious, but suggested that the mother occupy her son with toys, encourage him to urinate frequently, make sure that his clothes fit comfortably, and cleanse his penis thoroughly and often. Extraordinarily detailed instructions for cleaning uncircumcised penises followed all such discussions.[9] One mother, reassured by social worker Dr. Elizabeth Monahan that masturbation would not retard her four-year-old daughter's development, exclaimed, "I'm glad to know that doctors don't think it causes feeblemindedness. That's one less thing for me to worry about."[10]

Most mothers worried over how to explain anatomical sex differences to their children. Alliance women recommended occasional family nudity or viewing classical art. "The setting and atmosphere in the Art Galleries," social worker Frances Strain suggested, "gives the knowledge its proper tone and dignity." Seventeen of the approximately fifty mothers whose interviews were transcribed related that their children's sexual experiences had included another child's "undesirable" behavior. Most accounts involved boys undressing, harassing, fondling, or urinating in front of young girls. Others concerned older boys "handling," "trying to make use of," or requesting fellatio from younger boys. Alliance social workers, never revealing alarm, calmly encouraged troubled mothers to consider the possibility that the other child had acted on curiosity and ignorance rather than depraved desire. Speculating that proper sex education would remedy the problem, they promptly visited the delinquent child's mother, providing her with a carefully chosen set of pamphlets and three follow-up calls. By 1922, the alliance's tireless social workers had presented their sex education program to a remarkable 75 percent of all Minneapolis mothers, and by 1925, they had contacted each house in the city multiple times.[11]

Most mothers welcomed the alliance's sex education program. In fact, so many of these women—encouraged by social workers who assured them that meeting with other mothers would help them overcome embarrassment—attended sex education workshops in 1925 that alliance leaders had to close enrollments. The introductory series of sex education workshops consisted of eight weekly classes focused on physiology, using Galloway's *Biology of Sex*. Alliance social workers lectured during the first hour, then facilitated a half-hour group discussion. Advanced classes, held in sixteen similarly structured, two-hour sessions, dealt with relationships—including adolescent, courting, marital, and family relations—using Galloway's *Sex and Social Health* and *Parenthood and the Character Training of Children*. Workshop discussions sometimes reached a level of intimacy comparable to the home visits, as when Gilman mentioned a conversation with her husband about unfortunate women who became so adept at suppressing sexual desires that they lost the ability to achieve orgasm. A mother at another session shared a story involving her young son who confessed that he and two other boys had exposed themselves to each other. Her response, "Well, you were all alike," earned universal approval from the women gathered. The 4,559 women who attended alliance workshops by 1923 left little additional evidence of their discussions, but they clearly returned home with new information, new relationships, and a sense of themselves as members of a group struggling to rear sexually aware yet wholesome children in the midst of an increasingly vulgar commercial culture.[12]

Sexualized urban environments made sex education inevitable. One alliance bulletin bluntly asserted, "Parents have no choice as to whether or not children receive this education. Their only choice is from whom they receive it." In the absence of wholesome sex information, boys and girls would learn about sexuality through readily available commercial material.[13] Sex education might be acquired from parents, peers, or movies, but in a culture permeated with sexuality it could not be avoided, an approach that anticipated twenty-first-century billboards that urge parents, "Talk to your kids about sex. Everybody else does." Then, as now, Hollywood films did a lot of the talking, and Gilman hoped that "frank sex education" could "deprive the movie of the appeal of the mystery of sex."[14] Sexual material created for profit would, she believed, "incite lust rather than educate or restrain it," making commercialized sexual information anathema to the goal of curbing, or wholesomely channeling, children's sexual curiosity and impulses.[15] But even as alliance women decried the day's "pernicious sex influences," they blamed Victorian mystification of sex for causing widespread ignorance and generating unhealthy interests. Curiosity drove the innocent child "into the street for information," alliance women claimed, leaving "the way open for those whose distorted minds or sordid interests . . . pour forth a stream of filth."[16] Only "sex information—full, free, and undiluted" could satisfy and safeguard inquisitive children.[17] Mothers who incorporated sex education into their children's everyday lives, beginning in infancy, would, alliance leaders believed, cultivate in their children a healthy sexual nature while distracting them from unwholesome amusements. Reasoning that children who understood human sexual and excretory functions—including menstruation, nocturnal emissions, sexual intercourse, and reproduction—and knew the proper or scientific names for sexual parts and activities, would not use vulgar expressions or experiment with their own or others' bodies, they urged mothers to replace "birds and bees" analogies with a direct approach to human sexuality.

The alliance's anti-obscenity work may have helped to protect its sex education program from charges of indecency, but not from disapproval among some of the city's most influential citizens. Leading members of the Minneapolis Community Fund—the postwar municipal organization that provided public financing for social welfare agencies under the veiled supervision of the Citizens Alliance network—pressured the women to discontinue their sex education work, driving the alliance to withdraw from the fund in 1922. Among the alliance's elite critics was Alice Ames Winter, who, according to Gilman, expressed "antipathy to our social hygiene work." Mrs. Samuel Sewall actually canceled her alliance membership after concluding that Gilman "was perfectly obsessed with the idea of sex . . . talking about it on all occasions." Nor did all mothers appreciate the alliance's home visits or their sex education theories. "The more you tell children, the more curious they get," one mother of three young girls declared. "They run out and undress the first child they see." But while the alliance's innovative sex education program clearly stirred controversy in some quarters, its social workers reported negative reactions in less than 5 percent of their visits.[18]

By 1925, the alliance's sex education program began to achieve national prominence. Gilman summarized its work in an article for the *Journal of Social Hygiene*. The American Social Hygiene Association persuaded the Rockefeller Foundation to fund a five-year, $51,250 study of the alliance's sex education program, to be administered by the University of Minnesota and culminate in an instruction manual for use by other organizations. Within three years, the university offered a graduate course to train social work students in the alliance's sex education methods. Between 1928 and 1930, the alliance published a collection of sex education pamphlets for parents, most authored by Gilman, based on alliance women's own research with local mothers, and approved by leaders in the field of sex education. Ralph Bridgeman, director of the Philadelphia Parents' Council, commended "A Vocabulary for Family Use in the Early Sex Education of Children" as "the best of its kind," and Katherine Bement Davis, of the American Social Hygiene Association, recommended it for use in the General Federation of Women's Clubs Social Hygiene Project. Meanwhile, William Leonard, a local physician, predicted that "Early Sex Education in the Home: When? How? What?" would "overcome much prudery and ignorance." Most satisfying of all must have been Thomas Galloway's praise and use of Gilman's pamphlets in his own parent education classes at Columbia University.[19] Until the end of the 1940s, Gilman received requests for her pamphlets from juvenile courts, schools of social work, and child welfare institutes around the world. Unique among social hygiene agencies, the alliance made its main contributions to the field in its home visits, its collaboratively designed educational program, and its simultaneous commitment to anti-obscenity work.[20]

Alliance women's complex strategy of promoting sexually explicit educational materials while suppressing sexually explicit commercial ones made them pioneers in bringing together the distinct movements of sex education and anti-obscenity. During the late 1920s, Gilman cultivated relationships with activists in each movement, placing the alliance at what seemed to her the natural intersection of the two agendas. Gilman met her anti-obscenity ally William Sheafe Chase at the founding of the Federal Motion Picture Council in 1925. A well-known clergyman from New York who headed the conservative International Reform Federation, Chase supported both Prohibition and strict censorship, making him a virtual reincarnation of Anthony Comstock in the eyes of his critics. He and Gilman worked closely together on the Federal Council for over a decade. Gilman initiated a correspondence with Mary Ware Dennett, who became her sex education ally, after receiving a copy of Dennett's sex education pamphlet, "The Sex Side of Life." Written for the author's two sons in 1915, the pamphlet impressed Gilman as just the sort of graphic, wholesome, positive sex education that young people needed in the 1920s. Dennett's politics extended as far to the left as Chase's to the right, from the National Woman Suffrage Association to the Voluntary Parenthood League and the radical feminists of Heterodoxy.[21] Between 1925 and 1929, Gilman drew upon her relationships with Chase and Dennett to advance the alliance's sex education and anti-obscenity work. But her carefully balanced reform program began to tip when, at the end of the decade, discrepancies between federal obscenity law and an increasingly sexualized culture provoked a landmark court case that pitted anti-obscenity reformers and sex educators, generally, and Chase and Dennett, in particular, against each other.

"The Sex Side of Life"

In 1922, the U.S. Postmaster General declared "The Sex Side of Life" obscene, summarily banning it from the U.S. mail. Unable to ascertain the objectionable passages, Dennett ignored the ban and continued filling orders for her pamphlet. For seven years, she escaped prosecution by sending pamphlets only in response to specific requests, under the confidentiality of sealed envelopes and first-class postage. In 1929, after Dennett had distributed approximately twenty-five thousand pamphlets, a Washington, D.C., postal inspector entrapped her by soliciting a copy of "The Sex Side of Life" under the name of a female decoy in Virginia. After sending the pamphlet, Dennett was promptly indicted and summoned before federal district court on charges of mailing obscene material.[22]

Dennett's indictment attracted national attention, stimulating discussion and worry among sex educators who knew that the outcome of Dennett's trial would affect their work. Gilman watched the legal proceedings unfold from afar, sharing her hopes and fears in correspondence with friends and colleagues. Dennett's arrest angered Gilman, alerting her to her own vulnerability. Not only were many of her own pamphlets as explicit as "The Sex Side of Life," but at times she used the postal system to circulate them and Dennett's work. To Gilman, the government repudiated the alliance's reform program by prosecuting Dennett.

Far from obscene, "The Sex Side of Life" served as an antidote to obscenity, Gilman argued. Government prosecutors mistook the cure for the disease—or, as a contemporary journalist expressed it, their case resembled "the disease condemning its medicament." Fearing that courts would find sex educators an easy target, and—stymied by the ploys of well-capitalized obscenity dealers—would suppress materials designed for sex education while inadvertently permitting those created for salacious entertainment, Gilman and other sex educators discussed the possibility that commercial interests would monopolize information about sex. "Either the indecent material will be given right-of-way and the material prepared by mothers for their children will be considered obscene," Gilman wrote to a sister sex educator, "or the reverse situation will come to pass."[23]

As sex educators around the country contemplated the possible impact of Dennett's indictment on their work and, by extension, on the nation's children, a male judge and jury considered Dennett's case. After hasty deliberations, the jury returned a guilty verdict, convicting Dennett of the federal crime of mailing obscenity; the judge assessed a relatively light fine of three hundred dollars. Refusing, on principle, to pay a cent, Dennett filed an appeal with the assistance of the American Civil Liberties Union.[24]

Gilman's distress over the verdict equaled her dismay at learning that Chase had filed an amicus curiae brief that contributed to the judgment against Dennett. In an impassioned letter to Chase, Gilman emphasized her credentials as a fifteen-year activist against obscenity, reminding him of her simultaneous efforts to combat the ignorance that led to sex delinquency. Pamphlets like Dennett's, Gilman argued, provided children with facts that helped instill wholesome sexual attitudes and counter the misinformation of parents, peers, and the media. The men of the jury, she pointed out, observed street vendors peddling obscene literature to children daily. How could they, she demanded, declare Dennett's sex education mailings to parents obscene? In breathless praise of Dennett as "a martyr to a great cause for emancipation of youth from ignorance which has resulted in the double standard of morals, prostitution, white slave traffic and all of the accompanying evils," Gilman pled with Chase to recognize Dennett as an ally. Closing dramatically, she regretted that "the workers in whom I have the greatest confidence in this country are liable to be convicted for the same or similar offenses. This includes myself."[25]

Chase responded thoughtfully but firmly. He objected most vociferously to Dennett's glorification of sexual pleasure, particularly women's supposed pleasure in sexual intercourse, protesting that Dennett's "statement that the sex act furnishes the highest physical enjoyment is simply untrue because, as my wife says, it is not to be mentioned on the same day with the joy of nursing one's own baby." Chase did not rely on his wife's testimony alone, but cited Howard Kelly, a Johns Hopkins University professor emeritus of gynecology, who confirmed that Dennett's pamphlet erred scientifically since most women received very little pleasure from intercourse. In fact, Kelly explained with apparent satisfaction, "Many women are and remain utterly indifferent, and their participation is but a matter of complaisance." Sheer modesty must have prevented Chase from pointing out that "The Sex Side of Life" privileged women's pleasure over men's by treating the female orgasm as the prototype and describing it vividly as "a peculiarly satisfying contraction of the [vaginal] muscles," while calling the male counterpart simply "the expulsion of semen." Chase did, however, denounce Dennett's detailed rendering of the act of sexual intercourse, calling it a "verbal picturization of the sexual act." Indeed, using terms graphic by today's standards, Dennett's pamphlet explained that, during intercourse, "the man's special sex organ or penis, becomes enlarged and stiffened . . . and thus it easily enters the passage in the woman's body called the vagina or birth-canal . . . The penis and the vagina are about the same size, as Nature intended them to fit each other. By a rhythmic movement of the penis in and out, the sex act reaches an exciting climax or orgasm." Chase found this passage pornographic and worried that it would provide instruction and permission for children's fumbling attempts at intercourse. The fact that Dennett provided what he considered a virtual license to masturbate did not lessen his anxieties. Advising her male readers not to "yield to the impulse to handle the sex organs in order to relieve the pressure which may occasionally feel overwhelming," Dennett conceded that the frustrated boy might indulge if "you find that nature does not bring you relief during sleep." Chase argued that, in place of this scientifically flawed justification for self-abuse, children should be taught the evils of masturbation and encouraged to "bathe the parts with cold water when tempted to yield." Draconian to the end, Chase protested that Dennett's section on venereal disease said nothing of sores, blindness, and death, but, by informing the reader of treatments and cures, encouraged illicit sexual activity.[26]

Gilman challenged Chase point by point, revealing that even when the two sought similar results, they employed diametrically opposed strategies. A sense of propriety must have prevented Gilman from discussing women's sexual pleasure with Chase, but elsewhere she wrote that "women have just as much right as men to any possible form of sex satisfaction" and treated a woman's inability to attain orgasm as a remediable problem. She heartily approved of Dennett's frank description of sexual intercourse, so much so that she often quoted "Dennett's description of the sex act itself." Gilman agreed with Chase that children should not attempt intercourse. But, whereas he believed that vivid descriptions of intercourse would "incite lustful desires, especially among the young," Gilman insisted that graphic explanations would deter juvenile sexual experimentation. Chase preferred to reserve vivid description for the ravaging effects of gonorrhea and syphilis, but Gilman completely disagreed. Filling young people's minds with images of venereal lesions and "pathological matters" might terrorize them into celibacy, but would subvert her goal of restoring dignity to human sexuality.[27] "We will have less venereal disease," she asserted, "when parents can discuss wholesome sex attitudes in the presence of their infants."[28] Concurring with Chase that children should not masturbate, she once again objected to his gratuitous threats, explaining that she gently urged mothers not to scare their children with the old stories of masturbator-turned-pockmarked-blind-lunatic. Alliance workers acknowledged, in fact, that medical experts had declared masturbation "so common . . . as to actually border on the normal."[29]

Pondering ongoing debates over "The Sex Side of Life," Gilman noted that supporters and detractors usually divided along gender lines, with women more often advocating and men rejecting childhood sex education. Alliance social workers reported to Gilman, for example, that many women feared their husbands' disapproval of sex education. "The chief difficulty with most fathers," an alliance worker replied, "is that they don't think of the home side of sex education. They think chiefly of the dangers a boy may get into."[30] Hoping to help her sons avoid these dangers, Louise Sanford Fisher drafted a sex education pamphlet for her adolescent sons, but resorted to writing in secret after both her husband and brother disapproved of her work, calling its scientifically precise terminology indecent, unnecessary, and unpleasant. Covertly, she mailed the completed pamphlet to her sons at boarding school and, when she finally agreed to let Gilman publish it for the alliance's use, insisted that it appear under a pseudonym. In Dennett's case, a jury composed entirely of men convicted her; men authored ten of the eleven amicus curiae briefs filed against her, and the trial court judge, Warren Burroughs, remarked that he had been "excessively" shocked by "The Sex Side of Life." Never, he exclaimed, had he "seen such a term as Vagina in print." Gilman began to develop a hypothesis that young boys who learned about sex through furtive perusals of obscene materials could not, as grown men, conceive of sex as anything *but* obscene. "The reaction of middle-aged married men comes from the type of information they received as children," Gilman explained in a letter of comfort to Fisher. "It is difficult for them to overcome the inhibition to discuss a subject which has been so immersed in the filth of the streets." Gilman's male colleagues in sex education tended to agree. John Dewey, renowned philosopher and educator who wrote a letter of support for Dennett, asserted, "It is the secrecy and nasty conditions under which sex information is obtained that creates the idea that there is anything obscene in the pamphlet." Similarly, Morris Ernst, Dennett's attorney, suspecting the masculine psyche as Dennett's greatest enemy, crafted his statements to "release the jurors from whatever left-over sense of sex indecency they may have acquired in childhood."[31]

Chase, too, observed a gender difference in attitudes toward sex education, but he argued that women's widespread support for "The Sex Side of Life" indicated female naïveté regarding the lustful nature of the male animal. Dennett's pamphlet would inspire lewd thoughts in the mind of any red-blooded boy, he insisted. The federal prosecutor echoed Chase's anxiety, declaring that "on reading this book, there's nothing a boy could see . . . except a darkened room and a woman!" Striking an ominous tone, he told jurors that the first thing an "abnormally minded boy" would do after reading Dennett's pamphlet would be "to waylay a beautiful girl . . . and attack her!" Respectable women might have difficulty comprehending this sordid side of masculinity, Chase wrote Gilman, but they should heed men's warnings. Dennett "was thinking as a woman and of women, rather than of her boys as their father would think of them," he observed. Fathers, however, remembered from their own youths the dangers sexual information posed. "The mother who fails to realize this," he concluded ominously, "has failed her son most seriously, and endangered all girls and women."[32]

Gilman and Chase debated these issues for several months, exposing fundamental differences in their ideas about sexuality. Considering all children innocent, Gilman believed that providing frank and explicit information about sexuality would help them develop wholesome sexual characters. Chase, however, regarded males of all ages as innately lewd, needing women to help them escape temptation by avoiding graphic sexual discussions and other stimulants to male lust. Thus, while Gilman advocated using sex education to render women's and men's sexuality more similar, Chase declared women's and men's sexual natures antithetical. He conceded that men should adhere to women's strict standard of sexual morality, but argued that male chastity depended on warnings about sexual dangers and silence on sexual pleasures. Chase regarded as decent the vague sex education that emphasized sexual dangers and considered pornographic the explicit materials about sexual pleasure. These ideas might have gained him acclaim among nineteenth-century middle-class Americans. But in a culture increasingly suffused with sexually charged entertainment, "The Sex Side of Life" began to seem positively wholesome.

Vacating Victorianism

In 1930, the U.S. Court of Appeals for the Second Circuit reversed Dennett's conviction. The opinion, authored by Judge Augustus Hand, one of the nation's most distinguished jurists, echoed Gilman's reasoning as it overturned key aspects of the 1871 Comstock Law under which Dennett had been convicted. Hand departed from the Victorian "Hicklin standard"—a rule that declared an item obscene if it "had a tendency to deprave or corrupt" the most susceptible members of society—by focusing instead on the effect of the pamphlet on its likely and intended audience.[33] Referring to sex education's preventive potential, Hand asserted that, without accurate information about sex, "lascivious thoughts" would plague children, leaving them "in a state of inevitable curiosity, satisfied only by the casual gossip of ignorant playmates." Newspaper editors around the country echoed these sentiments in celebration of Dennett's victory.[34] Having been reproved by Gilman, Chase showed uncharacteristic restraint and made no public comment on Dennett's exculpation. The outpouring of support for Dennett and absence of condemnation for Hand's decision no doubt discouraged the prosecution from appealing. Dennett's victory stood as a landmark in obscenity adjudication and public discussions of sexuality. It simultaneously narrowed the scope of obscenity law and broadened the American Civil Liberties Union's free speech agenda to include issues of sexuality.[35]

Ironically, Dennett's court victory also marked the end of the Dennett-Gilman alliance. Following her bruising court battles and ultimate exoneration, Dennett used her remaining funds to found a new ACLU agency, the National Committee on Freedom from Censorship. Through this committee the ACLU expanded its purview beyond political expression to "motion and talking pictures, the radio, and the scientific discussion of sex." This widened scope embraced contraception, another issue dear to Dennett's heart. Through this new agency, Dennett's longtime support for free speech began to encompass a wide range of sexual expression, commercial as well as educational. Meanwhile, Gilman and the alliance returned to their sex education and anti-obscenity work. Ever vigilant in their two-front battle against commercialized sexual material and the "conspiracy of silence," they continued to use education to instill wholesome sex attitudes and the law to eliminate obscene influences. In the 1930s, however, Dennett and other reformers chiseled away at a new legal paradigm—one that disrupted the alliance's agenda by blurring the line between noncommercial sex education and commercialized sex exploitation, treating both as protected speech.[36] On this shifting terrain, Gilman and Dennett collided.

The hard times of the 1930s led motion picture producers and theater managers to explore more boldly the commercial possibilities of sex, giving rise to a new wave of anti-obscenity reform. Municipal officials and activists in Minneapolis, like those in other cities, noted that increases in juvenile delinquency paralleled the proliferation of obscene amusements. Recognizing that the Great Depression worsened both phenomena, they nevertheless hoped that juvenile delinquency would abate in the face of a crackdown on obscenity. Articulating these concerns in a 1932 speech, Minneapolis Mayor William Anderson connected juvenile crime to unemployment, explaining that young people with time on their hands and escape on their minds demonstrated a heightened susceptibility to criminal and indecent commercial appeals. Local lawyers, judges, social workers, educators, religious leaders, and alliance women who had fought against commercial obscenity as separate entities—testifying on the same side at the Gayety hearings, for example—now collaborated in forming an anti-obscenity coalition, the Committee of One Thousand, to publicize obscenity law infractions and prevail upon officials to enforce the law.[37] Gilman assumed the position of executive secretary and promptly entreated the mayor to remove five allegedly obscene magazines from local newsstands. After learning of the arrest of several belligerent news dealers, Gilman exulted in the administration's cooperation.[38] Soon, reformers and officials cast their nets beyond periodicals. When their reach extended to touring theatrical performances from New York City, Dennett's fledgling Committee on Freedom from Censorship intervened.[39]

In March 1932, performers in "Crazy Quilt," a New York musical revue, prepared to appear on the stage of Minneapolis's Metropolitan Theater. Having suffered an unsuccessful run in the East, in spite of an all-star cast featuring acclaimed comedienne Fannie Brice, producer Billy Rose hired a notoriously unscrupulous advertising agent to give the show a boost. The agent circulated publicity pictures of curvaceous nude women presented as "Crazy Quilt" cast members, and spread rumors that local officials would probably ban the show as obscene. This tactic attracted swarms of curious theatergoers and raised the

Fig. 6.1 This collage of seductively posed nude women represents one quarter of a large publicity poster for Chicago's showing of "Crazy Quilt," October 4, 1931. The promotional material circulated in Minneapolis has not survived, but according to Catheryne Cooke Gilman, it resembled this piece. Courtesy of the Billy Rose Theatre Collection, New York Public Library

ire of reform-minded citizens, including members of the Committee of One Thousand. When they convinced the mayor to confiscate the advertisements and cancel the show, the Committee on Freedom from Censorship rushed to the show's defense.[40]

Hatcher Hughes, chairman of the Committee on Freedom from Censorship, filed a protest with the mayor and Gilman, threatening legal action on behalf of "Crazy Quilt" and the Metropolitan Theater. Hughes accused the mayor and the Committee of One Thousand of illegally censoring the revue, arguing that "so controversial an issue as 'obscenity,' can be fairly determined only by the verdict of a jury." Gilman responded angrily, objecting to interference in midwestern affairs by East Coast "fanatical modernists," "overzealous" free speech advocates, and naïve proponents of the jury system. Since Hughes's letterhead listed member names, including Dennett's, Gilman noted that "there are members on your Committee whom I know have reason to be better informed." After forwarding a copy of her reply to Dennett, Gilman became immersed in a contentious exchange with her erstwhile ally.[41]

Both women expressed general disapproval of obscenity, but argued about the merits of various procedural methods for identifying it. While Gilman defended the right of municipal authorities to make this decision, Dennett echoed Hughes, naming the jury and the marketplace as the democratic forums for such decisions. Having studied the jury system in conjunction with various alliance projects, Gilman deemed juries neither just, intelligent, nor democratic. In local trials involving sex offenses against youths, she discovered that defense attorneys summarily dismissed potential jurors affiliated with the alliance, parent teacher associations, or school organizations. Equally important to Gilman, juries excluded women in nearly half of the states and discouraged them from serving in the others, denying any voice to a group that had special concerns about and insight into obscenity. Dennett's conviction, by a legally mandated all-male jury three years earlier, had only deepened Gilman's suspicions of such juries, especially in cases involving women's and children's welfare.[42]

Procedural methods for determining obscenity dominated discussions among Hughes, Dennett, and Gilman, but the source of their disagreement ran much deeper. If Gilman saw midwestern communities as casualties of eastern commerce, Hughes and Dennett perceived "Crazy Quilt" as a victim of midwestern moralists. Whereas Hughes and Dennett applied similar protections to commercial as to other types of expression, Gilman placed commerce in a separate, suspect category at odds with educational interests. She considered commerce a dangerous force, corruptive of youth and in need of regulation by a democratically elected government. Commerce aimed for private profit, while education sought the well-being of all. Sex vendors entertained and titillated customers, while sex educators informed and satisfied students. Commercial portrayals degraded, while educational materials venerated women's sexuality. No less important, men controlled commerce, while women supervised children's education. Gilman supported a free press but, like the Supreme Court, did not consider commercial imagery and performance protected by the First Amendment. "We cannot see eye to eye on this as we have on other things," she wrote in her final letter to Dennett, "including your own valiant struggle for freedom of education and the press."[43]

Banned in Minneapolis, "Crazy Quilt" promptly relocated to St. Paul, within reach of interested Minneapolis citizens. Those who attended the show defended it as cleaner than most. Several residents protested the mayor's ban and condemned "a certain narrow-minded women's organization."[44] In retrospect, the press agents for "Crazy Quilt" clearly misrepresented the show's sexual content and, in so doing, succeeded in attracting nationwide attention and a sell-out audience to a mediocre show while exposing previously concealed fault lines between Gilman and Dennett. In her 1929 support of Dennett, Gilman had advocated freer sexual discussion as a way to counter Victorian prudery and modern prurience—a way to preempt entrepreneurial attempts to exploit sexuality's salacious potential for commercial gain. She defended "The Sex Side of Life" for the same reason that she opposed "Crazy Quilt"—to counter efforts to manipulate sexuality for profit.

As battles over "The Sex Side of Life" demonstrated, ideas about sexuality, obscenity, and censorship became polarized in the 1920s and 1930s as civil libertarians, like Dennett, and purity crusaders, like Chase—representatives of competing historical trends—established the parameters of the debate. Caught in the middle, Gilman's carefully woven reform agenda combining sex education with obscenity repression began to unravel. Gilman and the Women's Cooperative Alliance used explicit sex education as a tool for divesting obscene amusements of their allure. In doing so, they inadvertently helped liberate the commercial forms of sexual expression they fought against. Ironically, by extending protection to graphic educational information even while continuing to suppress sexually explicit commercial material, Gilman and the alliance helped dismantle existing obscenity law in ways that fueled the growing free speech movement that would eventually undermine the law's usefulness for fighting obscenity. In 1932 Americans could practically count the remaining days of Victorian obscenity law. The eastern vice societies that had dominated anti-obscenity reform for three generations had dwindled into obsolescence, and anti-obscenity advocates around the country struggled against emergent free speech liberalism and each other. Increasingly liberal court decisions, following the precedent set by Dennett's successful appeal, narrowed the scope of obscenity law, while reformers' inability to agree on a definition of *obscenity* further undermined Victorian notions of the term. Even as Gilman and her allies won these battles over "The Sex Side of Life" and "Crazy Quilt"—securing federal court approval for explicit sex education and a local municipal ban on what promised to be an obscene show—they were losing their war.

CHAPTER SEVEN

"Sinful Girls Lead"

Crises in Women's Motion Picture Reform, 1932–1934

"Never were the words 'Women's Co-operative Alliance' sweeter or more significant than at this moment when we realize that our beloved organization is slipping from our grasp," began Mrs. Wilkin. Some women dabbed at their eyes while others searched their handbags for handkerchiefs. Fifteen years after opening its doors, unable to meet its budget under the desperate financial conditions of the worsening depression, the Women's Cooperative Alliance of Minneapolis closed with this poignant eulogy. From a peak of $46,157 in 1927, the alliance's income steadily declined, falling below $27,000 in 1932. Memberships and small donations actually increased during these years, but the alliance lost to the stock market crash the contributions of its most generous benefactor, Kate Koon Bovey. Unwilling to continue the work without adequate funds, Catheryne Cooke Gilman resigned as director, effective January 1933. "The organization should do what it promises to do or remove itself from the community," she explained. Several members, recalling the prevalence of "the underworld" and the unpopularity of women's reform before the alliance, implored leaders to consider alternatives, all of which—like rejoining the Minneapolis Community Fund or parceling out their work to other organizations—promised to compromise the alliance's autonomy. Gilman could not accept this, and Bovey refused to go on without Gilman, whom she called "the soul of the organization." "And the courage of it. I wouldn't have the courage," Bovey confessed quietly. After Mrs. Paige moved that the alliance be dissolved, Mrs. Bemis added a second, and the motion carried. Transformed by the vote from president to coroner, Bovey pronounced the alliance officially dead.[1]

The demise of the alliance left Gilman without secretarial help, an office, or an income—but not without employment. She remained president of the Federal Motion Picture Council, stepped up her involvement with the board of the Motion Picture Research Council—an organization that spearheaded studies of the impact of movies on youth—and became motion picture chair for the National Congress of Parents and Teachers. These offices, though less costly than the National Council of Women chairmanship she vacated in 1930, like it, provided no income. Moreover, in 1932 Gilman's husband accepted a 20 percent pay cut as director of the struggling Northeast Neighborhood House.[2] Under these difficult economic circumstances, Gilman received a job offer from Will Hays's general counsel, Charles Pettijohn. After reading about the closing of the alliance, Pettijohn hoped Gilman "would consider doing some work for him." With no immediate job prospects and great financial worries, Gilman must have been tempted, although she did not show it. To friends she confessed only to being "offended at Mr. Pettijohn's effrontery but not surprised." In a gracious letter to Pettijohn, she declined the offer, explaining that her support for federal motion picture regulation and her work on the Federal Motion Picture Council and National Congress of Parents and Teachers conflicted with the Hays Office agenda. The job offer, however, suggested that Hays's appointment of Alice Ames Winter as Woman's Ambassador to the motion picture industry had not provided the long-term panacea he sought. To be sure, by dividing organized women, Winter's appointment prevented them from uniting behind federal motion picture regulation while creating for Hays a solid core of female supporters. But the resulting fractures also gave rise to a very angry and determined group of opponents who, under Gilman's leadership, welcomed and enticed defectors from Hays's camp.[3]

The deepening Depression and Franklin Roosevelt's response added new dimensions to the decade-old feud between Gilman and Hays. Unemployed and anxious about her family's well-being, Gilman decried Roosevelt's promise to repeal Prohibition even as she rejoiced in his pledge to assume "responsibility for the welfare of all" and hoped that the emerging New Deal would elevate federal concern for public welfare over private profit. Hays, confronting a depressed motion picture market, reduced income from producers, and the first Democratic president in more than a decade, worried about losing his job. Still, he anticipated that Roosevelt would prove more effective than his predecessor at reviving the economy and trusted that his patrician roots would keep the new administration's policies in line with business interests.[4] On this unfamiliar economic and political terrain, Gilman and Hays each saw prospects and pitfalls; neither could forecast victory.

At the same time, emerging economic and political debates sharpened public disagreements between Gilman, who advocated federal motion picture regulation, and Winter, who promoted industry self-regulation, pulling female motion picture activists into the vortex of polarizing New Deal politics. Aired anew in debates over the National Recovery Administration's Motion Picture Code, their arguments begged a historic question: would organized women's ability to wield political, economic, or cultural power on behalf of womanhood survive the 1930s?

Motion Pictures in a New Era

By 1930, financial, political, and technological developments inspired Will Hays to draft a new moral code for motion pictures. During the prosperous twenties, producers had gone deeply into debt to expand their operations and convert to sound, but when the stock market crashed in 1929, they braced for the motion picture industry's collapse. In the short run, dire predictions proved ill-founded. The year after the crash, exhibitors logged ninety million ticket sales per week, nearly double the number of admissions in 1926, the last year of the completely mute motion picture. "Talkies" stimulated motion picture attendance for a while, but they also provided new vehicles for vulgarity, conveying to illiterate audiences, including children, meanings that intertitles would have concealed. Censors could snip away at silent movies without leaving noticeable gaps, but they found talkies nearly impossible to alter. Sound attracted the attention of reformers as well as patrons, contributing to a revival of the Federal Motion Picture Council, a series of harshly critical articles about Hays in the national Protestant Episcopal weekly *The Churchman*, and two new federal motion picture regulation bills sponsored by Congressman Grant Hudson (D-Mich.) and Senator Smith Brookhart (R-Iowa). At the same time, the Department of Justice initiated a major antitrust investigation of the motion picture industry. Will Hays responded quickly to these new threats, sending lobbyists to Washington and agents to disrupt meetings of the Federal Motion Picture Council, while recruiting supporters among Protestant clergy and filing a libel suit against the editors of *The Churchman*. He also capitalized on the upsurge in motion picture attendance and producers' attendant good humor to obtain industry support for a motion picture code that forbade nudity, limited references to illicit sexuality, and respected religion, law, and the sanctity of marriage. The Hays Code, as it was called, grew out of Hays's discussions with two Catholic acquaintances, Martin Quigley, a layman and editor of *The Motion Picture Herald*, and Daniel A. Lord, a clergyman who advised Hollywood producers on religious films. Perhaps, as some historians have suggested, Hays consulted these men in an attempt to woo the Catholic Church in compensation for his worsening relations with Protestants. But the Hays Code also promised to strengthen Hays's control over producers, quash the rising demand for censorship, earn the adulation of Winter and her followers, and undercut Gilman and other advocates of federal regulation.[5]

Meanwhile, Gilman and her allies on the Federal Motion Picture Council campaigned for the Hudson bill, cursing Hays for once again threatening to derail federal motion picture regulation with belated promises of reform. As Gilman wrote to several associates, motion picture producers always pledged to improve moral standards in years that saw the introduction of promising motion picture bills, but they never achieved noticeable improvement in movie morality, and she anticipated nothing different from this code. The Hudson bill read like a Federal Motion Picture Council wish list, declaring the motion picture industry a public utility and providing for its regulation by a Federal Motion Picture Commission of nine appointed members—including four women—charged with ensuring that motion pictures adhered to the moral standards formulated under Will Hays. The bill also allowed exhibitors to choose their movies free from the restrictive trade practices of block booking and blind selling. Hoping to expand their support base while discrediting Catholic women who cooperated with Hays—especially the International Federation of Catholic Alumnae—Gilman and William Sheafe Chase, general secretary of the Federal Council, courted Jewish and Catholic leaders. Gilman also joined Maude Aldrich, of the Women's Christian Temperance Union, in collecting two thousand resolutions and petitions bearing thirty-two thousand signatures, and Aldrich presented them to congressmen in a three-month Washington lobbying effort. Hoping for a public hearing on the bill, Gilman tried, without success, to acquire recent films in order to prepare an exhibition of scenes illustrating the inadequacy of the new Hays Code. To greater effect, she and Aldrich sought publicity for the bill, placing articles in such periodicals as *The Parent-Teacher Broadcaster, The Woman's Journal, The Union Signal, The Ladies' Home Journal,* and *The Christian Century.*[6]

But Hays's new moral code received even greater and more laudatory exposure, including favorable comment in *The Literary Digest* and the *New York Times.* Even producers left off counting their profits long enough to applaud the new morality code. In addition, Winter's regular mailings celebrated motion picture improvements under the new code and declared the Hudson bill a censorship measure, while Michigan theaters reportedly exhibited newsreels against Hudson. Felled by a one-two punch, Hudson lost his motion picture bill and his campaign for reelection by the end of 1930. Hudson and his faithful supporters,

The New Broom

Fig. 7.1 As this cartoon suggests, by 1930 the popular press continued to use domestic imagery to depict moral reform, but now a competent man, Will Hays, wielded the broom. *Rochester Times-Union*, April 3, 1930

Gilman and Aldrich, wondered whether to attribute their losses to flaws in the bill, legitimate opposition to federal motion picture regulation, the naïveté of the electorate, divisions among organized women, lack of sufficient Jewish and Catholic support, or the power and cunning of Will Hays.[7]

The demise of the Hudson bill coincided with a sharp economic downturn for the motion picture industry. In 1931, weekly ticket sales plummeted by one-third, to sixty million, as recent increases in movie attendance faded with the novelty of talking pictures and Depression-induced cuts in moviegoers' entertainment budgets. When their business capsized, exhibitors struggled to stay afloat, slashing admission prices and introducing gimmicks like double features and free dishware. Filmmakers, meanwhile, turned to increasingly sensational themes and scenes, jettisoning the Hays Code as mere ballast. In defiance of the code's provision that "illicit sex," for example, "must not be explicitly treated or justified, or presented attractively," producers portrayed prostitution as an unfortunate but understandable employment option for women. In movies such as *Susan Lenox: Her Rise and Fall, Blonde Venus, Faithless,* and *Call Her Savage,* filmmakers cast Greta Garbo, Marlene Dietrich, Tallulah Bankhead, and Clara Bow, respectively, as admirable women who prostituted themselves to support their families. The profusion of such films prompted *Variety* to announce, "SINFUL GIRLS LEAD IN 1931," and a friend of Gilman's to write that every movie she had seen in the past six months featured a prostitute as the leading lady. In another demonstration of producers' willingness to trade the Hays Code for box office success, Paramount hired Mae West, making her one of the few "sex goddesses" to transition successfully from the burlesque stage to the silver screen. When ticket sales soared in 1930, Hays had persuaded producers not to hire West. But by 1932, profits had sunk so low that everyone in the industry, including Hays, looked West-ward for relief. Financial failure posed a far greater menace than government interference and the potential profitability of West's films more than offset ensuing demands for censorship. Hays's influence subsequently declined and complaints about movie immorality escalated.[8]

Hays and Winter faced recurring public relations crises as racy new releases furnished reformers with fresh ammunition. Winter tried to deflect criticism of the industry through her monthly bulletins, reporting "progress, with plenty yet to do." After receiving several of Winter's upbeat missives, Gilman penned a sharp reply. "We have been hoping that your association with the Motion Picture Producers and Distributors at Hollywood would begin to show results here in Minneapolis," she began. During the past year, however, "the consensus of opinion" is that movies "are on the whole more obscene, more distasteful, more wanton in their violations" of the Hays Code. Chastising Winter for betraying the women who thought "you would be able to change the leopards' spots or in case you could not, would be unwilling to continue as a party working to lower cultural standards," Gilman informed Winter that her followers had lost confidence in her. "Women regret it," she concluded, "because you are a woman and because of your former position." Winter's reply foreshadowed what would become her stock public stance. She joined Gilman in condemning several recent productions but blamed the public for making them profitable. "I could wish," she remarked pointedly, "that Minneapolis showed its appreciation of good pictures," but commendable films such as *Disraeli* and *Abraham Lincoln*, "which have drawn good audiences in other places through the support of people who want good pictures . . . have been conspicuous failures in Minneapolis." Winter's insinuation could hardly have been more clear: Gilman and other motion picture activists had failed in their duty to make good movies pay.[9]

In private correspondence with Hays, Winter's tune changed to complaints about "vulgar," "unwholesome," and "demoralizing" motion pictures. Such movies as *Iron Man*, featuring a scantily clothed Jean Harlow, "leave a bad taste in the mouth and suggest coarse and low standards of social life," she wrote. Winter continued to issue optimistic reports and movie lists, but her confidence flagged as criticism grew louder, movies more daring, and her own and her husband's health deteriorated. She submitted her resignation to Hays in 1932. Obviously disturbed, Hays assured Winter that "under no circumstances could I or would I accept your resignation." Echoing her frustration, he acknowledged that the Depression triggered "a tendency to forget the Code." But with promises that "we are starting in a more earnest pursuit of high purpose right now than ever before," Hays persuaded Winter to stay on.[10]

"Movie-Made Children"

Gilman, meanwhile, continued fighting for federal regulation. Since 1928, she had worked with the Motion Picture Research Council, a national, New York–based organization committed to studying the impact of motion pictures on children. Recruited by the council's energetic director, William Short—who considered her "the best informed, most experienced, most level-headed student of motion pictures in this country," readily offered travel funds, and, at her behest, imposed an organization-wide ban on cooperation with Will Hays— Gilman joined an impressive board, including prominent social workers Jane Addams, Julia Lathrop, and Jessie Binford. With them, she helped to administer an enviable budget that exceeded $100,000, thanks to a Payne Foundation grant. Between 1929 and 1932, the Motion Picture Research Council awarded research grants to leading scholars at prestigious universities—among them, the University of Chicago, Ohio State University, the University of Minnesota, and Harvard—to study the impact of motion pictures on young people. Board members anxiously awaited the results as sociologists, psychologists, and education specialists subjected reformers' theories to cutting-edge social science methods and state-of-the-art research equipment.[11]

Confident that science would substantiate his suspicions about movies, Short explained to Gilman that scholarly studies would enhance motion picture reformers' credibility. Gilman concurred even as she admitted to skepticism about the ability of "modern methods" to "tabulate anything as subtle as the lowering of the standards of modesty and good taste," values that she considered crucial to the wholesome sexual development of young people. Anxious to appropriate the cultural capital of science but wary of its limits and biases, Gilman exerted as much influence as possible over the studies, counseling researchers on their questions, methods, and eventually their conclusions. For example, she cautioned Dr. Mark May of Yale University against using particular questions about sexual relationships in his attitude tests with fifth graders, noting that such questions would mystify most children. Upon learning that Dr. Charles Peters, of Pennsylvania State College, planned to investigate movies depicting "kissing and lovemaking by women," Gilman grumbled that he "certainly might have selected a more important category" to study and offered a list of issues she thought more pressing, including cruelty to animals and people and attitudes toward law and marriage.[12]

Making meaning of the results provoked even more disagreement between and among reformers and researchers. Where researchers found movies harmless or even beneficial, some reformers expressed relief but others skepticism. Gilman and Short, for example, doubted one scholar's finding that movies had little or no impact on young viewers and that "movie-going children" actually read books, sought parental approval, supported Prohibition, opposed crime, valued peace, and respected marriage as much or more than children who rarely attended movies. By contrast, Gilman and Short believed findings that children retained a higher percentage of information obtained from movies than from any other educational source; their emotional responses to movies exceeded adults'; their sleep suffered after viewing motion pictures; they imitated the behavior and dress of film stars and characters; they exhibited marked disrespect for women and girls after watching certain types of movies; and they explained their sexual fantasies, masturbation, and premarital sexual activity as direct responses to suggestive motion pictures. Gilman and Short knew that, coupled with surveys that indicated "an increase in sex pictures, pictures of violence, racketeering and crime of all kind," studies indicating motion pictures' profound impact on young people could, if managed carefully, galvanize their motion picture reform movement.[13]

Reformers actually left few fingerprints on the nine books published by the

Fig. 7.2 A few of the countless young motion picture patrons that female anti-obscenity reformers strove to protect. Minneapolis, 1930. Courtesy of the Minnesota Historical Society

Payne Fund researchers. In contrast, a dusting of Henry James Forman's popularized one-volume *Our Movie-Made Children*, commissioned by the Motion Picture Research Council, would reveal handling by an activist with an agenda. Where researchers perceived ambiguity and charted plans for future research, Forman, like Gilman and Short, jumped to conclusions, oversimplifying complex results and linking movies directly to premarital sex, prostitution, and rape. "The road to delinquency," Forman observed ominously, "is heavily dotted with movie addicts." Several researchers condemned the best-seller as unbalanced, prejudiced, and, from the title forward, not at all the sort of measured, objective summary text they could endorse. But even as scholars decried the book as unscientific, Gilman and other reformers celebrated it for translating to the general public scientific proof that movies harmed children. "Our opponents may be able to sneer at our moral views," the Texas Congress of Parents and Teachers declared triumphantly, but "they cannot laugh off such an important array of facts as have been set forth by the Payne Foundation Studies of the movies."[14]

The Payne Fund studies, as they were called, attracted a great deal of attention. Most reports commented positively on the studies themselves even as they recommended widely divergent policy responses. *McCall's* editors, for example, condensed and serialized Forman's work, highlighting the dangers of movies, but explicitly advising against "additional censorship" or even keeping children "away, to any appreciable extent, from their cherished movies." Instead, the magazine simply offered "some ammunition for the mother" trying to resist her child's demand to see three movies each week. In a similar vein, several newspapers treated the studies as a charge to—and sometimes an indictment of—American mothers; if movies exercised such influence over young people, mothers should exercise more diligence. "That is what a mother is for," insisted Edith Johnson in the *Daily Oklahoman*. Other newspapers lambasted the Payne Fund studies for attributing too much power to movies. The *St. Paul Dispatch*, for example, accused the studies of "dumping at the studio door all the ills of society from crime to vanity that have at other times been blamed upon co-education, the bunny-hug, jazz music, French novels, high heels, the split skirt, one-piece bathing suits and so many other things." Many reporters and letters to the editor called the studies "bunk" and "tripe," and one pointed out that the Bible contained more sex and violence than the movies. Still, readers of most middle-class periodicals, including the *Saturday Review of Literature, Parents' Magazine, Christian Century, Survey Graphic, Literary Digest*, and the *New York Times*—which declared: "EFFECT OF MOVIES ON CHILD FOUND BAD"— learned that researchers considered movies potentially dangerous to youth.[15]

This unprecedented scholarly assault worried motion picture industry representatives, who tried to discredit the studies. The editor of *Motion Picture Daily*, a trade journal for exhibitors, searched for evidence that Gilman and other board members of the Motion Picture Research Council had tampered with the research. Will Hays assiduously monitored the impact of "the Payneful Studies," as they were known in his office, tracking opinions in editorials, articles, and letters to the editor, while collecting names of scholars who offered rebuttals. Reluctant to attack the studies directly for fear of appearing unwilling to accept "a scientific appraisal" of movies, Hays refused to acknowledge them publicly. But in private, he marveled at and fretted over the publicity they attracted, attributing it to the financial resources and zealous membership of the Motion Picture Research Council, the scholarly status of the researchers, and the Depression "psychology of the time with the public willing to try any new deal." During the next year, Hays plotted behind the scenes, quietly recruiting his own academic support team to dismantle the studies. In 1934, he released a compilation of "Authoritative Statements Concerning the Screen and Behavior"—essentially, criticisms of *Our Movie-Made Children* by newspaper editors and researchers—and began to collaborate with Mortimer Adler, a University of Chicago philosopher and specialist in crime and juvenile delinquency. At Hays's request, Adler attended the 1934 National Conference on Crime and Juvenile Delinquency, called by the attorney general of the United States, for the express purpose of defending movies against accusations that they contributed to crime and delinquency. During the next two years, Adler wrote *Art and Prudence*, an anticensorship tome that Raymond Moley—a New Deal administrator and consultant to Hays—summarized in *Are We Movie Made?*, a direct attack on the Payne Fund studies.[16] While Hays carefully planned and vigorously implemented this defense, Gilman plotted a new offensive.

Child Welfare and the Free Movie Menace

Gilman's newest base of operations, the National Congress of Parents and Teachers, grew fivefold in the 1920s, replacing the General Federation of Women's Clubs as the leading women's organization in the United States. This flourishing thirty-seven-year-old association coordinated the work of thousands of local Parent and Teacher associations to promote "the interests of children." Officers sensitized by the Payne Fund studies to the powerful influence of motion pictures over children and disenchanted with the motion picture industry's pleas for cooperation, proclamations of morality, and production of objectionable movies, elected Gilman as their motion picture chair in 1932.[17]

Gilman developed a three-part plan that promised to transform the motion picture work of the National PTA by expanding and extending the organization's traditions. The National PTA already endorsed various federal laws—among them, the Sheppard-Towner Maternity and Infancy Act and the federal Child Labor Amendment—but not until Gilman became motion picture chair did it actively support federal motion picture legislation. Similarly, the National PTA had produced occasional educational films, but under Gilman's plan it would convert this sporadic activity into a systematic visual education program of noncommercial movie production and exhibition. These changes required significant but relatively gradual and uncontroversial shifts in National PTA motion picture policy. The third component of Gilman's plan, however, brought a swift, far-reaching, and, to many, unsettling change; it terminated the ten-year-old movie review section in the National PTA monthly magazine, *Child Welfare*.[18]

Because Gilman equated movie reviews with advertisements, she considered printing them a violation of the National PTA's own rule against endorsing commercial enterprises. Referring to "the commercialization of the General Federation of Women's Clubs," Gilman explained to the editor of *Child Welfare* her goal "to avoid any such charges being made against the National Congress of Parents and Teachers because of my work." National PTA officers agreed, asking only that Gilman prepare subscribers before abolishing the reviews. Elegantly interweaving the strands of her plan, Gilman explained to readers that, under the motion picture industry's ongoing trade practices of block booking and blind selling, "previewing amusement films, publishing evaluation lists, promoting the best pictures and ignoring the rest" could not improve motion pictures. In fact, well-meaning women engaged in such work effectively subsidized the commercial motion picture industry by advertising its products, encouraging children to attend movies, and providing parents with a false sense of security. Even the most careful selection of motion pictures could not protect children from the indecent shorts and violent newsreels that accompanied feature films, Gilman explained. Moreover, parents who supported Hollywood pictures and the better film committee work sanctioned by the Hays Office actually stunted the growth of the noncommercial film industry by diverting attention from it. Thus, in place of the movie reviews published in *Child Welfare*, Gilman announced that she would report on legislative progress and discuss developments in the National PTA visual education program.[19]

Complaints immediately poured into the *Child Welfare* editor's office. "*Ever so many* people want the reviews back again," importuned one emphatic state motion picture chair. Another wrote that many parents subscribed to *Child Welfare* for the film reviews alone, and yet another—who simultaneously chaired the better films committee for the Daughters of the American Revolution—called Gilman's charges against better film committees "slanderous." Demanding a personal apology and a public retraction, she informed the editors, "Miss Gilman can have no real knowledge of the value of these reviews." Gilman's policy rested on the principle that women's groups should not promote commercial motion pictures. But in practice, parents around the country relied on the reviews to guide their children's motion picture viewing. Three months after the magazine dropped the reviews, in March 1933, subscriptions had dropped by three thousand, inciting a flurry of letters among the editor, the circulation manager, and the National PTA president, Minnie Bradford—all of whom assumed that read-ers' desire for movie reviews had caused the nosedive in subscriptions. Gilman suggested other factors, including the insidious influence of motion picture in-dustry agents and the "financial hysteria" precipitated by the recent change in the country's presidential administration. The decline in subscriptions paled be-side membership losses—totaling 200,000 by 1934. Increasingly, economic trou-bles seemed to blame. Gilman weathered the storm by offering to resign, solic-iting letters from supporters, repeating rumors of a Hays Office plot against her plan, reporting several state motion picture chairs who were inciting rebellions against her plan, and graciously accepting the forthcoming rush of support from President Bradford and the *Child Welfare* staff.[20]

Encouraged, Gilman renewed her commitment to the National PTA and began to rally state motion picture chairs behind the second element of her agenda, visual education. Like her sex education program, Gilman's visual edu-cation plan aimed to replace commercial with educational, or noncommercial, material. Convinced that motion pictures and sex, independently but especially together, exercised a powerful influence over human behavior, Gilman resisted leaving them in the hands of commercial interests concerned only with profit. She dreamed of creating a national film institute—a federal agency to produce, distribute, and exhibit movies in the public interest. In the short term, she planned to develop the educational potential of movies by helping state motion picture chairs tap government and nonprofit sources of wholesome non-commercial films, acquire motion picture equipment for use in schools and other civic spaces, and create motion picture programs for children. Conveying this ambitious plan in a pre-convention mailing to state motion picture chairs, Gilman invited conventioneers to attend a kick-off exhibition of sixteen-millimeter educational films.[21]

Gilman debuted as motion picture chair at the 1933 National PTA conven-tion in Seattle, with mixed success. While most state motion picture chairs fully endorsed her national plan, chairs from Missouri, Indiana, Georgia, and Cali-fornia refused to abandon their movie review work and better film committees. Gilman expected as much from California delegates. The California PTA had cooperated directly with the Hays Office since Winter's appointment as Woman's Ambassador to the motion picture industry in 1929, sponsoring a pre-view committee in Hollywood that led many to believe—and Winter occasion-ally to claim—that the *National* PTA worked with Hays and Winter. California delegates took Gilman by surprise, however, when they protested against her educational motion picture exhibition, claiming that Gilman's films posed a fire hazard. Taken aback, Gilman yielded, later discovering that sixteen-millimeter films were not printed on flammable stock.[22] Her disappointment over this lost opportunity and suspicions of California delegates soon gave way to doubts about the National PTA leadership itself.

Gilman returned home to find a letter from the new National PTA president, Mary Langworthy. Langworthy, who authorized correspondence distributed by the national office, refused to approve Gilman's correspondence until purged of all references to Winter and Hays, including assertions like: "Mrs. Winter was not appointed by the organized women of America nor is she employed or *paid* by them." Not only might such statements incite legal action, Langworthy argued, but they inappropriately muddied the motion picture issue—an issue of principle—with "personalities." Gilman conceded grudgingly, wondering "why we should treat Mrs. Winter with any consideration since she has so deliberately misrepresented us in all her publications." When Gilman learned that the just-published *Parent-Teacher Manual* failed to incorporate her new program, instead reprinting the old plan of endorsing movie reviews, she began to suspect a Hays-backed conspiracy to undermine her National PTA motion picture work.[23]

Gilman's work unsettled Hays, and he watched her closely, collecting daily reports on her speeches, travels, interviews, and meetings, and monitoring Parent Teacher Associations, on the national and local level, as diligently as he had the Payne Fund Studies. Hays saw in the National PTA both promise and peril for his work. Visions of creating a national network of better film councils out of the National PTA's "eighteen thousand communities," thereby transforming troublesome critics into paying customers, tantalized Hays. He cultivated relationships with state PTA leaders, predicting that, when Gilman's "short-sighted policy" of visual education collapsed, state and local PTAs would turn in disappointment to the more practical better film council work of reviewing and listing approved commercial movies.[24]

As Gilman suspected, Hays wanted the National PTA. But she did not realize that his plan for getting it rested less on conspiracy than on her own missteps. Hindsight traces those missteps back to a moment that looked, to Gilman, most auspicious. Several months after the National PTA convention, she plucked a victory from her canceled motion picture exhibit when enthused local PTA leaders bombarded her with requests for sources of noncommercial films. Gilman scurried to accommodate them, initiating a distribution network through university film departments and redoubling her efforts to obtain exhibition rights to a series of independent productions. But Gilman found herself woefully unprepared to satisfy the sudden demand for noncommercial films and ended up directing correspondents to borrow films from the U.S. Bureau of Mines. That a federal agency produced motion pictures and operated a lending library came as unexpected and welcome news to many PTA leaders—but disappointment soon followed. The mining, metallurgical operations, and manufacturing processes documented in *From Mountain to Cement Sack* and *Refining the Crude* lured few youths away from *Blonde Venus* or *King Kong*. Instead, these films may have turned Gilman's unexpected victory into one of her worst blunders when many disenchanted PTA leaders concluded, rightly under the circumstances, that noncommercial films clearly could not compete with, let alone replace, Hollywood motion pictures.[25]

In an apologetic letter to a frustrated PTA leader, she admitted that she had probably "overrated government and educational sources of films" in an effort to fuel demand and thereby production. Aware that sparking a demand she could not meet threatened to sabotage her visual education program, Gilman hastily developed a fateful compromise solution that harkened back to her 1920 settlement house community theater project. She encouraged PTA leaders to procure carefully selected commercial films and exhibit them on a not-for-profit basis in noncommercial venues like school auditoriums and church fellowship halls.[26] Ironically, Gilman's visual education strategy relied upon economic reasoning that she herself had criticized—the same economic reasoning employed by Hays and Winter: stimulating public demand for particular films would encourage production of them.

Gilman's original plan to exhibit noncommercial films had attracted scant attention from motion picture interests, but when local PTAs, unable to obtain noncommercial films, began to show commercial motion pictures, movie men protested loudly. Local exhibitors indicted a PTA in New York for competing with "the legitimate motion picture trade" and convinced the local board of education to terminate the PTA's motion picture program. In the national press, Gilman's erstwhile exhibitor allies turned against her. Pete Harrison—whose widely read trade paper *Harrison's Reports* supported Gilman's crusade against block booking, blind selling, and Will Hays—condemned Gilman's "mercenary" efforts to "put churches, schools, and civic organizations on a business basis with motion picture theaters."[27] A competing publication, *The Motion Picture Herald*, censured the National PTA for "contemplating forcible entry into the motion picture business." Gilman's rejoinder addressed peripheral issues: The National PTA could neither be mercenary—it sought welfare, not profit—nor enter the motion picture business—that would violate its policy of noncommercialism. But such arguments offered little reassurance to exhibitors alert to competition from every quarter as they struggled to stay afloat in the depressed 1930s. On this issue, exhibitors enjoyed the support of Will Hays, who decried the "Free Movie Menace." To show motion pictures "either free or at a low price or at whatever price, in school or church," he informed an assembly of clubwomen, "is to set up an altogether unfair, unjust and uneconomic competition to the theater owner."[28] All contenders would soon find a new forum for their debate under the wings of the New Deal's Blue Eagle.

Motion Pictures under the Blue Eagle

A year of Depression-era prosperity followed by reduced admissions, two-for-one tickets, free silk stockings, and several racy box office hits could not save the major production studios from tumbling into financial chaos in 1933. Three of the biggest—Paramount, RKO, and Fox—had plunged into receivership by the time Roosevelt took office, and the rest slashed employee wages by 50 percent in the months thereafter. Will Hays responded to Roosevelt's election with ambivalence. As a loyal Republican who boasted extraordinary connections within the GOP, he supported Herbert Hoover for president. Still, the deepening Depression and its recent devastating impact on the motion picture industry prepared him to trade partisan preferences for economic recovery. Upon Roosevelt's election, Hays offered his full support, calling upon citizens to follow Roosevelt as loyally as a warring army its commander. Even so, rumors that a Democratic administration would force Hays out of office spread throughout the national press; editors at the *Tampa Morning Tribune* and the *Los Angeles Times* even named his successors. They may not have realized that Hays's personal and professional networks extended into the Democratic Party, linking him closely with such leading Democrats as Joseph Kennedy, a Roosevelt intimate, and Charles Pettijohn, Hays's general counsel, who accompanied Roosevelt on his western campaign.[29] Nevertheless, nothing like the chummy letters that Hays exchanged with Harding, Coolidge, and Hoover appear in his rare correspondence with Roosevelt. Hays, more than anyone, knew that he was entering uncharted political waters in 1933.

So did Roosevelt. Desperate to arrest the economy's rapid downward spiral, he hurried the National Industrial Recovery Act into effect, inviting leaders of the nation's industries to develop and submit for his signature "codes of fair competition" to stabilize corporate structures and aid recovery through reduced competition. NRA director Hugh Johnson insisted on one code for motion picture producers, distributors, and exhibitors, leaving the Hays Office and independents to square off. After each submitted a separate code, the NRA motion picture code administrator, Sol Rosenblatt, threatened to write the code for them if they could not cooperate. The broad issue of contention—rights of theaters operated independently versus those owned by producers affiliated with the Hays Office—involved matters, including block booking and blind selling, of great concern to motion picture reformers. Gilman and her colleagues hoped that, in bringing the bankrupt motion picture industry under the purview of the federal government, the NRA would impose the sort of regulation envisioned by the ill-fated Hudson bill. They became alarmed, however, by news that the code written by Hays and affiliated producers contained only a feeble morals clause and nothing about block booking or blind selling, while the independent exhibitors' version prohibited movie rentals to tax-exempt institutions such as settlement houses, churches, and schools. Fearing that Hays and exhibitors would use the NRA to obtain federal sanction for unfair trade practices and hijack the National PTA visual education program, Gilman dispatched a letter of protest to Hugh Johnson and anxiously awaited developments.[30]

When public hearings on the NRA motion picture code opened in Washington, D.C., in September of 1933, dire financial straits and a family health emergency prevented Gilman from attending. Nor could Winter be found among the 209 reformers and motion picture men in attendance. Will Hays may have been just as glad. Just two months earlier, Winter had again attempted to resign from her position as Woman's Ambassador, pronouncing her efforts to influence the moral standards of motion pictures "quite useless." She agreed to hang on only after learning of the NRA motion picture code, in which she saw the "possibility of swinging the whole mass of pictures into more satisfactory relations with the public." Against her deep Republican loyalties, Winter privately hoped "that the 'new deal' would clear things up" by enhancing the public's influence over motion pictures. Hays, who aimed to minimize governmental interference with the motion picture industry, probably did not encourage the disgruntled Winter to attend the hearings.[31]

Ever the master of ceremonies, Hays opened the hearings with a pledge of support for the NRA, a pointed reference to Hollywood's $100 million annual tax payment, and a disingenuous claim that his organization represented all of

"the units and elements of the industry—producer, distributor and exhibitor."
With a philanthropic final flourish, he proclaimed his association united with the
NRA in prioritizing the public interest over corporate profits. Testimony by
fourteen reformers who claimed to represent the public interest followed. All—
including representatives of the General Federation of Women's Clubs, better
film councils, and International Federation of Catholic Alumnae—entreated
NRA administrators to redraft the motion picture code to include Hays's 1930
code of moral standards. William Sheafe Chase, representing the Federal Motion Picture Council, supported this suggestion but accused the women who testified of hypocrisy. Their cooperation with the motion picture industry had thus
far discouraged the sort of federal regulation that could have enforced Hays's
moral code, he argued. After Chase declared the NRA a historic opportunity to
reverse that damage, Deputy Administrator Sol Rosenblatt interrupted him,
charged him with advocating federal censorship, and hurried him off the floor.[32]

Tensions ran high at the NRA motion picture code hearings as reformers demanded changes that code administrators considered unfeasible or irrelevant to
the goal of economic recovery. The *New York Times*, however, reported no disagreements, announcing, rather, "Chase praises efforts," "women uphold 'moral'
sections of tentative agreement," and "women witnesses were unanimous in support" of the NRA code. Gilman, who knew better, sensed the Hays magic at
work and scrambled to stop it, urging friends and colleagues to convey their dis-
satisfaction with the motion picture code to Eleanor Roosevelt—"a power in the
Administration" who shared women's interest in "home, school, and community" and will protect children "against an industry which has exploited them."
Thousands of women answered her call, registering their objections by signing
petitions, penning simple one-sentence postcards, composing choppy telegrams,
or typing lengthy letters, many signed with their husbands. Most echoed leaders of the Motion Picture Research Council, the National PTA, and *The Christian Century*, who signed telegrams, en masse, entreating Roosevelt to withhold
his approval of the NRA motion picture code until, at minimum, it abolished
monopolistic trade practices by prohibiting block booking and blind selling and
protecting citizens' rights to exhibit motion pictures in nonprofit institutions.
Evelyn Patterson, president of a Women's Republican Club, "composed largely
of mothers," begged Eleanor Roosevelt to remember the Payne Fund studies
and resist government attempts to grant the motion picture industry a "monopoly right in motion pictures."[33] Other women copied Gilman's suggested word-
ing, asking that the NRA motion picture code eliminate any provisions that

could prevent "schools, churches, museums and other non-theatrical agencies from renting and exhibiting current films in their auditoriums either with or without fee."[34]

These efforts made little or no impact on the motion picture code signed by Roosevelt on November 27, 1933. Roosevelt and NRA administrators cared about economic recovery, not motion picture morality. They intended, not to eliminate the cartels and restrictive trade practices that offended reformers, but to encourage economic stability through industry self-regulation much like that already promoted by the Hays Office. While reformers longed to invigorate competition and revive their own influence over local motion picture exhibitors by abolishing block booking, NRA officials considered block booking a useful measure to reduce the cut-throat competition they blamed for destabilizing and depressing the economy. In addition, the enforcement mechanisms employed by NRA administrators—industry leaders' cooperation and the coercive potential of public opinion—ensured that Hays would prevail over reformers.

As a politically powerful Republican and head of a major, self-regulated industry that controlled the nation's most effective communication system, Hays and his support for the NRA proved invaluable. No industry could more effectively display the Blue Eagle, identifying itself as an NRA supporter and equating patronage with patriotism, than the motion picture industry. Gilman understood this. Roosevelt's political career depends on "an unscrupulous industry," she wrote to several friends. "The motion picture industry could, with its screen facilities defeat the N.R.A., the F.R.C., the A.A.A., the C.W.A. or the administration itself if he opposed them on so fundamental an issue as 'block' and 'blind' booking." Hays and Hollywood producers played their supporting roles well, promoting the NRA, the New Deal, and Roosevelt himself through motion pictures, slides, posters, and lobby cards. Partisanship became virtually irrelevant, prompting one critic to observe, "The Roosevelt and Hoover administrations have vied with one another in granting favors to Will Hays." Along with a variety of labor regulations, the NRA motion picture code approved by Hays and signed by Roosevelt incorporated only a vague morals clause, preserved block booking and blind selling, and prevented distributors from leasing pictures to noncommercial institutions if local exhibitors objected.[35]

The success of the NRA codes required public as well as industry support, something Motion Picture Code Administrator Rosenblatt heeded when crafting responses to the correspondence piling up in his office. To those who demanded a strengthened morals clause, Rosenblatt wrote that Hays had rededicated the motion picture industry to the Hays Moral Code. To citizens worried about block booking and blind selling, Rosenblatt guaranteed that the NRA motion picture code would allow exhibitors to cancel 10 percent of their blocks—a sufficient amount, he maintained, to permit the elimination of all salacious films. But complaints that the code would prevent noncommercial interests from exhibiting motion pictures seemed genuinely to confuse Rosenblatt. The code "contains nothing," he insisted, "which acts in any way adversely to the interests of schools, churches, museums and other religious or educational institutions."[36]

Rosenblatt's repeated assurances that the NRA would not inhibit noncommercial motion picture exhibitions bore no relationship to the code's actual implementation. In most cases, NRA code authorities—the staffers of grievance boards and arbitration committees under the motion picture code—represented various elements of the industry itself, from producers and distributors to exhibitors. The few seats reserved for representatives of the "public" or "consumers" attracted a great deal of attention from Gilman's longtime foes, several of whom vigorously angled for these positions. Mrs. Piercy Chestney, president of the Macon Better Films Committee, Mrs. Alonzo Richardson, of the Atlanta Board of Review, and Eunice McClure, motion picture chair for the General Federation of Women's Clubs, each suspected that Rosenblatt would appoint, at most, one woman as an NRA code authority. Vying to become that woman, Chestney and Richardson each informed Rosenblatt that her credentials exceeded those of the other. Several women wrote similar letters on McClure's behalf. An amused Rosenblatt assured each one that her candidate would receive full consideration "in the event that it is determined that a woman should be appointed as one of the administration members upon the Motion Picture Code Authority." Rosenblatt did, in fact, appoint a woman to the Code Authority—not one suggested by organized women, but Mabel E. Kinney, the Hays Office nominee.[37] Such industry-chosen boards interpreted and enforced the NRA motion picture code.

According to Rosenblatt's lawyerly reading, the motion picture code posed no hindrance to noncommercial motion picture exhibitions in schools, churches, and clubs. But the code's contradictory and ambiguous language allowed significant latitude to code authorities, and in their deliberations, the code's provisions against noncommercial competition with "an established motion-picture theatre" trumped all others. By 1935, 4 percent of all complaints under the NRA motion picture code concerned noncommercial competition, and, Rosenblatt's expectations to the contrary, not a single noncommercial interest won. Louis

Nizer, an attorney who conducted an exhaustive study of the motion picture code's actual operation in 1935 concluded, "The Code Authority has zealously enforced this provision of the Code to protect the Industry."[38]

While NRA motion picture code authorities decided case after case on behalf of commercial interests, producers prevented many more cases from ever receiving a hearing by summarily canceling orders destined for noncommercial institutions. Shortly after Roosevelt signed the code, Rosenblatt received a letter from Dr. Frederick Gamage, Headmaster of Pawling School in New York, who complained that Paramount, Warner Brothers, Fox Film Corporation, and MGM had abruptly terminated film service to his school. Upon further inquiry, Rosenblatt learned that the producers had received a veiled threat from a local commercial exhibitor who argued that, by continuing to license their product to Pawling School, the producers generated unfair competition with his business in violation of the NRA motion picture code. Similar incidents recurred in cities and small towns around the country as noncommercial motion picture programs at fairs, parks, gymnasiums, farm bureau meetings, churches, and schools closed, unable to procure films or forbidden by NRA grievance boards to exhibit them.[39]

Gilman's hometown of Minneapolis proved no exception. Several months after the NRA motion picture code took effect, the principal of Jefferson Junior High School informed Gilman that he would have to discontinue his school-sponsored motion picture programs; Warner Brothers refused to rent films to the school because "the local theater men objected." When Gilman appealed, the local NRA grievance board secretary told her, "Schools, churches, and other non-theatrical, non-licensed, and non-tax-paying agencies were to receive pictures *unless the local theater men objected.*" Since local exhibitors had complained that motion picture shows "in school auditoriums reduced materially the attendance at theaters," the local NRA code administrator forbade such shows.[40]

Gilman had initially welcomed the National Recovery Administration as a program that could restore local control through federal power. The NRA motion picture code, however, brought the federal government into her community and communities around the country in ways she never anticipated and deeply resented. Far from curbing motion picture producers' quest for profits at all costs, the code protected restrictive trade practices that reduced community influence over local exhibitors. Perhaps even more disappointing, code authorities undercut Gilman's effort to circumvent the commercial distribution system, leaving her no choice but to oppose the NRA motion picture code.[41]

Varieties of Womanhood and Limits of Sisterhood

While the NRA aimed to revive industry through regulation, Hollywood continued to seek salvation in sex, churning out a steady stream of racy movies for Winter to defend. In 1933, Paramount featured Mae West—"the finest woman who ever walked the streets"—at her hump-walking, double-talking best, trading sex for diamonds and crooning for "A Guy What Takes His Time" in *She Done Him Wrong*, and playing "a girl who lost her reputation and never missed it" in *I'm No Angel*. Publicly, Winter began to condemn the recent release of "sex films" and "dirty" pictures but indicted patrons, especially mothers, for making unwholesome movies profitable.[42] Privately, she complained to Hays that Warner's *Baby Face* and RKO's *Bed of Roses* glamorized prostitution by starring screen idols Barbara Stanwyck and Constance Bennett as femme fatales who seduced men and raided their wallets. Even worse, in Paramount's *The Story of Temple Drake*, neither love nor money motivated sexual encounters between a rape victim and the perpetrator with whom she fell in love. Columbia's *So This Is Africa* contained sexual situations and innuendos "that even ten year old children" will understand. "The constant flow of these pictures leaves me with mental nausea," Winter wrote to Hays. While she remained convinced that the previewing and listing activities conducted under her supervision rendered a valuable public service, she considered her efforts to influence moral standards "even more than useless." Unable, in good conscience, to continue, she assured Hays that she would tell no one the true reason for her departure but would blame it on her age. In November 1933, Winter again tendered her resignation, but Hays talked her out of it. Three months later, she remained on the job, repeating to Hays, "the machinery isn't working as it ought to do for the purposes for which you created it," and declaring "the situation here desperately unsatisfactory."[43]

Despite Gilman's and Winter's objections, many women enjoyed the so-called "sex films," and entertainment magazines like *Variety* raced to announce it. "DIRT CRAZE DUE TO WOMEN" screamed the headline of a front-page article, claiming that women favored movies with sex and "bad women. The badder the better." As if to explain the presumed slump in female morality, the paper continued, "That's what women go for besides voting since given their much abused suffrage."[44] Gilman and her friends rejected the logic that linked female immorality to political empowerment, but they too noted a disturbing trend in women's motion picture tastes. The Minnesota PTA motion picture chair liked *The Story of Temple Drake*, Gilman noted, a film "in which sex degeneracy and

Fig. 7.3 Suggestive advertisement for "So This Is Africa," a
1933 movie condemned by both Catheryne Cooke Gilman and
Alice Ames Winter. *Variety*, January 17, 1933

underworld vice and crime occupies every scene and line." Equally troubling was
a friend's observation that "a large class of women choose Mae West and her
crowd." Even the General Federation of Women's Clubs noted in its annual motion picture report, "Groups condemn the Mae West productions, but they fill
the theatre." West, a physical caricature of womanhood with an insatiable libido,
offended many female spectators who recoiled from her hard-bitten sexuality
and dreaded seeing girls imitate her lurching gait, flamboyant dress, and
clenched-teeth one-liners. Worse, they feared that her movies would encourage young people to associate wealth and ease with wanton living.[45]

But West possessed an undeniable intergenerational appeal. Younger women thrilled to West's insistence on her own pleasure. Depression-era actresses often portrayed pathetic characters who "endured a fate worse than death for the sake of their children," but West played a woman who enjoyed sex for its own sake as well as for its exchange value. She confidently flaunted her sexual charms, shaping a distinctly modern style of female autonomy that included traditional male sexual prerogatives. Many older women enjoyed watching West disarm male sexuality, challenge the double standard, and revive an outdated model of female sexual attractiveness—the tightly corseted hourglass—traditionally associated with fecundity. No less an authority than the Central Association of Obstetricians and Gynecologists declared West "a boon to motherhood" for bringing back "plump female figures," while Dorothy Dix, the noted journalist, praised West for resisting modern women's efforts to "desex themselves" with "bobbed heads and mannish clothes." "Mae West has been a benefactress to womanhood. More power and more curves to her," cheered Dix. Meanwhile, a Kansas City newspaper reported that "perfectly respectable matrons" delighted in West as a "picture of woman triumphant, ruthlessly and unscrupulously triumphant, over poor, blundering, simple-minded men." Even viewers who disapproved of her tactics enjoyed watching her win.[46]

Motion pictures attracted male and female fans of all classes and ages—but different women wanted to see different things on the silver screen. By the middle of the 1930s, even *Variety*'s male editors tailored movie reviews to various types of "fanettes"—from "flaps" to "matrons" to "femmes in the sticks."[47] Such sharp and public differences in female sensibilities made women who claimed to speak for womanhood, like Gilman and Winter, extraordinarily vulnerable. Striving to convey an image of unified womanhood in the face of clear evidence to the contrary left them feeling exposed and betrayed. Already disappointed by Will Hays and the NRA, they now discovered that the women they claimed to represent were as likely to approve of Mae West as to object to her brazen sexuality. But this disillusionment alone cannot explain why Winter and Gilman, whose shared taste in films and passion for motion picture reform might have made them allies, became bitter enemies, drew other women into their disputes, and ultimately undermined women's leadership of motion picture reform.

Crisscrossing lives and values set Winter and Gilman on explosively intersecting reform trajectories. College-educated women, transplanted from the East to Minnesota at the behest of bridegrooms, ambitious leaders of local women's organizations and major national associations—these women lived lives very sim-

ilar in outline but dramatically different in detail. Because Winter wed a prosperous businessman and needed no independent income, she could join, contribute to, and devote her life to the unpaid work of women's clubs. Ready-made
family connections exceeded even her ample financial resources, tying her into
celebrated eastern reform communities, the Republican Party leadership, and—
through the Citizens Alliance network and the Public Safety Commission—powerful Twin Cities business elites. In contrast, Gilman's marriage to a settlement
house director placed middle-class advantages of daycare, medical care, and private schooling for her two children beyond reach without her salary. She received
an income as the executive secretary of the Women's Cooperative Alliance, an
organization dependent upon wealthy benefactors for its budget. Gilman's hum-
ble lineage required that she assemble, piece by piece, a network of relationships
with donors and other reformers.[48] Thus, at the outset, financial and social resources guided Winter and Gilman along divergent paths.

Partisanship joined class to divide the two women further. Winter, whose
deep Republican roots embraced the Hooverian tradition of voluntary cooperation, worried that newly enfranchised women in the 1920s would use their electoral power to legislate morality and inflate government. Hoping to do just that,
Gilman, a political independent with a solid progressive faith in government regulation, fashioned legislative solutions to social problems from juvenile delinquency and prostitution to obscene burlesque and motion pictures. So persuaded
was Gilman of the efficacy of law, that she even explored the possibility of suing
the motion picture industry for group libel against American womanhood.
Gilman's celebration of the New Deal's national approach to public welfare con-
trasted sharply with Winter's warning against "the danger of heaping all our
problems on the federal government." While Winter, a wealthy Republican,
wielded power beyond government at the local level and through partisan chan-
nels and private industry in the national arena, Gilman strove to obtain influence
within democratically elected bodies, especially in the federal government,
where, she believed, personalities, money, and social status held less sway.[49] Thus
Gilman's activism led her to the state legislature and halls of Congress, while
Winter's brought her into private, cooperative alliances with business leaders and
associations.

Individual personality traits intensified differences between the two women.
By all accounts, Gilman lacked a sense of humor while Winter took great pride
in hers, advising a gathering of clubwomen, for example, to avoid being "so Puritanical" that they failed to "have a good time in life and see a joke."[50] Winter

set out to charm men in this equal suffrage era of the so-called "sex war," renaming the 1920s "the age of chivalry" and calling "the men of today" most "splendid specimens."[51] Gilman, by contrast, distrusted men, and family and friends noted that she disliked "even the looks of a man."[52] A notable exception was her husband, Robbins—with whom she shared a passion well beyond their partnership in reform. When, seventeen years into their marriage, a transatlantic separation prompted a daily exchange of romantic letters, Gilman wrote, "If you were near I should kiss you even tho [*sic*] the world looked on—moral or glasses notwithstanding."[53] Overall, though, Gilman lamented the degeneracy of modern men, blaming them for abusing and failing to protect women and children. "At the hands of men lawyers, men judges, and men juries," she asserted, female and juvenile victims would "never receive justice."[54] Thus, while Winter consistently denied any special female morality, maintaining that, as equally moral beings, women and men should tackle social problems together, Gilman identified male immorality as the source of most social ills and female moral authority as the remedy.

Both Gilman and Winter relied on female solidarity to sustain their work, but each conceived of it differently. To Gilman, moral superiority and conflict with men forged the bonds of female unity. Virtuous and embattled, women must parlay their moral superiority into authority through reform and political activism. In contrast, Winter discouraged women from organizing around feminine moral sensibilities, since "women are not more ethical or moral than men."[55] She admitted that home responsibilities sensitized women to certain issues, conceding that this made men's perspective *different* from women's, but neither innately nor insidiously so. While Winter discouraged sex antagonism in favor of communication and cooperation, Gilman expected conflict with men and encouraged women to replace them in positions of power.

Beneath Gilman and Winter's public debate over motion picture reform lay common concerns but starkly divergent financial, class, and personal circumstances. At the center of their disagreement lay a pressing question for Americans in the 1930s: How could democracy survive a capitalist, consumer-driven economic system? Gilman argued that unrestrained mercenary corporations suffocated democracy. The motion picture industry, in particular, corrupted American values, subordinating children's welfare to private profit and competitive ideals to monopolistic business practices. Only federal regulators, appointed by democratically elected officials, could protect democracy from the excesses of capitalism, defend public welfare against corporate greed, and preserve morality against the onslaught of Hollywood vice. In equally dualistic logic, Winter declared that federal motion picture regulation would corrupt American democracy by imposing "the heavy hand of censorship" and giving the federal government dictatorial power over speech and private industry. Issues of federalism stood at the heart of these arguments. Gilman believed that mighty cartels like the motion picture industry could be restrained only by a greater power. The federal government, she reasoned, could shift the balance of power from corporations and the mass culture they shaped back to parents and communities. In contrast, Winter argued that "federalization" undermined local authority, vesting responsibility and control in a distant, oppressive bureaucracy.[56]

When Winter and Gilman debated whom to hold accountable for the growing salaciousness of Hollywood productions, each reproached the group with which she identified least and sought to empower the group with which she identified most. Winter blamed consumers and "the public," while Gilman indicted producers and private industry. Winter touted the virtues of industry self-regulation and a laissez-faire economy, while Gilman celebrated federal regulation, pronouncing market-based efforts to influence producers worse than useless under current industry trade practices. Winter enjoyed a degree of financial, social, and political influence at the municipal and state levels that she could not hope to enjoy in a more pluralistic national arena. Locally, the Winter and Ames families wielded expansive private and public power through social contacts, employers' associations, and political clout. Lacking such local status and power, Gilman lamented that her success depended on the inclinations of current municipal officials. Suspecting, often rightly, that entanglements between businessmen, politicians, and city government undermined her reform efforts, she advocated federal remedies. "The Federal authorities," Gilman noted, "are not so susceptible to local politics."[57]

Winter assumed that parents controlled their children's motion picture attendance; ticket sales reflected consumers' desires, and public will guided filmmakers. Her ideas conflated capitalism and democracy, assuming the existence of a commercial democracy by treating consumer and citizen, box office and voting booth, ticket and ballot as interchangeable elements. In such a system, consumers shaped motion picture morals. As evidence, Winter cited theater managers' efforts to assist parents by creating children's programs, grouping their most child-friendly movies together for Saturday matinees. Castigating parents for failing to make such programs profitable and forcing exhibitors to "go back to the haphazard selection, with no reference to the child audience," Winter declared, "Mother and father have got to put thought and sanity and guidance into child life." By attributing to patrons the power to shape motion picture production, Winter delineated a form of commercial citizenship complete with civic duties; good citizens bought tickets to good movies. In Winter's commercial democracy, votes were not just for sale—they had to be bought.[58]

Gilman rejected Winter's reasoning, disputing the notion of a citizen's obligation to purchase movie tickets and arguing that because block booking and blind selling prevented exhibitors from selecting their programs, individual patrons exercised little or no influence over local theater showings. Producers, far from simply responding to moviegoers' desires, actually shaped them, creating a market for unwholesome movies by tantalizing and exploiting latent appetites for salaciousness and violence. Several elements prevented parents from exercising effective guidance over their children's movie consumption, she explained. Unwholesome "shorts" and advertisements appeared in conjunction with wholesome movies, making it impossible for parents to control the quality of their child's entire movie experience. Furthermore, since theater lobbies displayed indecent advertising, youthful patrons witnessed it no matter which feature they attended. Theater managers "know that if children see the good pictures and the lurid advertisements for coming attractions," Gilman argued, "a large portion of the adolescent group will manage in some way" to see the unwholesome films advertised. Indeed, because she considered the motion picture industry a monolith, Gilman held parents who purchased tickets for "good" movies responsible for inadvertently financing production of "bad" ones.[59] Only the federal government could transfer control over motion picture content to the public, Gilman concluded.

Although Winter and Gilman did not know it, by 1933 their ideas about and positions within motion picture reform briefly converged as each confronted the limits of her chosen approach. Winter, increasingly disenchanted with industry self-regulation, momentarily but privately defied her Republican allegiances to endorse moral reform under the NRA motion picture code. Gilman too hoped the NRA would achieve motion picture reform. But disappointment with the profit-oriented motion picture code returned Winter and Gilman to their conflicting reform strategies.

Winter stayed on as Woman's Ambassador to the motion picture industry even as producers paid less and less attention to her suggestions, turning to her mainly for promotional assistance. The upbeat monthly missives she sent in 1929 had recommended individual movies and celebrated women's reform efforts, but

Fig. 7.4 This cover of a brochure published in the 1930s by the Motion Picture Research Council portrays motion picture industry trade practices—specifically, block booking and blind selling—as a brick wall that prevents the public from freely choosing its motion pictures. Courtesy of the Robbins Gilman and Family Papers, Minnesota Historical Society

by 1934 these had disintegrated into semiannual reports of exemplary movies that the hypocritical public had turned into box office failures. Rebuking audiences for patronizing Mae West's *I'm No Angel* instead of *Alice in Wonderland*, Winter concluded one letter bitterly, "The cleansing of the movies seems well under way. Can we clean up the demand?"[60] Disillusionment with industry self-regulation and the inability of market forces to reform motion pictures did not divert Winter from the reform course that defined her public persona and had already absorbed more than a decade of her energies.

Gilman, likewise, continued pressing for federal motion picture regulation even after discovering, through her experience with the NRA motion picture code, the ease with which corporate interests captured federal policy and turned it against reformers. Initially, Gilman hoped the Roosevelt administration would use federal power for the public good, eliminating monopolistic trade practices, exposing corporate greed as the cause of the Depression, and holding motion picture producers accountable for the moral quality of their products. More immediately, she anticipated that children with reduced entertainment budgets would gladly avoid expensive, salacious, commercial theaters to attend wholesome free movies in the local school gym. Instead, at this crucial historical juncture when the Depression might have helped noncommercial compete with commercial enterprises for children's attention, NRA motion picture code administrators ruled such competition unfair. As implemented, the code inverted Gilman's logic regarding trade practices, treating block booking and blind selling as fair, and noncommercial competition as unfair. From Gilman's perspective, it provided federal sanction for monopolistic trade practices, ignored the issue of moral standards, and undercut the National PTA's ambitious visual education plan. But Gilman's commitment to federal remedies did not dim; in March 1934 she testified before Congress on behalf of federal motion picture regulation, before embarking on a whirlwind, 23-state, 259-lecture tour.[61]

Thus, while Winter quietly accepted her increasingly marginal role in motion picture reform, Gilman made one last effort to direct the movement toward government and away from industry self-regulation, using the national lecture circuit to lambaste the NRA, Will Hays, and the women who supported him.[62] Gilman's new wave of attacks would open the final chapter of women's anti-obscenity leadership.

CHAPTER EIGHT

"'Catholic Action' Is Blazing a Spectacular Trail!"

The Collapse of Women's Anti-obscenity Leadership, 1934–1935

In 1934, Catheryne Cooke Gilman butted heads with Eunice McClure, the new motion picture chair for the General Federation of Women's Clubs. As Gilman redoubled her efforts to lead the motion picture reform movement and McClure launched her chairmanship, each eyed the other's followers. Gilman counted on widespread disgust at the previous year's movies to help her incite a rebellion among clubwomen, turning them, once and for all, against Will Hays and Alice Ames Winter. McClure, by contrast, aimed to bring the National PTA and the Women's Christian Temperance Union into cooperation with Hays and Winter through her campaign to build better film councils around the slogan: "Be Better Motion Picture Buyers." She scored a major victory when the WCTU's *Union Signal* circumvented its own motion picture chair—Gilman's ally, Maude Aldrich—to publish the General Federation plan. McClure also attended state and local PTA meetings, promoting her program and spreading rumors that Gilman had resigned as National PTA motion picture chair. Fearing that McClure would dupe the PTA rank and file with her warmed-over version of "Boost the Best and Ignore the Rest," Gilman alerted state motion picture chairs and ordered McClure to stop misrepresenting her. A contentious exchange ensued.[1]

In private correspondence, McClure implored Gilman to set "personalities" aside and help her work for better movies. "Personalities," Gilman replied, had nothing to do with her contempt for "women who are mothers" and yet cooperate with an industry that "proclaims its right to exploit public welfare for private gain." Gilman vowed never to work with such women. She suspected, in fact, that McClure received funds from Hays and that her interest in the National PTA derived from her desire to gain movie customers from among its membership of young mothers. "The General Federation is composed of older women," Gilman wrote a colleague. "Mrs. McClure must interest the Parent Teacher Associations because they have the children."[2] Failing to hear back from McClure, she took a veiled version of her argument to the pages of *Child Welfare*, warning readers that, contrary to clubwomen's claims, better film councils could not reform movies by reviewing, advertising, and patronizing them. Not only did block booking and blind selling stand in the way; the Hays Office subsidized better film councils because they increased ticket sales and producers' profits. In a public rejoinder, McClure abandoned her usual efforts to cloak what she called personalities, rebuking "Mrs. Robbins Gilman" for attacking "the soundness and integrity" of the General Federation, arguing that, not only did better film councils operate independently of the Hays Office, but they helped parents choose appropriate movies for children and encouraged filmmakers to create more such movies.[3]

Many women joined the fray; most accused each other of accepting money from the Hays Office. Front and center was Frances Diehl McClure's predecessor as General Federation motion picture chair, Gilman's successor as National Council of Women motion picture chair, and a close friend of Will Hays. Diehl circulated inquiries about Gilman's earlier relationship with Hays, asking several of Gilman's coworkers to confirm rumors that in 1922 Hays had paid Gilman to help him defeat censorship in Massachusetts. The editor of *Child Welfare* relayed this accusation to Gilman, requesting an explanation. Replying with a detailed account of her work with Hays, including his financial support, Gilman admitted that Hays tried to "secure my services to exploit women's organizations." After discovering this, she explained, "I refused to have anything further to do" with him, despite his repeated offers of employment.[4] Gilman reciprocated with a casual inquest of her own, repeating gossip that producers purchased movie scenarios from Diehl at a rate of $25,000 apiece. An indignant Diehl denied the rumor, declaring that she accepted money only from family members, and fared quite well on an $800 monthly allowance from her husband, Ambrose, vice president of the United States Steel Corporation.[5]

As internecine warfare eroded women's efforts to reform motion pictures, Catholic Church leaders created the Legion of Decency to fill the emerging void. By taking up anti-obscenity reform, the Legion challenged women's leadership, promising to replace women with men and Protestants with Catholics at the head of the anti-obscenity movement. After Gilman and her allies had struggled for over a decade to control motion picture reform from within women's organizations, one might expect them to reject Legion men as interlopers who threatened to upset twenty years of women's efforts. On the other hand, given their disillusionment with organized women by 1934, one can imagine them embracing Legion men who adopted their reform agenda. That neither of these scenarios occurred raises questions about how Legion leaders reshaped the anti-obscenity movement and the reaction their work elicited from female activists. The answers shine a bright light on women's troubled history as anti-obscenity activists and political actors in the 1920s.

The Legion of Decency and the International Federation of Catholic Alumnae

American Catholic concern about motion picture morality did not appear suddenly in 1934. However, earlier examples of Catholic reform have often escaped scholars' notice, because the embattled insularity that characterized the Church's efforts to cope with anti-Catholic prejudice—through its extensive parochial school system, for example—also assured that early Catholic reform efforts focused not on American society broadly but on the church community. The Catholic Theatre Movement, for example, founded in the 1910s, monitored stage plays, creating a "white list" of approved performances, but it limited itself to shaping the entertainment choices of parishioners. By all accounts, World War I and the simultaneous resurgence of the virulently anti-Catholic Ku Klux Klan initiated a dramatic shift in Catholic reform strategy, convincing Catholic leaders to take a more active role in national affairs. In the early 1920s, soon after taking office, Hays courted the Catholic clergy, winning the support of the National Catholic Welfare Conference and the long-term cooperation of the International Federation of Catholic Alumnae several years before he collaborated with two Catholic leaders to develop the 1930 Hays Code. Hays's successful recruitment of Catholic leaders encouraged Gilman to redouble her efforts to build alliances with the Church. Her efforts bore fruit, convincing the influential Bishop Michael Curley of Baltimore and the National Council of Catholic Women to endorse federal motion picture regulation.[6] Thus by the 1930s Catholic leaders had endured more than a decade of efforts by motion picture activists and industry representatives to enlist their support in disputes that occurred chiefly among Protestants.

No longer content to play a supporting role, in 1934 a group of Catholic prelates and laymen set out to take control of motion picture reform, declaring the Hays Code ineffective, creating the Legion of Decency, and using it to launch a nationwide motion picture boycott. Within a few months, Catholic leaders had earned their new movement's moniker by recruiting hundreds of thousands of parishioners to sign "The Pledge of Decency." Most promised only to avoid indecent motion pictures, but Cardinal Dennis Dougherty of Philadelphia, Pennsylvania, instructed his followers to avoid motion pictures altogether. Movie attendance in Catholic areas plummeted, making Hays and his staff tremble at the thought of losing the patronage of American Catholics—all twenty million of them—"enough to put one awful dent in motion picture attendance," noted a Hays staffer. More disturbing still, the possibility of a budding motion picture reform alliance between Catholics, Protestants, and Jews indicated that the boycott might exceed Hays's worst fears.[7]

A range of emotions washed over Gilman as she watched the swelling ranks of the Legion of Decency. "The 'Catholic Action' is blazing a spectacular trail," Gilman wrote to a friend excitedly, "one that is alarming the producers." In her more optimistic moments, she anticipated that the Legion would ally with her against Will Hays and Alice Ames Winter. Since 1922 Hays had enjoyed the co-operation of the International Federation of Catholic Alumnae, an organization that, under the leadership of Rita McGoldrick, created the system of movie previewing and listing that Winter now supervised. With the Legion's help, Gilman hoped to bring McGoldrick and the Catholic Alumnae to heel. But even as she celebrated the Legion of Decency and congratulated Jewish and Protestant groups that emulated its work, she betrayed an underlying distrust of Catholic leadership and lamented that Protestant ministers had failed to initiate such a "courageous" mission. Fearing also that the Legion of Decency might eclipse and neglect its debt to her own work, she devoted several of her public lectures to tracing the Legion's roots to the National PTA's "pioneer efforts," urging women to launch a national boycott of their own.[8] Most of all, however, Gilman worried that the Legion of Decency would succumb to the same Hays strategies that had divided and disarmed organized women.

Discussing this with motion picture reform allies, Gilman pointed out that, by supporting a selective boycott of indecent movies rather than a blanket boycott of all movies, as Philadelphia Catholics under Cardinal Dougherty had, Legion leaders begged from their followers the fateful question: Which movies must we avoid and which ones may we attend? Gilman feared the answer. Legion leaders who responded with the obvious "we will list them" would become yet another cog in Hays's public relations wheel, offering free advertisements for Hollywood movies along the lines of the ineffectual International Federation of Catholic Alumnae, General Federation of Women's Clubs, and Alice Ames Winter. Such a result seemed likely not only as a response to a selective boycott and an extension of the work begun by the Catholic Alumnae but also pressure from the Hays Office. "My fear," Gilman wrote one friend, "is that the industry will approach the leaders with a proposal to let them censor or preview films and publish estimates," creating "the same situation which we have had with the women's clubs."[9]

Publicly, Hays applauded the Legion of Decency, thanking its leaders for assisting his efforts to clean up the movies. Privately, he strove to regain control, knowing that his job security depended on safely shepherding the motion picture industry through threats of state censorship, insolvency, federal supervision, and now a massive boycott. Public demands for his resignation only added to his worries. As Gilman suspected, behind the scenes Hays plotted to neutralize the movement by pulling a Legion leader into his system of industry self-regulation. He did not need to look far. Hays would have preferred to recruit a member of the Catholic clergy, but he already employed a Catholic staff member—Joseph Breen—with very strong ties to Legion leaders. Breen had helped to craft Hays's 1930 moral code and served faithfully with Winter on his Studio Relations Committee, while demonstrating great ambition and a real knack for Hollywood politics. As the Legion crisis deepened, Hays promoted Breen into positions of increasing visibility and power. By summer 1934, he had replaced the Studio Relations Committee with the Production Code Administration and placed Breen at the helm, charged with enforcing the Hays Code. Unlike his predecessors, Breen approached his task armed; all films produced by studios affiliated with the Hays Office had to earn the Production Code Administration "seal of approval" and display it with each showing. Violators would pay a hefty $25,000 fine. Within a few months, many Legion supporters applauded Breen's work, noting a marked improvement in films released under him.[10]

Gilman saw the appointment of Breen as Hays's first step toward neutralizing the Legion of Decency. In an effort to save the Legion from cooptation while simultaneously unseating her old adversaries in the Catholic Alumnae, she sent carefully crafted letters to three Legion leaders—the Rev. James Cummings, of the National Catholic Welfare Conference, the Rev. John T. McNicholas, archbishop of Cincinnati, and the Rev. John Cantwell, bishop of Los Angeles. Has the Catholic Church, she asked, authorized the International Federation of Catholic Alumnae to represent it? If so, she continued, Legion leaders should know that the Catholic Alumnae's close cooperation with the Hays Office had tarnished its image among motion picture reformers. Her message could not have been more clear: Denounce the Catholic Alumnae or remove it from the Hays Office and earn the support of veteran motion picture activists. "I fear more than I can say," Gilman wrote a colleague in reference to the Legion, "that they will be approached, flattered and pledged until they will fall into the trap" of previewing and listing motion pictures. "If I were financially able," Gilman sighed, "I should go to them and sit on the sideline until I convinced them" not to cooperate with Will Hays.[11] Instead, she looked on anxiously, hoping that the Legion would depose the motion picture bureau of the Catholic Alumnae.

Like Gilman, several Legion leaders suspected the International Federation of Catholic Alumnae of benefiting financially from its close relationship with Hays. Among its harshest Catholic critics, Bishop Michael J. Curley, one of Gilman's supporters, accused the Alumnae of accepting money and "courtesies" from motion picture producers. Rita McGoldrick, chair of the Catholic Alumnae Motion Picture Bureau, passionately denied the charges, insisting that neither she nor her coworkers had accepted or been offered as much as one dollar from the producers or the Hays Office. To be sure, McGoldrick may not have charged mink coats and diamond rings to Hays's account but, as Gilman and Legion leaders knew, her motion picture reform agenda clearly depended on Hays's financial support. Not only did the Hays Office pay McGoldrick's travel expenses when she delivered motion picture–related talks, but it also covered printing and mailing costs for the group's movie lists.[12]

Although many Legion leaders shared Gilman's contempt for the Catholic Alumnae, most also disagreed with Gilman on several counts. In contrast to Gilman and Curley, the vast majority of Legion leaders—hoping to avoid empowering a potentially anti-Catholic state—approved of the Catholic Alumnae's active opposition to government intervention with motion pictures, including its rejection of regulations regarding industry trade practices.[13] The issue of motion picture lists broke three ways. Under McGoldrick's leadership, the Catholic Alumnae published lists of endorsed motion pictures known as white lists. McGoldrick, who refused to blacklist movies because she feared that doing so would only attract curious young people, championed Hays's favored slogan: "Boost the best and ignore the rest."[14] Gilman, who equated motion picture lists with advertisements and opposed them all, white and black, argued that women's organizations should not boost filmmakers' profits by encouraging children to attend movies. Especially under the restrictive trade practices of block booking and blind selling, "patronizing the best," Gilman argued, "means subsidizing the rest." Most Legion leaders, including Curley, however, sanctioned lists but insisted on a combined black and white list. A black list, they argued, would assist pledge signers in their efforts to avoid indecent movies while preventing the Legion from becoming a promotional arm of the Hays Office. As Curley put it, let's boost the best and "damn the rest."[15]

Bishops vying among themselves for leadership of the Legion of Decency pressured the Catholic Alumnae to change its policies. Priests based in Chicago generated a list of approved and forbidden motion pictures to rival the Catholic Alumnae's white list, while priests in New York agreed to support the Catholic Alumnae only if it would produce a black list along with its white one. McGoldrick appreciated the Legion's efforts but refused to change her review policy and ultimately resigned under escalating pressure. The rise of McGoldrick's assistant, Mary Looram, correlated with her acceptance of Legion directives. Soon after replacing McGoldrick as chair of the Catholic Alumnae Motion Picture Board, Looram announced that the organization would publish a black list. She also moved the Catholic Alumnae out of the Hays Office and into the New York Legion of Decency Office, where a team of priests and laymen began to supervise the women's work. The Chicago Legion, declaring itself satisfied with the new arrangement, agreed to abandon its list and support the New York Legion.[16] The women's subjection thus laid the groundwork for the men's reunion.

A few Catholics ridiculed Legion leaders' treatment of the Catholic Alumnae. Father Edward Schwegler, a well-known writer for the Catholic press, scoffed at "the air of vast age and experience assumed" by Legion leaders, whose interest in motion pictures had surfaced so recently. "The only group of people who can really speak in this matter with an air of experience and venerableness," Schwegler wrote, is the International Federation of Catholic Alumnae. *The Brooklyn Tablet*, too, proclaimed solidarity with the Catholic Alumnae, and *The Brooklyn Catholic Actionist* asserted that "the Motion Picture Bureau of the International Federation of Catholic Alumnae should play the role of national arbiter" in Catholic motion picture matters. In stark contrast, Gilman applauded Legion leaders' exercise of priestly prerogative, because it dethroned and separated from the Hays Office a women's organization she had long opposed, even as it unified the Legion leadership.[17]

Legion leaders contended with ongoing internal divisions, but they achieved an image of unity and with it commanded a level of respect that, by 1934, eluded organized women. They began with the ultimate trump card for American Catholics of the 1930s: apostolic benediction. Early in the campaign against indecent motion pictures, Pope Pius granted American bishops his blessing, encouraging them to invoke his name in their efforts. After Legion officials in Chicago and New York collaborated to bring the Catholic Alumnae under their supervision, consolidating Legion men's leadership in the process, they became more effective at using the hierarchical structure and disciplinary apparatus of the Catholic Church to contain and conceal divisions. With formal reprimands, demotions, transfers, and dismissals, Legion leaders could exercise a degree of control unavailable to organized women. For example, when the National Council of Catholic Women testified on behalf of a federal motion picture law that the Legion opposed, two archbishops instructed them to "be silent" to preserve "unanimity of thought and unity of action within our ranks." After one Legion official, Father Joseph Daly, exposed internal disagreements and made impolitic public statements, the bishops reassigned him to a less visible post. Legion officials enjoyed significant influence over parishioners as well. Not only could they instruct priests to administer the Pledge of Decency to their congregations, but Legion leaders in some dioceses employed more coercive tactics, reporting to the local priests which members of their congregations patronized theaters showing condemned movies.[18]

Meanwhile, Hays and motion picture producers hastened to appease or neutralize the Legion of Decency by placing Breen at the head of the new Production Code Administration and instituting a stringent process of internal censorship. These dramatic moves represented Hays's response to the Legion's façade of unity and apparent authority both inside and outside the Catholic Church. A unified Legion, accompanied by organized consumer muscle-flexing, endangered the motion picture industry's profits at a financially vulnerable moment. Furthermore, reports of Protestants and Jews joining the Legion campaign, signing pledges, and boycotting movies, caused Hays special concern. Not only did this coalition expand an already sizable movement, but it signaled unprecedented—and alarming, from Hays's perspective—cooperation among the three major American religions. Protestant anti-obscenity reform dated back to Anthony Comstock and focused heavily on state action, including censorship and efforts to obtain the sort of federal motion picture supervision advocated by Gilman. Although Catholic leaders opposed government intervention, Hays feared that, by forming an alliance with Protestants, the Legion would inadvertently encourage Congress to consider federal motion picture regulation.[19]

Jewish involvement in motion picture reform had emerged recently, inspired, in part, by ominous foreign and domestic developments. A 1934 *New York Times* front-page headline declared: "THREE-FAITH GROUP FORMED HERE FOR A CITY-WIDE MORAL CLEAN-UP." Next to it, another announced: "NAZI LEADER HERE DEFENDS DRILLING AND BAN ON JEWS." The first article reported the Catholic-Protestant-Jewish motion picture reform alliance forming under the Legion of Decency. The second explained that the American pro-Nazi group, "Friends of the New Germany," conducted military drills under a swastika and pledged allegiance to the anti-Semitic policies of the German Nazi Party. Meanwhile, the *Jewish Advocate* announced that Rabbi Morton Goldberg supported the Legion, castigating "Jewish movie producers who bring disgrace upon the Jewish people." A few days later, the paper published a letter declaring that "in self-defense and out of self-respect every Jew must back up the Roman Catholic clergy's" motion picture reform. Similarly, Rabbi Sidney Goldstein told the *New York Times* that "as Jews, we are more interested than others" in motion picture reform because of the large number of Jewish filmmakers and public perceptions of Jewish responsibility for indecent motion pictures.[20] Aware of the Nazi threat at home and abroad, many Jewish Americans felt more vulnerable than Will Hays in 1934, and their leaders joined the Legion of Decency campaign at least partly as a preemptive strike against American anti-Semitism.

The Disintegration of Women's Motion Picture Reform

Organized women did not simply surrender the anti-obscenity movement to priests, rabbis, and other Legion of Decency leaders in 1934. Women's Christian Temperance Union leaders, in fact, resisted the Legion's dominance of motion picture reform, anticipating that the "drinking pictures" they despised would fare rather well under Catholic reformers. With Maude Aldrich at its head, the WCTU's motion picture department continued to collaborate with Gilman's Federal Motion Picture Council in support of federal legislation. In 1939, however, Aldrich's successor, Augusta Urquhart, a Hays protégé, reshaped the WCTU motion picture department into a quasi–better film council, encouraging members to attend motion pictures and send their assessments to producers. The impoverished and discredited WCTU exercised little influence after the repeal of Prohibition in 1933, however, and in 1945 it disbanded its motion picture department altogether.[21]

In contrast to Aldrich, Gilman encouraged cooperation with the Legion of Decency even as she continued to work for federal regulation and visual education in her capacity as executive board member of the Motion Picture Research

Council, motion picture chair for the National PTA, and president of the Federal Motion Picture Council. But in 1934 her influence within each organization and the clout of the organizations themselves began to slip.

Gilman's authority on the Motion Picture Research Council suffered a severe blow when, after the Payne Fund studies exhausted the organization's budget, director William Short secured financing for the reform phase of the work from two socially and politically prominent women—Eleanor Robson Belmont and Pauline Morton Sabin—both founders of the recently victorious Women's Organization for National Prohibition Reform. Belmont and Sabin, who helped to defeat Prohibition by mobilizing a group of women to argue that it endangered maternal and child welfare, promised to ward off a federal motion picture commission in the same way. Under their leadership, the Motion Picture Research Council encouraged parents to guide their children's motion picture selection and advocated narrow legislation to abolish the motion picture industry's restrictive trade practices. In 1935 it joined with exhibitors to endorse a bill sponsored by Representative Sam Pettengill (D-Ind.) to eliminate block booking and blind selling. Gilman and Iva White, another board member, who considered the Pettengill bill weak, inadequate, and even "pernicious," supported a rival bill, championed by Representative Francis Culkin (R-N.Y.), an antimonopoly activist who drafted his bill in consultation with Gilman and the Federal Motion Picture Council. When the Motion Picture Research Council came out against the Culkin bill, Gilman and White bemoaned their lost influence. "If I were rich," White grumbled, "I too might be recognized a little more." "When I cannot contribute and they can," Gilman echoed, "I am silenced." Both women resigned from the council in 1935, rejoicing to see it dwarfed by the Legion of Decency.[22]

Even as Gilman extricated herself from the Motion Picture Research Council, Mary Bannerman, the National PTA legislative chair, joined it, setting these two National PTA coworkers on a sure collision course. The confrontation came quickly. In 1935, without consulting the other or obtaining authorization, the two women committed the National PTA to conflicting legislation. Gilman, as National PTA motion picture chair, publicly endorsed the Culkin bill, and Bannerman, as legislative chair, publicly supported the weaker Pettengill bill. Gilman learned of the mix-up when she received from President Langworthy a reprimand for acting without official approval. Under these awkward circumstances, Langworthy and Gilman agreed that the National PTA would simply have to endorse both bills. Gilman feared not only that the PTA would appear ridiculous for supporting rival bills, but that the feeble Pettengill bill would prevail, preventing the more robust Culkin bill from passing. Meanwhile, Bannerman, who considered the Culkin bill too radical but the Pettengill bill moderate enough to pass, mistakenly—or cunningly—ascribed these sentiments to Senator Francis Culkin himself in a letter to state PTA presidents, and a furious Senator Culkin apprised Gilman of Bannerman's maneuver. When Gilman learned, soon thereafter, that the National PTA executive committee refused to safeguard her work against a repeat of this fiasco and failed to allocate funds for her motion picture correspondence, she submitted her resignation. Remaining in place as motion picture chair would, Gilman believed, merely allow Bannerman to "continue her work of undermining my work." Still, she hoped to prevent the position from going to one of her opponents and recommended that Langworthy ask Dr. Edgar Dale, one of the Payne Fund researchers, to replace her. He "has access to money to do what I have wanted to do," she explained.[23] Gilman's selection of Dale as her successor in 1935 represented a culmination of several painful realizations. The growing importance of wealth, or access to it, and the diminishing potential for female unity on political or moral issues left her disillusioned with womanhood and ready to accept a male replacement—just as she had welcomed the rise of the Legion of Decency.

Gilman remained president of the Federal Motion Picture Council, a position to which she had recently been reelected, ironically, "because this work is really a woman's work." So said Canon William Sheafe Chase when nominating Gilman over her male rivals. Under her leadership, the council maintained its support for federal motion picture legislation, even after the disappointments of the NRA Motion Picture Code and the failures of both the Pettengill and Culkin bills. But by 1936 Gilman had become little more than a figurehead for a nearly defunct organization. Sporadic correspondence and board meeting minutes trace the Federal Motion Picture Council's protracted demise to 1947, but more than a decade earlier the organization had ceased to have a significant voice in motion picture reform.[24]

The General Federation of Women's Clubs, also on the wane, reinvigorated its motion picture program through the Legion of Decency and the National PTA. "The Film Shopper's Guide"—a new page in its recently renamed magazine, *The Clubwoman*—represented the General Federation's main contribution to motion picture reform in 1935. With this new feature, Eunice McClure placed age-graded movie reviews at the center of the organization's motion picture work, inaugurating clubwomen's active cooperation with the Legion of Decency even as she credited clubwomen with the Legion's success. As McClure ex-

Fig. 8.1 Fifteen years after agreeing to preside over the Motion Picture Producers and Distributors of America, Will Hays had survived the Arbuckle scandal, women's organized protests, the country's worst depression, Franklin Roosevelt's New Deal, and, most recently, the Catholic Legion of Decency. Here he strikes a typical pose while working his legendary magic, cultivating a relationship or negotiating a deal. 1937. Courtesy of the Indiana State Library

plained, the General Federation motion picture program had long focused on the power of the purse, directing women to reform movies by registering their preferences at the box office. The Legion's selective boycott validated their work by making "the world conscious of the value of the box office dollar." The "entire world," McClure concluded grandiosely, is now "putting into practice our slogan." In 1936, under a new motion picture chair, Mrs. William C. Brown, clubwomen joined the National PTA in advancing one of Gilman's favorite agendas, visual education. By declaring the National Recovery Act unconstitutional in 1935, the U.S. Supreme Court had freed clubwomen from the motion picture code constraints that had frustrated Gilman's efforts. Moreover, clubwomen found Edgar Dale, the new National PTA motion picture chair, more cooperative than Gilman had been. Working together, the General Federation and National PTA facilitated the installation of audio-visual equipment in public schools and the creation of film libraries and film lending services.[25] By the end of the 1930s, their motion picture work cemented public perceptions that women should reform motion pictures through consumption and education, rather than political action.

Alice Ames Winter maintained close ties to the General Federation and, thanks largely to the Legion of Decency, remained with the Hays Office throughout the 1930s. As the Legion peaked in June 1934, Winter admitted to Hays that its "hue and cry" caused her some discomfort. "Nevertheless, I feel as you must," she wrote, "that it is reinforcing just the attitude that we would like to see taken by the studios themselves." By "cleaning up" from the inside, she noted, the industry would protect itself from investigation and regulation from the outside. In public, Winter rarely mentioned the Legion, instead praising organized women, better film councils, and "public opinion" for improving motion pictures. When she finally retired, in 1942, at the age of seventy-seven, Hays's handling of her position bespoke the diminished status of women in motion picture reform. In 1929, Hays had endeavored to appoint the most prominent leader of organized women as Woman's Ambassador to the motion picture industry; upon Winter's departure, he awarded the job to Alice Evans Field, Winter's longtime assistant, a woman unknown among organized women.[26]

The Legion of Decency Triumphant

In its heyday, the Legion of Decency exercised a profound influence on motion pictures, indirectly preventing the production of, and prompting alterations in, many Hollywood films. Its classification system, backed by boycott threats and an automatic Church ban on any condemned movie, guided Breen's decisions to award or withhold the industry seal of approval. Through this process, the Legion accomplished many reforms that would have pleased female motion picture reformers—from taming Mae West (*Klondike Annie*, 1935), to eliminating female nudity (*Pygmalion*, 1938), to securing dignified portrayals of Catholics (*Going My Way*, 1943).[27] But because Legion leaders and organized women approached motion picture reform with different goals, Legion successes did not necessarily achieve the objectives of organized women.

The Legion targeted for condemnation several types of motion pictures that many organized women supported, including sex education films. For example, in 1933, before the Legion emerged, the American Social Hygiene Association sponsored *Damaged Lives*, a public health film about the devastating impact of venereal disease on a young married couple. When the filmmaker approached the National PTA for an endorsement, President Langworthy turned for advice to Gilman in her capacity as a motion picture chair and a prominent sex educator. Concluding that, because the independently produced film would run in commercial theaters on a for-profit basis, the National PTA could not endorse it, Gilman nonetheless agreed to preview the film. She approached the screening skeptical about any "mass attempt to teach social hygiene," especially in the setting of a commercial motion picture theater, but she emerged from it deeply impressed with the film's educational possibilities. To be sure, she still worried that a commercial environment would distort the audience's reception of such delicate information and wished that it could be delivered in community and school auditoriums. But she realized that "the young people of this country have been exposed to the most degraded sex situations. It will not hurt them," she concluded, "to see the subject handled from the point of view represented in *Damaged Lives* and I am convinced that it will probably be very helpful." In 1937, a very similar independent production, *Damaged Goods*, delighted the Catholic Alumnae Motion Picture Bureau chair, Mary Looram, but nonetheless incurred Legion censure. Looram hoped that young people would see the film, but Archbishop John McNicholas of Cincinnati announced the Legion's official position: "Sex instruction does not come within the function of the motion picture theater." The film would appear on the Legion's condemned list. Thus, with regard to sex education films, the Legion worked at cross-purposes with many organized women.[28]

Political convictions also distinguished the Legion's motion picture reform from Gilman's, particularly regarding attitudes toward Communism. In the late 1930s, Legion leaders accused left-leaning Hollywood producers of disseminating Communist propaganda and, by the end of the decade, imposed a blanket condemnation on all Russian-made films. The Legion's suspicions of motion pictures received congressional sanction in the House Un-American Activities Committee (HUAC) investigations of Hollywood in 1947. To Legion applause, HUAC interrogated directors and producers of such films as *Song of Russia*, a 1943 movie censured by some Catholic leaders as Communist propaganda. Gilman vehemently disagreed, calling the movie "a beautiful portrayal of family and neighborhood life with a simple and wholesome romance." Legion leaders damned the movie for the same reason, considering its very beauty Communist propaganda because of its setting in Soviet Russia. Whereas Gilman urged her audience to recognize the movie's values as quintessentially American, pointing out that it was produced during the war, "when our government was wooing Russia," Legion leaders blacklisted the film.[29]

The Legion's agenda diverged from Gilman's in method as well. The Legion unequivocally opposed federal motion picture legislation, seeing in it the danger of political censorship rather than the promise of democratic regulation. To Gilman's chagrin, when Legion leaders discovered that the National Council of Catholic Women—a group that had worked with Gilman since its 1933 convention in Minnesota—had declared support for federal motion picture regulation, they pressured the women's organization to reverse its policy, forbidding it to issue public policy statements without first obtaining Legion approval. The Legion also adopted strategies Gilman had long considered counterproductive, from acknowledging Joseph Breen as its representative in the Hays Office to adopting the Catholic Alumnae's motion picture lists. "History is repeating itself," Gilman noted privately. The Legion of Decency has accepted "Breen as the Presbyterians accepted Mr. Will Hays . . . and the women Mrs. Winter." Had the Legion remained completely independent of the motion picture industry, Gilman believed it might have achieved permanent reform. Instead, she regretted that it would only accomplish "a temporary respite."[30] Of course, history cannot really repeat itself. Even as Gilman scribbled these words, motion picture reform was evolving, transforming in many ways that Gilman and her sister reformers initiated but did not necessarily intend.

Gilman and other female anti-obscenity reformers agreed on at least one thing: the harm of obscenity lay in its impact on children. And if they accomplished one thing, it was to embed this notion of children's vulnerability to obscenity deeply in the American consciousness. They did this by targeting as obscene only sexual material that children could see and understand, and by developing anti-obscenity strategies that used explicit sex education material to shape children's sexual development. But under the Legion of Decency, whose leaders also identified children as their main concern, notions of children's vulnerability to obscenity took the anti-obscenity movement down a new path.

Legion leaders insisted that they did not aim to turn "moving pictures into toys for the nursery." "There should be a distinction," asserted the Rev. Russell Sullivan, "in films for children and adults." With the help of the Catholic Alumnae, Legion leaders defined and institutionalized this distinction by categorizing movies as "family," "adult," or "condemned." Gilman considered such ratings insidious, functioning like a blacklist to heighten curiosity and ultimately twist a child's normal and healthy interest in sex into a prurient obsession with it. "There is something in the psychology of prohibition," Gilman mused, "which stimulates interest." But, as Gilman well knew, the Legion's commitment to a *selective* boycott required such categories.[31] To Gilman, the boycott spearheaded by Philadelphia's maverick Legion leader, Cardinal Dougherty, looked more promising, because, by placing a blanket embargo on motion picture attendance, it avoided lists altogether. To Gillman's dismay though, Dougherty's comprehensive boycott gave rise to the first industry rating system. The boycott inflicted such debilitating losses on Harry Warner, who owned most of the city's first-run theaters, that he agreed to try nearly anything to break it—including rating his own movies. "F" for families and "A" for adults did the trick; Warner Brothers earned public accolades in the local and national press, and the Philadelphia boycotters, apparently satisfied with the new ratings regime, gradually returned to motion picture theaters.[32]

This logical extension of women's theories about the harm of obscenity moved motion picture reform beyond their reach, even as it reaffirmed individual maternal accountability and rekindled paternalist notions of women's vulnerability to obscenity. Fans of the rating system praised it for holding parents responsible "for any ill effects, moral, physical, mental or otherwise, suffered by children attending movies meant primarily for adult audiences."[33] But celebration of parental responsibility slipped easily into accusations of maternal negligence, as demonstrated by New York City's Cardinal Patrick Hayes, who in 1934 upbraided "the mothers of America" for failing to control their children's motion picture attendance. Other Catholic clergymen urged women to use their "feminine influence over men" to keep them away from indecent shows. But even as Legion leaders encouraged women to exercise maternal and marital influence at home, they also treated women as uniquely vulnerable, identifying women and children as "the family audience" or simply defining "Class A" movies as those "suitable for women and children."[34] In so doing, the Legion returned to an earlier anti-obscenity paradigm, one that infantilized women and placed them under men's supervision even as it reinforced the notion—popularized by the General Federation and the National PTA—that with regard to motion pictures, women's authority best functioned in private, as wives, mothers, and consumers, not in public, through politics and collective action.

Catholic prelates and laymen rapidly transformed the anti-obscenity movement, displacing women as leaders for the next forty years. The Legion united three historically antagonistic religious groups in an intimidating national motion picture boycott while organized women splintered into hostile factions that posed little threat to Hays or filmmakers. Anti-obscenity reform enhanced Catholic moral authority inside and outside the Church even as it undermined the moral authority of women's organizations by provoking destructive struggles within and among them. As gatekeepers of heaven and guardians of an earthly flock, Catholic leaders possessed a level of influence that eluded organized women. They also *expected* to have to use it. Unlike Gilman and many other organized women in the 1920s and 1930s, Legion leaders did not anticipate unity among Catholics or even among Catholic clergy. In the face of disagreement, rather than retreating with hurt feelings or attacking with cries of "traitor," Legion leaders negotiated, compromised, and, when those strategies failed, repressed and disarmed. Intra-organizational conflicts derailed their work at times, leading to frustration and even anger but not disillusionment. Thus the Legion remained a vital force in motion picture reform through the 1960s, negotiating changes in films, preventing the production of others, and eventually giving rise to an industry rating system still in place today.

The Legion of Decency spelled the end of women's anti-obscenity leadership. As the Legion stepped into the power vacuum created by women's intra- and inter-organizational conflict, it stripped many women of the small measure of power they retained, reviving elements of the Victorian paternalism that had, for decades, shut women out of both electoral politics and anti-obscenity reform. Curiously, organized women who had battled each other for control of the movement welcomed the leadership of Catholic men—even when the men's goals diverged from their own. Gilman poses the greatest puzzle. For all that Gilman had earlier trumpeted the virtue of women, decried the wickedness of men, and stressed the vulnerability of children as the justification for women's anti-obscenity reform, she readily handed the movement over to Catholic men— even though by the end of the 1930s she saw little if any improvement in motion pictures, feared the effects of the emerging rating system, decried Catholic anti-Communist hysteria, lamented the Legion's success at keeping "public health films from the public," and grieved the Legion's willingness to sabotage its own work by cooperating with the motion picture industry. Gilman continued to champion the Catholic Legion of Decency long after it adopted motion picture reform strategies she abhorred, banned sex education films she admired, and achieved little that she considered worthwhile. Rather than branding the Legion's work worse than useless, as she had the very similar work of rival women's organizations, Gilman admitted, "Any effort is important and I hope they continue their crusade."[35]

That this maternalist activist with deep roots in women's reform culture brooked so little disagreement from female but so much from male anti-obscenity reformers returns us to the puzzle with which this chapter opened. Why did Gilman renounce organized women who employed slightly different methods but embrace Catholic men whose goals and methods diverged dramatically from hers? The modern concepts of essentialism and identity politics suggest a solution to this problem. Along with many, if not most, organized women of the early twentieth century, Gilman practiced a particular form of identity politics, one grounded in essentialist notions of womanhood. She identified herself first as a woman, considered women essentially different from men, and expected this shared essence to unite women with regard to maternal and moral issues. Her unswerving belief in womanhood led to unrealistically high expectations of female unity that left little room for differences among women. As a result, when Gilman encountered women who disagreed with her on maternal and moral issues, she perceived not rivalry but treachery—not differences of opinion but evidence of betrayal—not challengers but traitors. In contrast, because Gilman was neither Catholic nor male, she presumed that she had little in common with bishops and priests. Given no reason to expect that she and they might agree, Gilman appreciated any convergence in their perspectives and approaches—and she did not feel betrayed when they disagreed with her. Thus essentialist identity politics allowed Gilman to tolerate differences with Catholic men that she could not accept with women, leading her to help the Legion of Decency bring an end to women's twenty-year reign as leaders of anti-obscenity reform.

Anti-obscenity Reform and Women's History

In the 1910s organized American women drew upon widespread assumptions about womanhood to position themselves as arbiters of obscenity. Parlaying perceptions of female maternal expertise and moral superiority into public authority, they became leaders in anti-obscenity reform and won deference from men in the entertainment business. During the 1920s, women expanded on these strategies, expecting to accomplish even more now that they brandished ballots. For several years, they coasted on earlier successes and persistent notions of a united womanhood, moving their anti-obscenity leadership to the national stage and tightly focusing discussions of obscenity on material that appealed to and harmed youth. But by the middle of the decade, public disagreements among organized women exploded into internecine wars over leadership, strategies, and the very definition of obscenity. By the 1930s, organized women could not help but notice a steep decline in their own efficacy. Some understood that they had failed to adapt to change. "Our organizations," Catheryne Cooke Gilman mused in 1933, may "have developed techniques based upon conditions preceding the time when we had suffrage."[1] Ironically, many of those obsolete techniques derived from or depended on the same politics of womanhood that underwrote women's earlier anti-obscenity successes. Their failure signaled a major shift in women's history.

Women's Reform and the Politics of Womanhood

More than a century before American women assumed leadership of anti-obscenity reform, their foremothers constructed political roles rooted in female moral authority. The bases of that authority shifted over time, obtaining first from women's status as nonvoters. Revolutionary-era leaders argued that disfranchisement rendered female citizenship disinterested, motivated by community concerns in contrast to the enfranchised citizenship of self-interested, entrepreneurial men. Women, as disinterested citizens and republican mothers, would preserve the nation's civic virtue and convey it to their children while men pursued their own interests in the political and economic sphere. Republican motherhood, as contemporaries and historians labeled this ideology, disallowed woman suffrage even as it promoted women's private authority as custodians of civic virtue, for if electoral exclusion explained women's special political role, enfranchising women ran the risk of eliminating that role as well as the traits that made women's citizenship unique and valuable.

By the middle of the nineteenth century, changing gender roles and concepts of domesticity gave rise to true womanhood, a loose collection of ideals that replaced disfranchisement as the primary source of women's virtue. These qualities—domesticity, piety, submission, and sexual purity—removed as they were from issues of politics and citizenship, seemed even less likely than republican motherhood to afford women a political role. Nevertheless, astute women forged one. Reasoning that womanhood could civilize the public domain, they created a dizzying array of voluntary associations to uplift the poor, promote temperance, rescue prostitutes, and otherwise spread domestic values and virtues. These organizations, firmly rooted in the seemingly apolitical ideals of womanhood, moved women into the political sphere as signers of petitions, voices of moral suasion, and representatives of womanhood. To be sure, they excluded most women, particularly those who held different priorities and lacked leisure time and money. But influence could become power when sought on behalf of womanhood, and organized women strove to appear representative of their sex, capitalizing as they did so on assumptions that underlay the cult of true womanhood.

In the decades preceding passage of the Nineteenth Amendment, women in temperance and welfare reform proved especially adept at manipulating true womanhood to shape public policy, using it to achieve mandatory temperance education, dry laws, child labor legislation, and even a federal Children's Bureau. At the same time, the purity component of true womanhood initially impeded women's entrance into anti-obscenity reform, encouraging women to limit themselves—and male anti-obscenity reformers to limit women—to supporting roles in the movement as a way of protecting them from contamination. But as the possibilities of escaping exposure to obscenity diminished early in the twentieth century, so did rationales for excluding women from anti-obscenity reform. In fact, women discovered pressing reasons to take up this work, for if they could not avoid stumbling upon sexually daring amusements in public, neither could their children. The liberalizing sexual trend emancipated even the women it horrified, because the same sexual freedom that encouraged sexual expression released women to speak openly against sexual amusements. Thus female anti-obscenity reformers did not simply oppose sexual liberalization; they also seized upon its new permissiveness regarding sexual expression to voice their own concerns about it. In so doing, they revised true womanhood and inverted male activists' logic, arguing that female moral sensibilities translated not into vulnerability but into public authority.

Female anti-obscenity activists also claimed authority on the basis of maternalism. Echoing their counterparts in welfare reform by insisting on "putting children first," they argued that obscenity's danger stemmed from its harm to children and that, therefore, the common experience of motherhood uniquely prepared women for anti-obscenity work.[2] As maternal caregivers, they believed that mothers understood what types of sexual materials would harm children, and only mothers would exercise the sort of vigilance needed to control public amusements. Maternalism emerged out of women's experiences as mothers, beliefs about womanhood, and shrewd political choices as disfranchised activists. Reasoning that most women were mothers, that all mothers wanted the best for children, and that what was good for children was good for women, female anti-obscenity reformers anticipated broad female agreement on a program to combat what they called "indecent appeals to youth." Combined with the vote, they expected gender solidarity to propel their reform to certain victory.

Enfranchisement boosted women's reform even before the suffrage amendment passed, partly because women's issues rode the same progressive reform wave that brought woman suffrage to fruition, but also because politicians and businessmen began to woo prospective female voters long before they could actually vote. By 1919, the women's welfare reform network acquired two federal agencies in the Children's and the Woman's Bureaus, temperance activists celebrated the passage of federal Prohibition, and female anti-obscenity reformers, still new on the scene, persuaded burlesque and motion picture theater managers to eliminate profanity, nudity, and suffragette jokes. All benefited from the image of unity and moral authority that inhered in true womanhood, one that women would, presumably, now express at the ballot box.[3]

Female anti-obscenity reformers relied more heavily on the politics of womanhood than either temperance or welfare reformers, for a variety of reasons. Women became involved in temperance and welfare activism early in the nineteenth century, and by 1920 had already established their authority over alcohol and maternal and child welfare. Indeed, out of whole cloth they created laws, regulations, professional schools, careers, and bureaucratic agencies that reflected and enforced their values. In stark contrast, women who took up anti-obscenity reform in the 1910s entered territory recently the exclusive province of men. Struggling to assert and establish their new authority, they operated within an anti-obscenity regime fashioned by men. Its laws, judicial interpretations, and enforcement mechanisms targeted birth control, literature, and sex education texts—material that did not bother and often even appealed to female reformers, because they did not consider it harmful to children—but failed to deal seriously with items that children liked and understood, including sex magazines, burlesque shows, and motion pictures. By relegating enforcement of obscenity law to the courts and postal department, male preserves, this system effectively placed it beyond the reach of women. Female anti-obscenity activists faced men who challenged their authority, including their attendance at risqué shows, their definition of obscenity, and their proposed remedies. Thus women entered the anti-obscenity movement in a defensive position that they never fully transcended, and, lacking the sort of legal and bureaucratic infrastructure that temperance and welfare reformers had erected by the 1920s, female anti-obscenity activists bet everything on the politics of womanhood, wagering that a unified female voice and vote would trump their opponents.

Organized women could virtually coast on assumptions of female unity for the first few years after winning national suffrage. Politicians catered to them, hoping to capture the "woman vote" by backing "women's" legislation. Most notably, the Sheppard-Towner Infancy and Maternity Protection Act of 1921, sponsored by the Children's Bureau and unanimously endorsed by the ten national women's organizations that made up the affiliated women's lobby, passed easily, supported by legislators who imagined that a unified female constituency would exact revenge if the bill failed. Businessmen in a variety of industries, including munitions and motion pictures, also courted organized women, fearing that a solid female vote could undermine their industries. Motion picture executives diverted newly enfranchised anti-obscenity reformers from legislative action by inviting them to help the industry clean up motion pictures, subsidizing their reform work and appointing them to prominent positions. Under these auspicious conditions, female welfare and anti-obscenity reformers employed carefully crafted strategies. Julia Lathrop, who headed the Children's Bureau, exercised her legendary diplomatic skills to cajole congressmen, build coalitions among public health and labor organizations, and strike compromises, one of which limited Sheppard-Towner to a five-year renewable term. Under Catheryne Cooke Gilman, female anti-obscenity activists formed coalitions with motion picture interests, devoted their immediate energies to anti-censorship work, developed reform strategies in consultation with producers and exhibitors, and depended on their roles as envoys of womanhood to sustain their influence over businessmen. To many organized women in the early 1920s, the future looked bright indeed.

The outlook began to dim within a few years. When Sheppard-Towner went up for review in 1927, congressmen—knowing that women had not voted together in the 1924 elections and that the Equal Rights Amendment and Spider Web Charts provoked bitter disputes among them—no longer feared a woman's voting bloc. Nor did they worry that women might use the political parties to inflict reprisals, because women had acquired little influence within them. Sheppard-Towner went down in defeat even as women's anti-obscenity movement split over issues of strategy and representation, with Gilman now demanding federal motion picture regulation and Alice Ames Winter urging women to cooperate with the industry, and both claiming to represent womanhood.[4]

When Will Hays appointed the popular Winter as "woman's ambassador to the motion picture industry," he appropriated the politics of womanhood. His ploy attracted Winter's followers, alienated her critics, and aggravated disputes among organized women. But Hays did not single-handedly divide womanhood. Rather, by anointing Winter as woman's representative on an issue that sparked so much controversy among organized women, Hays forced women publicly to choose sides. This deepened and exposed divisions among them, belying the notions of female unity on which the politics of womanhood rested. For decades, organized women had quietly managed internal disagreements by concealing them and external ones by denying their authenticity. Although women fought on both sides of the suffrage battle, for example, female suffragists refused to acknowledge that some women sincerely opposed enfranchisement, characterizing female adversaries as fronts for the liquor interests, agents of big business, pawns of the Catholic Church, anything but women speaking in their own right.[5] But even if they had wanted to—and many of them did not—organized women could not easily conceal or deny Winter, a woman many of them had already elected to represent them, a woman whose fame now rivaled movie stars'.

Even as organized women divided over motion picture reform, women unaffiliated with women's organizations entered reform politics, admitted by the vote and often escorted by men who hoped to capitalize on or undermine the politics of womanhood. Women's exclusion from electoral politics had masked many female differences by amplifying the voices of organized women while silencing unaffiliated women. As potential voters or members of a constituency, however, individual women's opinions mattered, whether or not they belonged to an organization. As women whose class, ethnic, and other identities might very well overwhelm their sense of gender solidarity, unaffiliated women's opinions promised to expose the politics of womanhood as an illusion. Anti-suffragist Emily Bissell feared this very outcome when, in 1916, she celebrated unaffiliated women's exclusion from politics, declaring that without female suffrage, "we get the best and bar out the rest."[6] As she predicted, after 1920 the carefully woven tapestry of womanhood began to fray, revealing an underlying tangle of disagreement that permeated and extended well beyond women's organizations.

Rather than abandoning the politics of womanhood in the face of these new challenges to it, Gilman and her followers in the anti-obscenity movement fought hard to regain control over it. Schooled in the presuffrage politics of organized womanhood, they had grown accustomed to ignoring or discounting evidence of disagreements among women, and they entered the postsuffrage era ill prepared to accept or negotiate them. Female anti-obscenity activists found this new state of affairs especially disturbing, because it dissolved their primary source of political leverage—claiming to represent womanhood. But they were also bewildered, because many sincerely believed that women shared a basic sense of morality and maternal concern for children. Thus they assumed that women who disagreed with them—from those who occasionally enjoyed a racy burlesque show to others, like Winter, who shared their disgust at but not their methods for reforming such entertainment—must be traitors to womanhood. By lashing out against other women, even those with whom they agreed about ends, if not means, Gilman and her allies alienated women with whom they might have compromised, collaborated, and achieved a great deal. They also played directly into the hands of their opponents.

Women in welfare reform also experienced disappointments in the 1920s, but they avoided taking the destructive turn that tore women's anti-obscenity reform apart. Congressmen publicly attacked their patriotism, their femininity, their sexuality, and their looks, while "superpatriot" women accused them of bolshevism, but female leaders in the network did not strike out at each other. Why? In contrast to female anti-obscenity activists, who had only recently taken up their cause, welfare reformers were old-timers who had practiced politics in Washington for nearly two decades before 1920. They brought to their work a deep understanding of bureaucratic and electoral politics, a willingness to compromise, and two seasoned political leaders, Julia Lathrop and Grace Abbott.[7] In the 1920s, they pursued a tried-and-true agenda—the Sheppard-Towner Act and the

Child Labor Amendment—one that flowed from earlier Children's Bureau initiatives and enjoyed long-standing support from the major women's organizations, including the General Federation of Women's Clubs, National Congress of Parent-Teacher Associations, and Women's Christian Temperance Union. Their institutional power base in the Children's Bureau prevented them from relying solely on the politics of womanhood for their credibility. Perhaps most important, welfare reformers' opponents made no convincing claims to represent womanhood on welfare issues. During the previous twenty years, the women's welfare reform network, a veritable "female dominion," erected such a solid fortress of authority that no interloper could have broken in to crown a competing leader.[8]

In the short run, the Great Depression and the New Deal affected women's welfare and anti-obscenity reform in opposite ways. When Franklin Roosevelt's new administration assembled a team of experts to craft social security legislation, it recruited women from the welfare network who proceeded to write their vision for maternal and child welfare into law. Female anti-obscenity activists hoped that the coming of the New Deal and the financial collapse of the motion picture industry would revitalize their efforts to bring the motion picture industry under federal supervision and create alternatives to commercial movie theaters. Instead, the ever-pragmatic Roosevelt approved a program designed to restore industry profits by permitting restrictive trade practices, suppressing questions of morality, and forbidding competition from noncommercial exhibitors. Because the New Deal's expanded federal authority aimed to achieve financial relief and business recovery, it increased the influence of welfare reformers even as it reduced that of anti-obscenity activists.

By the end of the 1930s, men assumed authority over both welfare and anti-obscenity reform. Even as individual female welfare reformers ascended into policymaking positions, where they exercised a profound influence over the Social Security Act of 1935, their network lost its monopoly over maternal and child welfare; a male-dominated Social Security Board administered the new programs while the Children's Bureau and the "female dominion" disintegrated.[9] Anti-obscenity reformers had responded to their diminishing influence by viciously charging each other with bribery, immorality, and perfidy. Bitter and disillusioned, Gilman eagerly surrendered to Catholic men the anti-obscenity movement that she and other women had led for two decades.

Too late, Gilman wondered if organized women had employed tactics more appropriate to the period preceding women's enfranchisement. Their claims to represent womanhood rang true in the years just before and after 1920 but sounded hollow by the end of the decade, as female voices vigorously debated issues of sexuality, maternal duty, and government responsibility. Enfranchisement expanded the female chorus beyond middle-class women's organizations, adding untrained voices, creating dissonance, and revealing that the melodious chords sounded by organized womanhood had been struck by a select few; harmony had come at the cost of diversity. Even white, middle-class organized women were much less homogeneous than they themselves believed. While they agreed that obscene movies harmed children, they disagreed passionately over how to define obscenity and how best to protect children. Opponents rushed to exploit these disagreements, exposing as unfounded reformers' claims to speak for womanhood. Such tactics devastated reformers who staked their moral authority and political leverage so heavily on womanhood.

Under these conditions, the politics of womanhood not only ceased to benefit female reformers—it actually made them more vulnerable, weakening their cause by denying the reality of differences among women. At a time when the American political system admitted more diverse female participation than ever before, the politics of womanhood made a liability of women's multiple perspectives, turning them into signs of political weakness rather than evidence of engaged citizenship. At a time when many political observers feared a female voting bloc, the politics of womanhood raised the specter of one, leading opponents of women's reform to try to break up the bloc or expose it as a chimera by provoking, uncovering, and publicizing disagreements among women. In the end, female reformers who employed the politics of womanhood turned each other into their own worst enemies.

Many organized women entered the 1920s believing in women's solidarity and expecting great things from woman suffrage. Painfully disillusioned to discover that enfranchisement did not provide a new medium for deploying the values of womanhood but revealed and sharpened differences among them, many organized women turned their anger on each other. Disputes between and among Catheryne Cooke Gilman, Alice Ames Winter, Frances Diehl, Eunice McClure, Mary Ware Dennett, Betty Sippel, Maude Aldrich, Mary Bannerman, Rita McGoldrick, Iva White, and so many others emerged out of genuine political differences and personality clashes. But the bitterness and destructiveness of those disputes derived from unreasonable expectations and feelings of betrayal, all exacerbated by external provocations. In the end, womanhood, the major source of women's presuffrage political power, simply could not survive enfranchisement, a sexual revolution, anti-obscenity politics, and Will Hays. It splintered on the shoals of a pluralistic, competitive, political system, taking with it women's anti-obscenity leadership.

Intended and Unintended Consequences

In many ways, the story of women's anti-obscenity activism came full circle by 1934. As in 1910, men led anti-obscenity reform and, like their Victorian-era predecessors, articulated their mission in terms of protecting women and children. But this return to Victorian paternalism was far from complete. In the preceding twenty-five years, women's anti-obscenity leadership had, for good or for ill, profoundly altered the treatment of sexual material in the realm of reform, adjudication, and even commerce, initiating a paradigmatic shift that would have long-term consequences for debates over obscenity for decades to come.

Because female anti-obscenity activists challenged men's obscenity regime by focusing public concern about the impact of obscenity solely on children, they encouraged the removal of sexually explicit material from public places where children might view it. Thanks in part to women's work, we live in a nation of bifurcated information and amusements. Our movie rating system, adult bookstores, opaque covers, V-Chips, and "net nannies" all aim to shield minors from graphic violence and sex. But Gilman and other female anti-obscenity leaders would not have been pleased with these developments. They suspected that such devices would create taboos, whetting children's curiosity by surrounding sex with the aura of the forbidden. Moreover, parental carelessness and youthful ingenuity would, they knew, severely limit the effectiveness of age restrictions. They did not anticipate a more troubling development. Child-oriented regulations have given rise to a virtually unfettered adult entertainment industry. For if, as female anti-obscenity activists argued, the danger of obscenity lay solely in its harm to children, by extension, no boundaries need limit material reserved for adults. By narrowing concerns about obscenity to children's welfare, female anti-obscenity activists unintentionally stifled other arguments against such material, inadvertently helping to loosen restrictions on amusements reserved for adults. Due in part to their success, adult bookstores and strip clubs line city streets and dot country highways—a consequence that would have horrified women who battled against obscenity early in the twentieth century.

Female anti-obscenity activists would have proudly accepted credit for ending parental silence on sexual matters, cheering the frankness with which many mothers and fathers today discuss sex with their children. Equally pleased with the four-year-old girl who shamelessly utters the word "penis" and the ten-year-old boy who can explain the mechanics of heterosexual intercourse, female anti-obscenity activists would, nevertheless, have been saddened to learn that the vast majority of young people interviewed at the end of the twentieth century reported that their parents had not served as a significant source of information about sex.[10] They would have despaired to find that, with regard to sex education, some of their worst fears have been realized. Not only do most young men identify pornography as their first source of sex education, but a growing number of women celebrate pornography as their *sole* source of childhood sex information.[11]

Activists like Gilman and her friend Louise Sanford Fisher—women who fought against obscenity while helping to rescue sex education from the taint of obscenity—would have discovered, with regret, that free speech activists defeated their carefully nuanced approach to sexual material. Perhaps nothing shows this more clearly than *Defending Pornography*, a 1995 book by Nadine Strossen, president of the American Civil Liberties Union. In it, Strossen argues that women cannot have access to explicit sex education books like *Our Bodies, Ourselves* without accepting explicit sex magazines like *Penthouse*. In Strossen's free speech paradigm, one cannot oppose pornography without advocating censorship; nor can one boycott pornography vendors without engaging in "coercive tactics" with "censorial impact."[12] Honors students in a course at the University of Minnesota in 1997 highlighted the extent of Strossen's triumph when, one by one, each female student announced that, while pornography made her personally uncomfortable, she would never demand that her boyfriend or husband remove it from her home for fear of violating his right to free speech. By the end of the twentieth century, these students equated criticizing pornography with advocating censorship, eliding, in the process, critical distinctions between private behavior and state action.

Many twentieth-century developments in this nation's sexual culture—from age-oriented regulations, to unregulated new forms of media, to absolutist notions of the First Amendment—would have appalled female anti-obscenity activists. But one crucial development would have seemed all too familiar to them: vicious fights among women over the issue of pornography in the feminist sex wars of the 1980s.

Of course, there are lots of differences between women's anti-obscenity reform and feminist anti-pornography activism. Women who mobilized against pornography in the 1970s, for example, claimed, not that it harmed children, but that it objectified women by making inhumane treatment of women sexually enticing. The list of differences between these two movements could go on and on, but the similarities are striking. Having cut their activist teeth in the women's movement, anti-pornography feminists claimed to speak on behalf of women. That claim preceded the outbreak of open warfare among feminists. Some feminists embraced pornography as sexually liberating; others considered it harmless; and still others found pornography a relatively unimportant issue, given the multitude of economic and political problems confronting American women. The sex wars disrupted the women's movement throughout the 1980s. Anti-pornography women accused their feminist opponents of defending a male-dominated sex industry, seeking their own pleasure at other women's expense, and surrendering to a false consciousness bred of sexism. Women who resisted anti-pornography feminism returned the cutting accusations, calling their feminist opponents anti-sex prudes, feminist fundamentalists, victim feminists, and enemies of free speech. Each group debilitated the other, sinking barbs into Achilles heels visible only to each other.

Disillusionment with movement sisters led anti-pornography feminists to repeat, unwittingly, the strategy of their anti-obscenity foremothers, delivering their movement to right-wing activists—including James Dobson, president of Focus on the Family, and Edwin Meese, Attorney General under Ronald Reagan and sponsor of the 1985 Commission on Pornography—just as surely as Gilman handed women's anti-obscenity movement to the Catholic Legion of Decency. In both cases, activists who developed an alternative to mainstream America's commercialized sexuality lost their footing on the slippery politics of essentialism and identity. Expectations of unity, of a shared essence, led female anti-obscenity and anti-pornography activists to accuse women who disagreed with them of betrayal even as cynicism drew them into alliances with male-dominated groups whose broader agendas they abhorred.

Women's anti-obscenity activism may have left a legacy of intolerance, internecine warfare, and failed political strategy, but it also bequeathed us strong and imaginative female leaders who, at great cost to themselves, valiantly tried to rescue sex from Victorian suppression and profit-motivated stimulation at a moment charged with potential. As twenty-first-century technologies present new methods for commercializing sex, taking us further and further beyond the relatively innocent performances of Elsie La Bergère and Mae West, women's anti-obscenity reform reminds us of the possibilities in our past even as it warns against dangers intrinsic to a politics rooted in essentialist notions of identity.

Abbreviations

AAW	Alice Ames Winter
AAWC	Alice Ames Winter Collection, Hoover Institution (Stanford University)
AAW-BF	Alice Ames Winter, Biographical File, Minneapolis Public Library
AAW-CF	Alice Ames Winter, Clipping File, Minneapolis Public Library
AFP	Ames Family Papers, Minnesota Historical Society (St. Paul)
CCG	Catheryne Cooke Gilman
FMPC	Federal Motion Picture Council
GFP	Robbins Gilman and Family Papers, Minnesota Historical Society (St. Paul)
GFWC	General Federation of Women's Clubs Resource Center (Washington, D.C.)
MHS	Minnesota Historical Society
MJT	Minneapolis Journal and Tribune Newspaper Morgue, Minneapolis Public Library
MPAA	Motion Picture Association of America, Margaret Herrick Library, Academy of Motion Picture Arts and Sciences (Beverly Hills, California)
MPPDA	Motion Picture Producers and Distributors of America
MWD-MC	Mary Ware Dennett Microfilmed Collection
NBR	National Board of Review
PTA	Parent Teacher Association
RG9	Record Group 9, National Recovery Administration, National Archives (College Park, Maryland)
TH-MC	Theodore Hayes Microfilmed Collection, Minnesota Historical Society (St. Paul)
THSB	Theodore Hayes Bijou Theater Scrapbook, Minnesota Historical Society (St. Paul)
WCA	Women's Cooperative Alliance
WCM	Woman's Club of Minneapolis Archive
WCM-MHS	Woman's Club of Minneapolis Papers, Minnesota Historical Society (St. Paul)
WCM-MPL	Woman's Club of Minneapolis, Women's Clubs and Organizations, Minneapolis Public Library
WHH	William Harrison Hays
WH-MC	Will Hays Microfilmed Collection

WHP   Will Hays Papers, Indiana State Library (Indianapolis)
WK-BF   William Koenig, Biographical File, Minneapolis Public Library
WML   Frances E. Willard Memorial Library (Evanston, Illinois)
WWL-MPL   Woman's Welfare League, Social Agencies, Minneapolis
                Public Library

Notes

INTRODUCTION: Crossing the Great Divide

1. Mrs. Richmond Wheeler to CCG, 10 May 1934, and Gilman to Wheeler, 23 May 1934, GFP, box 77.

2. *Current Opinion* 55 (August 1913), 113–14.

3. Barbara Welter, "The Cult of True Womanhood, 1820–1860," *American Quarterly* 18 (1966), 151–74.

4. William O'Neill, *Everyone Was Brave* (New York: Quadrangle, 1969), offers an early example; see also Note on Sources.

5. See the work of Kristi Anderson, Sara Hunter Graham, Michael McGerr, and Elisabeth S. Clemens discussed in the Note on Sources.

6. I refer to the work of Melanie Gustafson, Jo Freeman, Kristie Miller, and Elisabeth Israels Perry, among others.

7. Robyn Muncy, *Creating a Female Dominion in American Reform, 1890–1935* (New York: Oxford University Press, 1991); see also the work of Molly Ladd-Taylor, Linda Gordon, Theda Skocpol, Seth Koven, Sonya Michel, and Robyn Rosen in Note on Sources.

8. This trend is beginning to shift; see references to Kim E. Nielsen and Kathleen Blee in Note on Sources. On women as consumers of and performers in popular amusements, see also references to Elizabeth Ewen, Kathy Peiss, Lauren Rabinovitz, Nan Enstad, M. Alison Kibler, Shelly Stamp, Angela Latham, and Susan Glenn.

9. In the 1870s, United States courts began to adopt the British common law decision in *Regina v. Hicklin* (1868). Elizabeth Hovey, "Stamping Out Smut: The Enforcement of Obscenity Laws, 1872–1915" (Ph.D. diss., Columbia University, 1998), 237–51.

10. Alison Parker, *Purifying America: Women, Cultural Reform, and Pro-Censorship Activism, 1873–1933* (Chicago: University of Illinois Press, 1997), and Andrea Friedman, *Prurient Interests: Gender, Democracy, and Obscenity in New York City, 1909–1945* (New York: Columbia University Press, 2000); see Note on Sources for further discussion.

11. My approach parallels that found in Belinda Robnett, *How Long? How Long?: African-American Women in the Struggle for Civil Rights* (New York: Oxford University Press, 1977), 14.

12. Ellen Carol DuBois and Linda Gordon, "Seeking Ecstasy on the Battlefield: Danger and Pleasure in Nineteenth-Century Feminist Sexual Thought," *Feminist Review* 13 (February 1983), 44–55.

ONE: "Protect the Innocent!"

1. Quoted in Paul Boyer, *Purity in Print: The Vice-Society Movement and Book Censorship in America* (New York: Scribner's, 1968), 17.
2. Nicola Kay Beisel, *Imperiled Innocents: Anthony Comstock and Family Reproduction in Victorian America* (Princeton, NJ: Princeton University Press, 1997), 72.
3. Helen Lefkowitz Horowitz, *Rereading Sex: Battles over Sexual Knowledge and Suppression in Nineteenth-Century America* (New York: Knopf, 2002), 299–306, 312–13, 317–18, 367–85.
4. De Robigne Mortimer Bennett, *Anthony Comstock: His Career of Cruelty and Crime* (New York: De Capo Press, 1971), 1010; Horowitz, *Rereading Sex*, 419–36.
5. Heywood Broun and Margaret Leech, *Anthony Comstock: Roundsman of the Lord* (New York: Albert and Charles Boni, 1927), 224, 240.
6. Beisel, *Imperiled Innocents*, 53, 57–75.
7. Shirley Burton, "Obscenity in Victorian America: Struggles over Definition and Concomitant Prosecutions in Chicago's Federal Court, 1873–1913" (Ph.D. diss., University of Illinois, 1991), 191, 220–21; Bennett, *Anthony Comstock*, 1016–17; E. C. Walker, *Who Is the Enemy* (New York: E. C. Walker, 1903), 11–12, 31–32.
8. Beisel, *Imperiled Innocents*, 71–73.
9. Parker, *Purifying America*, 6–8, 21–31; Hovey, "Stamping Out Smut," 81–83, 102, 155, 190–95, 355–56.
10. Barbara Stuhler, *Gentle Warriors: Clara Ueland and the Minnesota Struggle for Woman Suffrage* (St. Paul: Minnesota Historical Society Press, 1995), 19, 23–24; Theodore C. Blegen, *Minnesota: A History of the State* (Minneapolis: University of Minnesota Press, 1963), 224–25; William Watts Folwell, *A History of Minnesota* (St. Paul: Minnesota Historical Society, 1926), 32.
11. William Millikan, *A Union against Unions: The Minneapolis Citizens Alliance and Its Fight against Organized Labor, 1903–1947* (St. Paul: Minnesota Historical Society Press, 2001), 17–29, 74–86.
12. *Annual Report of the Minnesota Federation of Women's Clubs, 1920–1921* (Minneapolis, MN: W. E. Kranhold Co., 1921), 129–42; Stuhler, *Gentle Warriors*, 61–63; John E. Hayes, "Reformers, Radicals, and Conservatives," in Clifford E. Clarke Jr., ed., *Minnesota in a Century of Change: The State and Its People Since 1900* (St. Paul: Minnesota Historical Society Press, 1989), 361–62; Millikan, *A Union against Unions*, 44–46, 183–87.
13. Audley M. Grossman, "The Professional Legitimate Theater in Minneapolis from 1890 to 1910" (Ph.D. diss., University of Minnesota, 1957), 98.
14. *Minneapolis Tribune*, 8, 15, and 16 October 1911; THSB, reel 13.
15. Steven Ross, *Working-Class Hollywood: Silent Film and the Shaping of Class in America* (Princeton, NJ: Princeton University Press, 1998), 79–80; Nan Enstad, *Ladies of Labor, Girls of Adventure: Working Women, Popular Culture, and Labor Politics at the Turn of the Twentieth Century* (New York: Columbia University Press, 1999), 186–200; Miriam Hansen, *Babel and Babylon: Spectatorship in American Silent Film* (Cambridge: Harvard University Press, 1991), 60–66; Lizzie Francke, *Script Girls: Women Screenwriters in Hollywood* (London: British Film Institute Publishing, 1994), 5–26.
16. *Minneapolis Tribune*, 21 October 1911, THSB, reel 13; Ross, *Working-Class Hollywood*, 31.
17. *Minneapolis Tribune*, 8, 9, and 19 October 1911, THSB, reel 13.

18. Friedman, *Prurient Interests*, 25–40; Robert Sklar, *Movie-Made America: A Cultural History of American Movies* (New York: Vintage Books, 1994), 18–30; Nancy Rosenbloom, "Between Reform and Regulation: The Struggle over Film Censorship in Progressive America, 1909–1922," *Film History* 1, no. 4 (1987), 307–25; Nancy Rosenbloom, "In Defense of the Moving Pictures: The People's Institute, the National Board of Censorship, and the Problem of Leisure in Urban America," *American Studies* 33, no. 2 (fall 1992), 41–61.

19. *Minneapolis Tribune*, 13 October 1911; *Minneapolis Daily News*, 21 October 1911; THSB, reel 13.

20. Newspaper articles, THSB, reel 13.

21. First quote in Koenig to Herk, 21 July 1918; second quote in Koenig to Robert Schoenecker, 10 September 1917, TH-MC, reel 3.

22. "Fatima's Dance," 1893, *Sex and Buttered Popcorn: The Story of the Hollywood Exploiters* (Monterey, CA: A Samfilm Production, 1991), video.

23. "Untitled (Girl on a Rock)," 1910, *Sex and Buttered Popcorn;* Thomas W. Bohn and Richard L. Stromgren, *Light and Shadows: A History of Motion Pictures* (Port Washington, NY: Alfred Publishing Co., 1975), 180; quote from Al Di Lauro, *Dirty Movies: An Illustrated History of the Stag Film, 1915–1970* (New York: Chelsea House, 1976), 48–49.

24. Many Minneapolis residents may have seen a "Theatre Warning," posted and mailed in 1911 by a C. W. Arnold. The bright yellow broadside claimed that hundreds of young girls disappeared from motion picture and vaudeville theaters, presumably abducted by unscrupulous theater men. C. W. Arnold, "Theatre Warning," 1911, MHS.

25. *Minneapolis Journal*, 18, 25, 26 October 1911; *Minneapolis Tribune*, 8, 9, 10, 27, 28 October 1911; THSB, reel 13.

26. All but last quote from *Minneapolis Tribune* 9, 10, 13 October 1911, THSB, reel 13; last quote from Janet Staiger, *Bad Women: Regulating Sexuality in Early American Cinema* (Minneapolis: University of Minnesota Press, 1995), 93.

27. Laura E. Richards and Maud Howe Elliott, *Julia Ward Howe, 1819–1910* (Boston: Houghton Mifflin, 1925), 210, 328, 362, 366, 371, 412; Alice Ames Winter, ed., *Charles Gordon Ames: A Spiritual Autobiography* (Boston: Houghton Mifflin, 1913), v–vi, 161–229; Albert Nelson Marquis, ed., *The Book of Minnesotans* (Chicago: A. N. Marquis and Co., 1907), 16, 562–63; unidentified local newspapers, 22 and 23 June 1934, AAW-CF; Steven C. Trimble, *In the Shadow of the City: A History of Loring Park Neighborhood* (Minneapolis: Minneapolis Community College Foundation, n.d.), 117; *Dual City Blue Book* (St. Paul: R. J. Polk and Co., 1911–1912), 271; (1917–1918), 333.

28. Kathleen Kasprick, "Culture and Reform: The Women and Work of the Woman's Club of Minneapolis, 1907–1914" (unpublished seminar paper, MHS, 1997); Alice Ames Winter, *The Prize to the Hardy* (Indianapolis: Bobbs-Merrill, 1905), and *Jewel-Weed* (Indianapolis: Bobbs-Merrill, 1907); "Articles of Incorporation and By-Laws of the Woman's Club of Minneapolis," n.d., WCM-MHS; Jeannette Ludcke, "You've Come a Long Way, Lady!: The Seventy-Five-Year History of the Woman's Club of Minneapolis" (unpublished book manuscript, MHS, n.d.), 93.

29. Mary Belle (King) Sherman, *The Women's Clubs in the Middle-Western States* (Philadelphia: American Academy of Political and Social Science, 1906); Margaret Lansing, "Woman's Club Movement in Minnesota" (seminar paper, University of Minnesota, 1931), MHS; Alice Winter, *The Business of Being a Club Woman* (New York: Century, 1925), 221.

30. Ludcke, "You've Come a Long Way, Lady!," 8; *Annual Report of the Minnesota Fed-

eration of Women's Clubs, 1920–1921 (Minneapolis: W. E. Kranhold Co., 1921), 57–58, 134, 142; Sherman, "The Women's Club in the Middle-Western States," 44–45; first quote in Karen Blair, *The Clubwoman as Feminist: True Womanhood Redefined, 1868–1914* (New York: Holmes and Meier, 1980), 70; second quote in Stuhler, *Gentle Warriors*, 73.

31. "Minneapolis Homemakers Exposition Program and Directory," 4 December 1926; see also playbills, 1914–1916, Woman's Club Assembly File, Minneapolis Public Library; "Annual Frolic, 20 April 1915," WCM-MPL; first quote in Stuhler, *Gentle Warriors*, 55; second quote in Winter, *The Business of Being a Club Woman*, 221.

32. "Articles of Incorporation and By-Laws of the Woman's Club of Minneapolis," undated; and "The Woman's Club of Minneapolis Year Book, 1907–8, 1910, 1912," WCM-MHS; *Minneapolis Journal*, 2 March 1924; unidentified local newspaper article, 20 February 1928, WCM-MPL; Mildred White Wells, *Unity in Diversity: The History of the General Federation of Women's Clubs* (Washington, DC: General Federation of Women's Clubs, 1953), 83–87.

33. Maureen Flanagan, "Gender and Urban Political Reform: The City Club and the Woman's City Club of Chicago in the Progressive Era," *American Historical Review* 95 (October 1990), 1032–50; first quote in Ludcke, "You've Come a Long Way, Lady!," 93; second quote in Janice C. Steinschneider, *An Improved Woman: The Wisconsin Federation of Women's Clubs, 1895–1920* (Brooklyn: Carlson Publishers, 1994), 31.

34. Blair, *The Clubwoman As Feminist*, 58, 97; Theodora Penny Martin, *The Sound of Our Own Voices: Women's Study Clubs, 1860–1910* (Boston: Beacon Press, 1987), 131, 168; Ann Bowers, "White-Gloved Feminists: An Analysis of Northwest Ohio Women's Clubs," *Hayes Historical Journal* 4 (fall 1984), 42; quote in "Hints on Etiquette," *Dual City Blue Book*, 39–44.

35. Birgitta Zaar, "The Women's Movement for Suffrage in Minnesota, 1911–1919" (seminar paper, University of Minnesota, 1986); Stuhler, *Gentle Warriors*, 71; quote in "The Woman's Club of Minneapolis Minutes," 6 September 1912; 21 January 1914; 18 September 1914; 6 October 1914, WCM.

36. Quotes in "Woman's Club of Minneapolis Bulletin," bulletin 12 (October 1914), WCM; Steinschneider, *An Improved Woman*, 9–10. The General Federation endorsed woman suffrage in 1914; Ludcke, "You've Come a Long Way, Lady!," 52.

37. "Following Sound Principles," unidentified local newspaper article, 2 April 1924, WCM-MPL.

38. Trimble, *In the Shadow of the City*, 16, 130–31, 58, 122, 117; Citizens for a Loring Park Community, *Reflections in Loring Pond: A Minneapolis Neighborhood Examines Its First Century* (Minneapolis: Citizens for a Loring Park Community, 1986), 13, 47–48, 57; Marion Daniel Shutter, ed., *History of Minneapolis: Gateway to the Northwest* (Minneapolis: S. J. Clarke, 1923), 273–74.

39. Ludcke, "You've Come a Long Way, Lady!," 10–11; Kate Louise Roberts, *The Club Woman's Handbook of Programs and Club Management* (New York: Funk and Wagnalls, 1914), 141–42; Anna Steese Richardson, *A Manual for Clubwomen* (New York: L. C. Smith and Corona Typewriters, 1929), 12; Winter, *The Business of Being a Club Woman*, 10.

40. Kasprick, "Culture and Reform," 20–21; first quote in Wells, *Unity in Diversity*, 19, 451; second and third quotes in Stuhler, *Gentle Warriors*, 75, 99.

41. John D'Emilio and Estelle Freedman, *Intimate Matters: A History of Sexuality in America* (New York: Harper and Row, 1988), 188–201; Kathy Peiss, *Cheap Amusements:*

Working Women and Leisure in Turn-of-the-Century New York (Philadelphia: Temple University Press, 1986); "Women's Welfare League," n.d., GFP, box 23; "Annual Report of the Women's Welfare League," 27 January 1928 (quoting the 1912 annual report), WWL-MPL.

42. Between 1910 and 1930, the number of female workers exceeded the number of male workers migrating to the Twin Cities, in every age bracket. Elizabeth Faue, *Community of Suffering and Struggle: Women, Men, and the Labor Movement in Minneapolis, 1915–1945* (Chapel Hill: University of North Carolina Press, 1991), 23–24; Lynn Weiner, "'Our Sister's Keepers': The Minneapolis Women's Christian Association and Housing for Working Women," *Minnesota History* 46 (1978–79), 189–90, quote, 192.

43. Mary Beard, *Women's Work in the Municipalities* (New York: D. Appleton, 1915), 98; quote in Sherman, "The Women's Clubs in the Middle-Western States," 36–38.

44. "Report of the Year's Work," 13 October 1909, *Woman's Club of Minneapolis Yearbook* (1907–8), 15–17, and "Reports of Departments," 9 April 1912, *Woman's Club of Minneapolis Yearbook* (1911–12), 17, MHS; "Woman's Club of Minneapolis Minutes," 8 March 1910; 6 December 1910, WCM.

45. Priscilla Murolo, *The Common Ground of Womanhood* (Urbana: University of Illinois Press, 1997), 15–16; Ludcke, "You've Come a Long Way, Lady!," 27–28; *The Woman's Club of Minneapolis Year Book* (1911–12), MHS; "Articles of Incorporation and By-Laws of the Woman's Club of Minneapolis," undated, WCM-MHS.

46. Mary I. Wood, *The History of the General Federation of Women's Clubs* (New York: General Federation of Women's Clubs, 1912), 382–401.

47. Martin, *The Sound of Our Own Voices*, 179; "Articles of Incorporation and By-Laws of the Woman's Club of Minneapolis," undated, and *The Woman's Club of Minneapolis Year Book* (1907–8), (1910), (1911–12), MHS.

48. Wood, *History of the General Federation of Women's Clubs*, 382–401.

49. Parker, *Purifying America*, 27.

TWO: Dressing Elsie

1. I. H. Herk to William Koenig, 11 October 1915, TH-MC, reel 2.

2. *Minneapolis Sunday Tribune*, 24 October 1915.

3. "Woman's Club of Minneapolis Minutes," 6 December 1910; 14 March 1911; 9 February 1912; 10 May 1912; 13, 23, 26 September 1912, WCM.

4. "Woman's Club of Minneapolis Minutes," 15 December 1911, and "Reports of Departments," 9 April 1912, *Woman's Club of Minneapolis Yearbook* (1911–12), WCM.

5. Countryman, quoted in "Annual Report of the Woman's Welfare League," 27 January 1928, WWL-MPL.

6. "Annual Report of the Woman's Welfare League," 27 January 1928, WWL-MPL; *Minneapolis Journal*, 5 January 1913; "Minneapolis Homemakers Exposition," 4 December 1926, Woman's Club of Minneapolis Program and Directory, Minneapolis Public Library; *Minneapolis Tribune*, 2 March 1924 and 2 April 1924; quote from "The Linden Club," n.d., and "Little Lights on Linden Life," n.d., WWL-MPL; Joanne Meyerowitz, *Women Adrift: Independent Wage Earners in Chicago, 1880–1930* (Chicago: University of Chicago Press, 1988).

7. Randy D. McBee, *Intimacy and Leisure among Working-Class Immigrants in the United States* (New York: New York University Press, 2000), 82–114.

8. "Annual Report of the Woman's Welfare League," 27 January 1928, and "The Linden Club," undated Woman's Welfare League pamphlet, WWL-MPL; "Woman's Welfare League Minutes," 1912, GFP, box 23.

9. Quote from "Woman's Welfare League Minutes, 1912–1913," 22 November 1912, GFP, box 23; *Minneapolis Tribune*, 28 January 1913, THSB, reel 13.

10. "Reports of Departments," 8 April 1913, *Woman's Club of Minneapolis Yearbook* (1912–13), WCM; "Annual Report of the Woman's Welfare League," 27 January 1928, WWL-MPL.

11. "Annual Report of the Woman's Welfare League, Minneapolis," 27 January 1928, WWL-MPL; "Woman's Welfare League Minutes," 2 February 1912, 14 and 21 November, 1912, 3 January 1913, 3 April 1913, 8 May 1913, 1 December 1913, 9 January 1914, 22 January 1914, GFP, box 23; quote in "Woman's Club of Minneapolis Minutes," 13 December 1912, WCM; Ludcke, "You've Come a Long Way, Lady!"; *Minneapolis Tribune*, 28 January 1913, THSB, reel 13.

12. David Rabban, *Free Speech in Its Forgotten Years* (Cambridge: Cambridge University Press, 1997), 44–76; *Mutual Film Corporation v. Ohio Industrial Commission*, 236 U.S. 230, 243–44 (1915).

13. Carl Chrislock, *The Progressive Era in Minnesota, 1899–1918* (St. Paul: Minnesota Historical Society, 1971), 39–40; "Woman's Club of Minneapolis Minutes," 1 February 1910, 26 September 1913, WCM.

14. "Woman's Welfare League Minutes," 3 May 1912 and 24 May 1912, GFP, box 23. See also Mary Beard, *Women's Work in the Municipalities* (New York: D. Appleton, 1915), 124–25, 148–49.

15. "Woman's Welfare League," 1916, report by Motion Picture Committee Chair, Mrs. T. F. Kinney; "Woman's Welfare League Minutes," 7 May 1915, GFP, box 23.

16. Rosenbloom, "Between Reform and Regulation," 307–25; Rosenbloom, "In Defense of the Moving Pictures," 41–61; Sonja Marakoff, "Boards of Censorship or Review," December 1920, GFP, box 13; "Woman's Welfare League Minutes," 7 May 1915, GFP, box 23; Robbins Gilman to Mary Caldwell, 16 March 1925, GFP, box 15.

17. *The General Federation of Woman's Clubs Magazine*, March 1917, 20–21, and April 1918, 36–37; quote in Richard Koszarski, *An Evening's Entertainment: The Age of the Silent Feature Picture, 1915–1928* (New York: Scribner's, 1990), 208.

18. Theodore Hayes to "Dear Madam," 19 December 1912, and *Minneapolis Journal*, 29 October 1911, THSB, reel 13.

19. Ludcke, "You've Come a Long Way, Lady!," 39; William Koenig to Herk, 14 February 1918, quote in 16 December 1919, TH-MC, reel 3; "Woman's Welfare League," 1916, report by Motion Picture Committee Chair, Mrs. T. F. Kinney, GFP, box 23.

20. Miscellaneous local newspaper articles and unidentified newspaper article by Caryl B. Storrs, 23 April 1916, WK-BF.

21. In 1918 Koenig assumed management of the Star Theater in St. Paul and continued his clean-show policy there in hopes of convincing the entire burlesque circuit to follow suit. To Herk he wrote, "Dirty shows such as Kirk [the previous manager] let them run last season I think hurt the business instead of helping it and I hope I will be able to prove this to all the managers before this season is over." Koenig to Herk, 19 August 1918; Koenig to Herk, 8 June 1917, TH-MC, reel 3; Koenig to Herk, 13 and 15 January 1916, TH-MC, reel 2.

22. First quote in unidentified local newspaper article by Caryl B. Storrs, 23 April 1916, WK-BF; second quote in Koenig to Herk, 16 August 1917, TH-MC, reel 3; third quote

in Roy Weir testimony, "Public Hearing Regarding Gayety License: Women's Cooperative Alliance Transcript," 25 October 1928, GFP, box 57.

23. Quote in Robert Schoenecker to Koenig, 5 September 1917, Koenig to Schoenecker, 10 September 1917, Koenig to Herk, 8 June 1917, TH-MC, reel 3; Koenig to Herk, 13 January 1916, TH-MC, reel 2.

24. CCG to Josephus Daniels, 1 May 1917; CCG to Raymond Fosdick, 11 May 1917; CCG's notes from women's meeting in Dayton's tea room, 17 May 1917, GFP, box 13; WCA report, "Special Survey of the Moral Conditions Surrounding Girls and Young Women of Minneapolis and St. Paul," September 1917, AFP, box 14; *General Federation Magazine*, April 1918, 32–33, and August 1918, 28–29.

25. William Becker, *Ten Million Americans Have It* (Philadelphia: J. B. Lippincott, 1937), 185–87; Allan Brandt, *No Magic Bullet* (Oxford: Oxford University Press, 1985), 123–24. The New York State Board of Censors declared the film obscene in 1922.

26. *Union Advocate*, 3 August 1917.

27. Unidentified newspaper articles, 9 and 11 June 1914, 13 September 1914, 10 November 1918, AAW-BF; AAW, "What War Is Doing to Club Life," *General Federation Magazine*, November 1917, 5; Ludcke, "You've Come a Long Way, Lady!," 46–52.

28. AAW to Family, 5, 10, 14, 20, 25 April 1918, and 15 October 1918, AAWC; Faue, *Community of Suffering and Struggle*, 53–54.

29. AAW to Family, 2 and 12 June 1918, 18 July 1918, 5 November 1918, AAWC.

30. T. G. Winter to C. W. Ames, 20 September 1917, and Governor Joseph Burnquist to C. W. Ames, 4 December 1917, AFP, box 15; first quote in Millikan, *A Union against Unions*, 117; second quote in unidentified local newspaper clippings, *St. Paul Pioneer Press*, 30 September 1917, AFP, box 14; third quote in Koenig to Herk, 8 June 1917, TH-MC, reel 3.

31. Quote in Koenig to Herk, 8 June 1917; see also 9 and 12 April 1917, 17 December 1917, and undated, TH-MC, reel 3. One burlesque publication even suggested that managers aim for children's as well as women's patronage. Irving Zeidman, *The American Burlesque Show* (New York: Hawthorn Books, 1967), 79–81.

32. Koenig to Schoenecker, 21 September 1917, enclosing the quoted notice, dated 27 September 1917, and Koenig to Herk, 1 October 1917, 5 November 1917, TH-MC, reel 3.

33. *Minneapolis Journal*, 23 April 1916; Koenig to Herk, 19 August 1918, 16 December 1919, TH-MC, reel 3.

34. Koenig to Herk, 17 and 29 October 1918; 5, 14, 18, 26 November 1918; 27 December 1918; 20 January 1919; 6 February 1919; Herk to Koenig, 29 November 1918, TH-MC, reel 3; AAW to Family, 30 September 1918, 9 October 1918, 15 October 1918, AAWC.

35. Koenig to Herk, 19 March 1919, TH-MC, reel 3.

36. "Woman's Welfare League Minutes," 1911–1912, GFP, box 23; "Annual Report of the Woman's Welfare League," 27 January 1928, WWL-MPL.

37. Ibid.

THREE: "Censorship Does Not Protect"

1. Virginia Blythe, "The Origins of the Women's Cooperative Alliance Was on This Wise," n.d.; "Speech," n.d.; "Early History of the Women's Cooperative Alliance: Interview with Mrs. Gilman by Dr. Owings," 3 October 1927; 1917 fundraising letter, GFP, box 23.

2. Ibid.

3. Elizabeth Gilman, "Catheryne Cooke Gilman: Social Worker," in Barbara Stuhler and Gretchen Kreuter, eds., *Women of Minnesota: Selected Biographical Essays* (St. Paul: Minnesota Historical Society Press, 1977), 190–207; CCG, "History: Northeast Neighborhood House," vol. 1, Northeast Neighborhood House Papers, 55, 59, MHS.

4. Gilman, "Catheryne Cooke Gilman," 194–95; Robbins Gilman to Dr. Harry Dewey, 27 June 1914, 17 October 1914; "We Dare Not Say What We Think," unidentified newspaper editorial, 17 July 1914; Board of University Settlement Society to Robbins Gilman, 16 July 1914; Harry Dewey to Robbins Gilman, 30 September 1914, GFP, box 12.

5. Quote in Georgia Cooke to CCG, 21 October 1914; Aditha Cooke to CCG, 24 November 1914 and n.d.; Nina Cooke to CCG, 28 November 1914; Harry Dewey telegram to Robbins Gilman, 14 October 1914, GFP, box 12; "Woman's Welfare League Minutes," February 1915, GFP, box 23; Robbins Gilman to Mary Caldwell, 16 March 1925, GFP, box 15; CCG to Miss Clarice Wade, 10 June 1932, GFP, box 74.

6. CCG, "History: Northeast Neighborhood House," vol. 1, 55, 59, MHS; Woman's Welfare League Minutes, February 1915; "Woman's Welfare League," GFP, box 23; Gilman, "Catheryne Cooke Gilman," 190–207.

7. Virginia Blythe, "The Origins of the Women's Cooperative Alliance Was on This Wise," n.d.; "Speech," n.d., GFP, box 23.

8. "Minneapolis Council of Social Agencies Yearbook, 1919," Community Fund Handbook, MHS; CCG to Rev. W. K. Williams, 15 December 1920, GFP, box 13; "Minneapolis Council of Social Agencies," GFP, box 14; "Committee of Thirteen File," GFP, box 39.

9. By 1919, the Woman's Welfare League had begun to move away from antiobscenity work to focus on the Linden Club and its other facilities for working women. Winifred Wandersee Bolin, "Heating Up the Melting Pot: Settlement Work and Americanization in Northeast Minneapolis," *Minnesota History* 45 (1976–77), 58–69; CCG, "History: Northeast Neighborhood House," vol. 1, Northeast Neighborhood House, 55, 59, MHS; quote in CCG, Notes for Sponsor's Dinner, 24 March 1924, GFP, box 24; *Minneapolis Daily News*, 12 October 1922; "Women's Cooperative Alliance Annual Report," 1925, GFP, box 34; CCG, "A Cooperative Movement in Community Social Service," May 1923, GFP, box 23.

10. "Description of the Organization in Which the Experience for This Examination Was Acquired: The Women's Cooperative Alliance, Catheryne Cooke Gilman, Executive Secretary, 1916–1933," 11; "Women's Cooperative Alliance," 1923, GFP, box 23; CCG to E. S. Woodworth (Chamber of Commerce), 1 April 1919, GFP, box 13.

11. "Community Problems," WCA Publication, October 1928, GFP, box 34.

12. Unidentified correspondent to Mr. Scott, Motion Picture Board of Review, 1 September 1917; "National Motion Picture Board of Review Monthly Bulletin," September 1919, GFP, MHS, box 13. The board changed its name from "Censorship" to "Review" in 1915 to distinguish itself from proponents of state censorship. Robert J. Fisher, "Film Censorship and Progressive Reform: The National Board of Censorship of Motion Pictures, 1909–1922," *Journal of Popular Film* 4 (1975), 150.

13. "Report of Interview with Mr. E. S. W.," March 1919, MHS, GFP, box 13.

14. CCG, "Jane Addams, the Universal," lecture 1946, Women's International League for Peace and Freedom Minnesota Branch Records, MHS, box 28; CCG to Addams, 4 April 1927, 20 April 1927; Addams to CCG, 12 April 1927; Addams to "The Presidents and Secretaries of the Various Sections of the Women's International League," 10 May 1927;

CCG to Dr. Alice Salomon, 17 February 1930, GFP, box 69; CCG to Miss Loni Cahn, 24 November 1932, GFP, box 70; Mrs. L. Cass (Etta) Brown to CCG, 11 July 1933, GFP, box 75. Jane Addams, *The Spirit of Youth and City Streets* (New York: Macmillan, 1909).

15. First quote in Minnie E. Kennedy, *The Home and Moving Pictures* (New York: Abingdon Press, undated), 3, 14–15, 22–23, 28; CCG, "Mobilize for Wholesome Motion Pictures," undated, GFP, box 66; second quote in "Sixth Annual Women's Cooperative Alliance Report," 1921, GFP, box 48.

16. First quote in Mrs. Florence Wilson to the editor, 9 December 1920, GFP, box 13; second quote in *Minneapolis Tribune*, 8 December 1920, GFP, box 23.

17. First quote in "Motion Pictures Not Guilty: Verdict Based on Reports from Chief Probation Officers of Juvenile Courts throughout the United States on Relation of Motion Pictures to Juvenile Delinquency," New York, National Board of Review, 1920, GFP, box 66; second quote in "A Motion Picture Problem Solved: Constructive Community Programs for Young People and the Family," New York, National Committee for Better Films, 1920, GFP, box 64.

18. Cocks to CCG, 29 June 1920; Marion Kofusky to CCG, 2 July 1920, GFP, box 13. WCTU and settlement house leaders were among the first to recognize the reform potential of motion pictures and incorporate films into their educational and recreational programs. Harriet S. Pritchard, "Moving Pictures as Educators," National WCTU pamphlet, 1911,7, WML.

19. Quote in CCG to Orrin Cocks, 7 July 1920; CCG to Orrin Cocks, 24 June 1920; CCG to the National Board of Review, 21 July 1920; CCG to C. W. Hadden, 15 December 1920; CCG to Orrin Cocks, 21 December 1920, GFP, box 13; "Women's Cooperative Alliance: Featuring the Sunday Paper," 20 October 1920, GFP, box 23; "Better Movie Movement," June 1920; "Women's Cooperative Alliance Sixth Annual Report," 1921; "Women's Cooperative Alliance Seventh Annual Report," 1922, GFP, box 48; Cynthia Hanson, "Catheryne Cooke Gilman and the Minneapolis Better Movie Movement," *Minnesota History* (summer 1989), 209; "Women's Cooperative Alliance Sixth Annual Report," 1921; "Women's Cooperative Alliance Seventh Annual Report," 1922, GFP, box 48.

20. "Better Movie Movement," June 1920, GFP, box 48.

21. "The Minneapolis Better Movie Movement Plan and the Report of a Survey of the Minneapolis Motion Picture Houses," February 1921, 4–7, GFP, box 48; "Women's Cooperative Alliance: Better Movie Movement," January 1922; CCG to Miss M. E. Kennedy, 27 February 1922, GFP, box 14; CCG to C. W. Hadden, 15 December 1920, GFP, box 13.

22. CCG to Hon. Bryon S. Payne (attorney general, South Dakota), 13 May 1921, GFP, box 14.

23. CCG to Mr. Flynn, 18 December 1920, GFP, box 13; Miss Barber to Mrs. Earl Whitney, 24 March 1921; Barber to Miss Derr, 30 March 1921; Barber to Mrs. Walter Stout, 4 April 1921, GFP, box 14.

24. Quoted in Hanson, "Catheryne Cooke Gilman and the Minneapolis Better Movie Movement," 209–10.

25. First quote in CCG to Orrin Cocks, 24 June 1920; CCG to National Board of Review of Motion Pictures, 21 July 1920; second quote in CCG to Mr. Flynn, Resident Manager, Goldwyn Distribution Corporation, 8 December 1920; Cocks to CCG, 18 June 1920; CCG to Cocks, 24 June 1920, GFP, box 13; CCG, "The Minneapolis Better Movie Movement Plan," February 1921, 5, GFP, boxes 24 and 48; CCG to Mrs. Adele F.

Woodard, 3 May 1921; "Women's Cooperative Alliance: Better Movie Movement," January 1922, GFP, box 14.

26. Quote in CCG to Falk, 9 May 1922; CCG to Mrs. Chilson Aldrich, 25 February 1921; CCG to Mrs. Edgar Baird, 6 June 1921; CCG to Falk, 9 May 1922; CCG to Harold Berg, 19 June 1922, GFP, box 14. Paul Murphy, *The Meaning of Free Speech: First Amendment Freedoms from Wilson to FDR* (Westport, CT: Greenwood, 1972), 121; Rosenbloom, "Between Reform and Regulation," 317, 320; Samuel Walker, *In Defense of American Liberties: A History of the ACLU* (New York: Oxford University Press, 1990), 228.

27. First and second quote in CCG to Madam Laura Dreyfus-Barney, 23 March 1928, 30 December 1927; CCG to Mr. Matz, 2 August 1927, GFP, box 69; third quote in CCG to Bryon S. Payne, 13 May 1921, GFP, box 14; Catheryne Cooke Gilman, "Our Responsibility," 1922, GFP, box 83; CCG to Mrs. W. A. Starin, 15 February 1931; CCG to Maud Owens, 10 May 1932, GFP, box 84; "Women's Cooperative Alliance," 20 October 1920, GFP, box 23; "Newer Aspects of the Citizens' Solution of the Motion Picture Problem," February 1924, GFP, box 68.

28. Henrietta Starkey (proprietor of the Star Theatre) to CCG, 12 February 1921, GFP, box 14.

29. One local newspaper article even reported that Theodore Hayes turned down the position (later assumed by Will Hays) of MPPDA "motion picture czar." *St. Paul Pioneer Press*, 6 May 1945; *Minneapolis Sunday Tribune*, 6 May 1945. Memo from WCA worker to CCG, undated, GFP, box 14; E. A. Purdy telegram to Will Hays, 11 April 1922; E. A. Purdy to Hays, 13 April 1922, WHP, box 16; E. A. Purdy to Kirk L. Russell, 22 June 1922, WHP, box 17.

30. WCA investigator to CCG, 13 October 1919; CCG to Theodore Hayes, 27 October 1919, 20 January 1920; Theodore Hayes to CCG, 30 January 1920, GFP, box 13; "Better Movie Movement: The Minneapolis Better Movie Movement Plan and The Report of a Survey of the Minneapolis Motion Picture Houses," February 1921, 27–28, GFP, box 48; Kathy Peiss, *Cheap Amusements: Working Women and Leisure in Turn-of-the-Century New York* (Philadelphia: Temple University Press, 1986), 150.

31. Mrs. Evans to Theodore Hayes, 12 October 1921; Hayes to Evans, 13 October 1921; H. W. Plain to CCG, 17 May 1922; CCG to Plain 19, May 1922; 1921 undated memo from WCA worker to CCG, GFP, box 14.

32. CCG to Theodore Hayes, 12 March 1921, GFP, box 14; WCA Research and Investigation Department Memo to CCG, 3 April 1923; Cortland Smith to CCG, 18 June 1923, GFP, box 71; CCG to Smith, 14 June 1923, GFP, box 15.

33. CCG to Theodore Hayes, 13 January 1922; Hayes to CCG, 27 January 1922, GFP, box 71; Molly Haskell, *From Reverence to Rape: The Treatment of Women in the Movies* (Harmondsworth: Penguin Books, 1974), 75.

34. Quote in CCG to Theodore Hayes, 5 September 1922, GFP, box 71; CCG to Mr. Durgin, 24 January 1921, GFP, box 14.

35. CCG to Orrin Cocks, 31 January 1921; Pierce Atwater to Theodore Hayes, 8 February 1921; Atwater to CCG, 2 and 11 February 1921; Hayes to CCG, 16 February 1921, GFP, box 14; Mrs. Bert Barber to the *Motion Picture News*, 7 January 1920, GFP, box 13; "The Minneapolis Better Movie Movement Plan and the Report of a Survey of the Minneapolis Motion Picture Houses," February 1921, GFP, box 48; CCG, "Newer Aspects of the Citizens' Solution of the Motion Picture Problem," February 1924, GFP, box 68; quote in CCG to Theodore Hayes, 5 September 1922, GFP, box 71.

36. *General Federation Magazine*, January 1917, 29–30; February 1917, 24–25; March 1918, 4; quote in advertisement for "Womanhood, the Glory of the Nation," *General Federation Magazine*, May 1917.

37. Excerpts from the 1916 resolutions can be found in the *General Federation Magazine*, April 1918, 11–12; *General Federation Magazine*, March 1917, 20–21; April 1917, 31; quote in April 1918, 36–37. For summaries of motion picture discussions between 1916 and 1918 see the *General Federation Magazine*, September 1918, 3–5; May 1918, 24–25; June 1918; July 1918, 5.

38. See articles in *General Federation Magazine*, September 1918, 6–10, 20–25; October 1918, 29, and January 1919, 13–26.

39. A mixed-sex jury acquitted Arbuckle. Most who considered him innocent explained Rappe's death as the tragic consequence of chronic bladder problems caused by venereal infections and possibly even pregnancy—all results of the woman's sexual promiscuity. Robert Young Jr., *Roscoe "Fatty" Arbuckle: A Bio-Bibliography* (Westport, CT: Greenwood Press, 1994), 68, 70; David Yallop, *The Day the Laughter Stopped: The True Story of Fatty Arbuckle* (New York: St. Martin's, 1979), 158, 189; quote in Stuart Oderman, *Roscoe "Fatty" Arbuckle: A Biography of the Silent Film Comedian, 1887–1933* (Jefferson, NC: McFarland and Company, 1994), 196, see also 79, 192–93.

40. Sklar, *Movie-Made America*, 82; Young, *Roscoe "Fatty" Arbuckle*, 72–73; CCG to WHH, 20 April 1922, GFP, box 71; quote in Oderman, *Roscoe "Fatty" Arbuckle*, 199, see also 164–65. Apparently, no women's groups called for the removal of Virginia Rappe's films, even though, according to the women's reasoning, the scandal surrounding Rappe's death could have been interpreted as contaminating her work as well. The women may have refrained from commenting on Rappe's films because she was not a famous actress, or because, whatever happened on the evening of September 5, 1921, Virginia Rappe was, unquestionably, a victim. On the other hand, the Committee of Public Welfare of the Theatre Owners of America unilaterally decided to withdraw Rappe's films as well as Arbuckle's.

41. Quote in CCG to Theodore Hayes, 12 March 1921; CCG to Mayor Meyers, 12 March 1921; Pauline Barber to Mrs. Gilmore Scranton, 7 April 1921, GFP, box 14. Published movie reviews echo CCG's observations: *Variety Film Reviews, 1907–1920* (New York: Garland, 1983), 7 February 1919, 30 April 1920, and 7 December 1920; Frank Walsh, *Sin and Censorship: The Catholic Church and the Motion Picture Industry* (New Haven, CT: Yale University Press, 1996), 23–24; David Shipman, *Cinema: The First Hundred Years* (New York: St. Martin's, 1993), 66–76.

42. As an MPPDA envoy in Massachusetts wrote to Will Hays: "If a few more states pass [state censorship] we could not physically or mechanically do the cutting to suit the minds of the individuals on different boards which themselves change daily." WHH to Raymond Benjamin, 21 October 1922, WHP, box 18.

43. See for example, WHH, "Address before the General Federation of Women's Clubs, Chautauqua, N.Y.," Sixth Biennial Convention, 28 June 1922, GFP, box 65; "Certificate of Incorporation of Motion Picture Producers and Distributors of America, Inc.," 10 March 1922, WHP, box 16; quote in Walsh, *Sin and Censorship*, 25. Will Hays's papers chart an extended network that reached deeply into the politics of Washington and the General Federation of Women's Clubs, even though he vociferously denied using his political connections to benefit the movie industry. WHH to Ralph Hayes, 22 May 1922, WHP, box 17.

44. *Pittsburgh, Pennsylvania Gazette-Times*, 18 April 1922; *New York Times*, 12 March 1922; *New York American*, 12 March 1922, WHP, box 16; Ross, *Working-Class Hollywood*, 131–32, 234–35; Douglas Gomery, "U.S. Film Exhibition: The Formation of a Big Business," in Tino Balio, ed., *The American Film Industry* (Madison: University of Wisconsin, 1985); *The Public Relations of the Motion Picture Industry* (New York: Federal Council of the Churches of Christ in America, 1931), 11–12, 18.

45. WHH, "Inter-Office Communication," 18 April 1922, WHP, box 16. In the aftermath of the Arbuckle scandal, Paramount stock plummeted from ninety to forty dollars a share, while women sent Hays warm messages of gratitude after his announcement that producers and distributors would cancel all Arbuckle films. Oderman, *Roscoe "Fatty" Arbuckle*, 196; Young, *Roscoe "Fatty" Arbuckle*, 72; "Brief Resumé of Facts Pertaining to Affairs of the Committee [on Public Relations]," 22 March 1923; Lee F. Hanmer to WHH, 23 March 1923, WHP, box 19; Samuel Altman to WHH, 20 April 1922, WHP, box 16; MPPDA press release, 1 December 1922; memo for mass mailing, 6 December 1922, WHP, box 18.

46. "Report to the Honorable Will H. Hays In re: Meeting of Women's Organizations in Atlanta, Georgia, April 27–28, 1922," WHP, box 17; WHH, "I Learned a Lot from the Folks Back Home," *American Magazine*, 2 January 1923; Charles H. Cole to Will Hays, 8 March 1923, WHP, box 19; WHH to President Warren G. Harding, 27 February 1923, WHP, box 19.

47. "Too Many Laws Passed, Mrs. Winter Claims at Federation Convention," unidentified local newspaper article, 17 June 1921; "'Keep Personalities out of Politics,' Mrs. Winter Urges Women," unidentified local newspaper article, 3 November 1920, AAW-BF.

48. "Read Her Out of the Party," 18 November 1923, unidentified local newspaper article, AAW-BF. Where I have substituted "feminists," this article actually uses the term "Belmonters," or "feminists of the Belmont school," a likely reference to Mrs. Oliver Belmont, a radical suffragist and leader in the National Woman's Party.

49. "'Keep Personalities out of Politics,' Mrs. Winter Urges Women," unidentified local newspaper article, 3 November 1920, AAW-BF; Lydia Adams-Williams to WHH, 30 May 1922, WHP, box 17; WHH, *The Memoirs of Will H. Hays* (Garden City, NY: Doubleday, 1955), 410–11.

50. Lydia Adams-Williams to WHH, 30 May 1922; WHH to Adolph Zukor, 22 June 1922; George Christian to WHH, 22 June 1922, WHP, box 17. Hays also attempted to obtain a special letter of support from his friend and ally President Warren G. Harding, but Harding declined, explaining that federation officials had already obtained a letter from him, making the one requested by Hays redundant.

51. WHH, "Address before the General Federation of Women's Clubs," at Chautauqua, New York, 28 June 1922, GFP, box 65.

52. "Resolutions Passed by General Federation of Women's Clubs, Chautauqua, N.Y., June 30, 1922," WHP-MC, reel 5. Hays kept a copy of this resolution in his files. "Resolution on Motion Pictures passed at the Biennial Convention of the General Federation of Women's Clubs," filed with 9 February 1925 correspondence, WHP, box 26; quotes in WHH to Mrs. Percy Pennybacker, 1 February 1923, WHP, box 19.

53. The vast majority of the four hundred sponsoring organizations identified themselves as women's clubs. State Committee on Motion Pictures, "The Motion Picture Situation in Massachusetts," WHP, box 18; "The Massachusetts Verdict and Its Signifi-

cance," MPPDA pamphlet, GFP, box 71; quote in Henry G. Hogan to WHH, 29 October 1922; "Plan of Campaign for Boston," enclosure in Henry Hogan to WHH, 29 October 1922; Henry Hogan to WHH, 2 November 1922, WHP, box 18.

54. General Charles H. Cole to Will Hays, 5 October 1922; J. C. O'Laughlin to Will Hays, 6 November 1922, WHP, box 18.

55. J. C. O'Laughlin to WHH, 6 November 1922, WHP, box 18.

56. Address of Will Hays before the Men's Bible Class Annual Dinner, 23 January 1933, WHP-MC, reel 8.

57. Henry G. Hogan to WHH, 10 October 1922; quote in "Plan of Campaign for Boston," enclosure in Henry Hogan to Will Hays, 29 October 1922, WHP, box 18; Wells, *Unity in Diversity*, 471–73; Orrin Cocks to CCG, 8 February 1921, GFP, box 14; Charles H. Cole to WHH, 5 October 1922, WHP, box 18.

58. First quote in *Educational Screen*, December 1920; see also *Film Year Book, 1922–1923*, 400–401; Adele F. Woodward to Mrs. Leopold Metzger, 25 April 1921; second quote from Orrin Cocks to CCG, 8 February 1921; correspondence files, February through May 1921, GFP, box 14; President of Motion Picture News, Inc., to Mrs. Bert Barber, 26 November 1920, GFP, box 13. In 1921, countless women's organizations, clubs, and parent-teacher groups, as well as public officials from other cities and states, wrote to the WCA to request more information on the Better Movie Movement. See E. A. Purdy to WHH, 13 April 1922, WHP, box 16; Purdy to Kirk L. Russell, 22 June 1922; Russell to Purdy, 2 June 1922, WHP, box 17.

59. The NBR gave the meeting national exposure in its publication *Film Progress*, reporting that "the National Committee for Better Films is giving consideration to some important suggestions presented to it by Mrs. Gilman in the light of her experience." *Film Progress*, January 1923, GFP, box 15. For a collection of anti-referendum newspaper articles from around the country compiled by Will Hays's office, see "Motion Picture Censorship Un-American: Leading Newspapers and Foremost Thinkers Demand a Free Screen," undated, GFP, box 65. Several letters document CCG's consultation with Theodore Hayes before her meeting with Will Hays: Pauline Barber to Mrs. C. C. Bovey, 18 September 1922; Barber to Theodore Hayes, 18 September 1922, Will Hays to CCG, 19 September 1922, GFP, box 14.

60. CCG to Theodore Hayes, 3 October 1922, GFP, box 14; Charles H. Cole to WHH, 5 October 1922, WHP, box 18; quote in CCG to Theodore Hayes, 3 October 1922, GFP, box 14; J. C. O'Laughlin to WHH, 6 November 1922, WHP, box 18.

61. First quote in CCG to Valeria Parker, 25 October 1922; CCG to Elizabeth Newman, 11 October 1922, GFP, box 71; second quote in "Mrs. Robbins Gilman, Better Movie Movement: Statistical Report of Towns Visited in Massachusetts, 1922," GFP, box 71; third quote in J. C. O'Laughlin to WHH, 6 November 1922, WHP, box 18.

62. CCG to Miss Alice Belton Evans, 20 April 1923, GFP, box 15; quote in Mabel Parkhouse to CCG, 1 November 1922; "Better Movie Movement: Statistical Report of Towns Visited in Massachusetts, 1922," GFP, box 71.

63. "The Massachusetts Verdict and Its Significance," undated MPPDA pamphlet, GFP, box 71; *Boston American*, 26 February 1922; *Boston American*, 28 February 1922; *New Bedford Standard*, undated article in collection entitled "Motion Picture Censorship Un-American: Leading Newspapers and Foremost Thinkers Demand a Free Screen," GFP, box 65.

64. J. C. O'Laughlin to WHH, 6 November 1922; Henry Hogan to WHH, 6 No-

vember 1922; Henry Hogan to WHH, 2 and 4 November 1922; "Town and City Clerks Report on Sentiment," 4 November 1922; WHH to Raymond Benjamin, 21 October 1922; Henry Hogan to WHH, 7 November 1922, WHP, box 18.

65. Quote in CCG to Elizabeth Newman, 11 October 1922; Courtland Smith to CCG, 9 November 1922; CCG to Smith, undated, GFP, box 71.

66. WHH to R. G. Tucker, 10 November 1922, WHP, box 18; "Address of Will H. Hays before the Men's Bible Class Annual Dinner—Baptist Church," 23 January 1923; WHH to Honorable Channing Moore, 12 March 1923, WHP, box 19; WHH, *The Memoirs of Will Hays*, 331–33; *Film Year Book, 1922–1923*, 1–5; Gregory Black, *Hollywood Censored: Morality Codes, Catholics, and the Movies* (Cambridge: Cambridge University Press, 1994), 32–33.

67. *Independent* 86 (22 May 1916), 265.

FOUR: "Woman vs. Woman"

1. AAW, *The Business of Being a Club Woman* (New York: Century, 1925), 228, 229–30; "'Keep Personalities out of Politics,' Mrs. Winter Urges Women," unidentified local newspaper article, 3 November 1920, AAW-CF; CCG, "Organizing the Women of Local Communities for Moral Welfare," undated notes, GFP, box 80.

2. Chapter 6 discusses the WCA's sex education program.

3. "Report of Interview with Mr. E.S.W.," March 1919, GFP, box 13; "A Statement to the Members of the WCA," 1921; "Recommendation to the Board of Directors," 16 February 1921; CCG to Pierce Atwater, 19 February 1921; Atwater to CCG, 23 February 1921; CCG to Dr. James Freeman, 20 April 1922; CCG to A. E. Zonne, 12 June 1922, GFP, box 14; Kate Koon Bovey to Mr. Carstens, 15 November 1924, GFP, box 15.

4. Millikan, *A Union against Unions*, 213–16; Committee of Thirteen Minutes, 15 February 1919; CCG to Charles G. Davis, 25 January 1922, "Manager's Quarterly Report to Board of Directors," 8 June 1922, GFP, box 39; Correspondence in Subject Files: Research and Investigation—Prostitution, 1926, GFP, box 57.

5. "WCA Executive Committee Meeting Minutes," 5 June 1924; CCG to Mrs. Gemmell, 8 June 1931, GFP, box 17; "WCA Minutes," 17 September 1925, GFP, box 25; quote in CCG to William Marston Seabury, 30 November 1932, GFP, box 84.

6. CCG to Miss Edna Chandler, 16 December 1921, GFP, box 14; "Woman's Club of Minneapolis Minutes," 6 October 1921, 3 November 1921, 17 November 1921, 5 December 1921, WCM.

7. MPPDA press releases, WH-MC, reel 4; WHH to Arbuckle, 3 June 1922; Minta Arbuckle to WHH, 20 June 1922, WH-MC, reel 5; J. Homer Platten to WHH, 3 January 1923; Thomas G. Patten to WHH, 4 January 1923; WHH to Thomas G. Patten, 9 and 11 January 1923; Kirk Russell to WHH, 6 and 11 January 1923; Frank Rembusch to WHH, 11 January 1923; Joe Schenck to Nicholas Schenck, 22 January 1923; Mae Wackenhuth to Courtland Smith, 23 January 1923; Smith to WHH, 25 January 1923; MPPDA Committee on Public Relations Resolution, 1 February 1923, WHMC, reel 8; Mrs. Bert Barber to WHH, 23 December 1922, GFP, box 14; Courtland Smith to CCG, 25 January 1923, 8 February 1923, 30 April 1923; Jason Joy to Mrs. Bert Barber, 20 February 1923; WHH to Mrs. Metzger and Mrs. Bert Barber, 23 February 1923; CCG to WHH, 27 February 1923, GFP, box 15; WHH, *The Memoirs of Will Hays*, 360–62.

8. "Women Launch War for Uniform U.S. Divorce Law," unidentified local news-

paper article, 22 January 1923, AAW-CF. Searches through myriad film catalogs and bibliographies turned up only one reference to AAW's film, describing it as a two-reel film, part one of the "American Home Life Series," directed by Arthur J. Zelner, of the Aralma Film Company, copyrighted January 11, 1923. Walter E. Hurst, *Film Superlist: Motion Pictures in the United States Public Domain, 1894–1939* (Hollywood: Hollywood Film Archive, 1994), 857, 1223; Fred Beetson to WHH, 16 November 1923; WHH to Beetson, 17 November 1923; Beetson to Hays, 21 November 1923; WHH to Beetson, 26 November 1923, WHP, box 22; quote in "Mrs. Winter Is Delighted with Hollywood Tour," unidentified local newspaper article, 25 November 1923, AAW-CF.

9. Millard to CCG, 13 March 1923; CCG to Millard, 22 March 1923, GFP, box 71; CCG to Smith, 30 October 1924; Smith to CCG, 5 November 1924, GFP, box 15.

10. Research and Investigation Department Memo to CCG, 3 April 1923, GFP, box 71; CCG to Theodore Hayes, 24 July 1924, 17 September 1924; Theodore Hayes to CCG, 16 August 1924, 19 September 1924, GFP, box 15; *Harrison's Reports*, 5 April 1924, 28 June 1924, 5 July 1924, 2 August 1924, 8 November 1924.

11. Margaretta Reeve to Mary Caldwell, 9 March 1925; Robbins Gilman to Caldwell, 16 March 1925; CCG to Caldwell, 23 March 1925, GFP, box 15; CCG to George P. McCabe, 8 May 1926, GFP, box 16; CCG to Wilton Barrett, 8 and 19 July 1924; Barrett to CCG, 25 July 1924, GFP, box 63. See also Charles Matthew Feldman, *The National Board of Censorship (Review) of Motion Pictures, 1909–1922* (New York: Arno Press, 1977), 168–82.

12. Eileen Bowser, *The Transformation of Cinema, 1907–1915* (New York: Scribner's, 1990), 45–47; CCG, "Newer Aspects of the Citizens' Solution of the Motion Picture Problem," February 1924, GFP, box 68; "Preliminary Report of Arthur Butler Graham on Trade Practices Existing in the Motion Picture Industry in the United States of America to the Committee on Research of the Motion Picture Research Council together with a Brief Discussion of the Development of the Industry," undated, GFP, box 72.

13. CCG's testimony, *Hearings before the Committee on Education, House of Representatives*, 14, 15, 16, 17, 27 April and 4 May 1926, 115, GFP, box 66; quotes in CCG to Mrs. Martha Sprague Mason, 7 April 1934, GFP, box 77; CCG to Miss Alice Belton Evans, 20 April 1923, GFP, box 15.

14. The following letters document Hays's contacts with motion picture men in Minnesota, including Theodore Hayes: Ed A. Purdy to WHH, 22 June 1922, WH-MC, reel 5; William A. Steffes to WHH, 11 May 1923, WH-MC, reel 10; quotes in J. C. O'Laughlin to WHH, 6 November 1922; Henry Hogan to WHH, 6 November 1922, WHP, box 18.

15. Gaylord Davidson to WHH, 18 May 1923, WH-MC, reel 10; Ralph Hayes to WHH, 3 October 1922, WHP, box 18; "Memorandum to W.H.H.," 22 March 1923; George Gleason to Thomas Patten, 23 March 1923, WH-MC, reel 9.

16. Courtland Smith to WHH, 9 February 1925; Jason S. Joy to WHH, 10 February 1925; "Memorandum for Mr. Courtland Smith," 11 February 1925; Courtland Smith to Julia Kelly, 12 February 1925; "Memorandum for Colonel Joy," 15 February 1925, WHP, box 26.

17. Quote in "Memorandum for Mr. Courtland Smith," 11 February 1925; Courtland Smith to Julia Kelly, 12 February 1925; Jason Joy to WHH, 24 February 1925, WHP, box 26; *New York Evening Post*, 28 April 1925; "Women Quit Hays's Film Committee," unidentified newspaper; Fred Beetson to WHH, 30 April 1925, WHP, box 27.

18. "Women Quit Hays's Film Committee," unidentified newspaper, 28 April 1925, WHP, box 27; Federal Motion Picture Council pamphlets, GFP, box 80; Federal Motion Picture Council Minutes, 10 July 1925; quote in FMPC "Minutes of the Special

Meeting of the Board of Directors," undated; FMPC "Minutes," 10 July 1935, GFP, box 81; address by Grant M. Hudson, "Digest of the Sixth National Motion Picture Conference, November 26–27, 1928," 2, 11, GFP, box 65. Most advocates of federal movie regulation supported prohibition as well, demonstrating a categorical readiness to invest the federal government with power over private industry. Like the Prohibition Amendment, federal motion picture regulation would protect Americans from businessmen who "exploit the weaknesses of human nature" and combat the industry centralization that left local controls impotent.

19. First quote in "Vital Movie News," 21 November 1934, GFP, box 81; Chase to CCG, 17 October 1927, GFP, box 81; FMPC Minutes, 19 March 1934, GFP, box 80; second quote in CCG testimony, "Proposed Federal Motion Picture Commission: Hearings before the Committee on Education, House of Representatives," 14–17 and 27 April and 4 May 1926, 105–6, see also 113, GFP, box 66; CCG testimony, "Hearing before the Committee on Interstate and Foreign Commerce, House of Representatives," 19 March 1934, 31, GFP, box 64; "Preliminary Report of Arthur Butler Graham on Trade Practices Existing in the Motion Picture Industry . . . ," undated, GFP, box 72; CCG to Dr. F. J. Kelly, 3 December 1930, GFP, box 84; "Report of the Chairman [CCG] of the Motion Picture Committee of the National Council of Women, U.S.A. to the Motion Picture Committee of the International Council of Women Meeting," 7–17 June 1927, GFP, box 68.

20. First quote in "Digest of the Sixth National Motion Picture Conference, November 26–27, 1928," 15, GFP, box 65; CCG to Edgar Dale, 20 June 1935, GFP, box 80; second quote in CCG testimony, "Proposed Federal Motion Picture Commission: Hearings before the Committee on Education, House of Representatives," 14–17 and 27 April and 4 May 1926, 94, GFP, box 66; CCG, "Motion Pictures and Morals," *Civic Forum*, February 1925, GFP, box 67.

21. *Literary Digest*, 12 April 1930; *Public Service Magazine*, May 1930, GFP, box 65; Hatcher Hughes to Mayor William A. Anderson, 5 April 1932; Hughes to CCG, 6 April 1932; Mary Ware Dennett to CCG, 7 May 1932, 25 May 1932, GFP, box 39. Andrea Friedman refers to this as an ideology of democratic moral authority. Friedman, *Prurient Interests*, 176–81. As late as 1942, nearly half of the states barred women from jury service and most of the others provided a female exemption. Not until 1973 did all states permit women to serve on juries, and in nineteen of these they were still granted special sex-based exemptions. Joan Hoff, *Law, Gender and Injustice: A Legal History of U.S. Women* (New York: New York University Press, 1991), 225.

22. CCG, "A Survey of the Motion Picture Problem," 10 February 1926, GFP, box 73; "Hearings before the Committee on Education, House of Representatives," 4–17 and 27 April and 4 May 1926, GFP, box 66; quote in FMPC "Minutes of the Special Meeting of the Board of Directors," undated; FMPC "Minutes," 10 July 1935, GFP, box 81; "Dear Friend" form letter, 28 September 1927, GFP, box 16; "Report of the Work on the Upshaw Bill," undated, GFP, box 63; CCG, "The Club Woman's Movie Problem—A Solution," 19 March 1928, GFP, box 72.

23. Federal Council of Churches memo, 1925, GFP, box 15; "Digest of the Sixth National Motion Picture Conference, November 26–27, 1928," 16, GFP, box 65; CCG to Clifford B. Twombly, 21 October 1930; "Extracts from Mrs. Gilman's Files for the Federal Council of Churches," September 1930, GFP, box 83; Wells, *Unity in Diversity*, 340–42; *The Public Relations of the Motion Picture Industry*, 106–7.

24. First quote in "Motion Picture Research Council Directors Reports," 6–9 July

1928, GFP, box 70; second quote in CCG to Mary Sayers, 12 June 1929, GFP, box 82. WHH presented the General Federation with gifts of films and motion picture equipment. See notice dated 27 June 1925, GFP, box 15.

25. WHH to Jason Joy, 18 October 1922, WHP, box 18; news releases, 11 and 15 February 1925, WHP, box 26; WHH, "Motion Pictures and the Public," to the Women's City Club of Philadelphia, 20 April 1925; "For Immediate Release," 21 April 1925, WHP, box 27; "Admirable Work of Will H. Hays: Woman's Progress Shown in Special Film," 11 February 1929, MPAA, reel 1.

26. Pettijohn to Hays, 5 November 1926; C.E.M., "Memorandum for Mr. Hays," 26 November 1926, WHP, box 31; Jason Joy to WHH, 5 January 1926, WHP, box 29; Lola Gentry to Jason S. Joy, 27 September 1927; Joy to Charles Pettijohn, 30 September 1927, WHP, box 35; "Assistant to the Secretary" to Mrs. Malcolm MacCoy, 18 December 1930, MPAA, reel 1. The Hays Office even instructed Mrs. Malcolm MacCoy, a New York club leader, to repress another clubwoman who publicly blamed motion pictures for juvenile crime.

27. "Interview with Mrs. A. C. Tyler, Chairman Motion Picture Committee, General Federation of Women's Clubs, Evanston, Illinois," 6–9 July 1928, GFP, box 70; MPPDA press release, 9 January 1930, WHP, box 41; Chase to CCG, 2 August 1928, GFP, box 82. FMPC leaders had hoped to move one of their members into position as General Federation motion picture chair.

28. Black, *Movie-Made America*, 167; newspaper clippings on block-booking, 8 May 1929; Rembusch to Sidney Kent, 8 May 1929; John Lord O'Brien to WHH, 8 October 1929, WHP, box 40; Frank Rembusch to WHH, 16 December 1925, WHP, box 29.

29. WHH, "Memorandum," 28 August 1929; Hays to "Chief" (President Herbert Hoover), 28 August 1929; WHH to Hoover, 25 September 1929, WHP, box 40.

30. FMPC conferences disturbed Hays so much that he took extraordinary measures to disrupt the 1928 meeting, sending delegates to interrupt the proceedings and issuing his own press releases about the conference. MPPDA press release, 11 May 1929; "Minister Lauds Movies' Power," unidentified newspaper article, 31 May 1929; press release, 31 May 1929; Frank Rembusch to Sidney Kent, 8 May 1929, WHP, box 40; CCG to C. G. Twombly, 19 January 1929; CCG to Smith Brookhart, 19 January 1929, GFP, box 82; "Digest of the Sixth National Motion Picture Conference," Washington, D.C., 26–27 November 1928, GFP, box 65; National Conference on Motion Pictures, *The Community and the Motion Picture Report of National Conference on Motion Pictures Held at the Hotel Montclair, New York City, September 24–27, 1929* (New York: Motion Picture Producers and Distributors of America, 1929); WHH, *Memoirs of Will Hays*, 407–9.

31. National Conference on Motion Pictures, *The Community and the Motion Picture*, 13, 64, 81–82; press release, 28 September 1929, WHP, box 40; *Baltimore Sun*, 12 June 1930, GFP, box 63; Wells, *Unity in Diversity*, 86, 341–42; "Public Relations and the Motion Picture Producers and Distributors of America, Inc.: Mrs. Winter's Work," January 1932, GFP, box 66; CCG to Mrs. L. Cass Brown, 7 July 1933, GFP, box 75; "Facts Concerning the Withdrawal of Various Organizations from the Joint Previewing Committee at Hollywood," c. 1933, GFP, box 84; AAW, "Women's Organizations and the Films," undated, GFP, box 17.

32. "Mrs. Winter to Aid Films," unidentified local newspaper, Associated Press date: 27 September 1929; "Mrs. Winter Will Try to Reform Film Colony of Stupidity," unidentified local newspaper, Associated Press date: 6 October 1929, AAW-MPL; Lamar Trotti

to Governor Milliken, 19 September 1928, General Federation of Women's Clubs File, Motion Picture Producers and Distributors of America Microfilmed Collection.

33. Quote in *Minneapolis Journal*, 4 June 1924, AAW-CF; Wells, *Unity in Diversity*, 83–87; Sonja Marakoff, "'Taming the Budget' Will be Discussed," n.d.; unidentified newspaper articles, 24 March 1928; 4 June 1928; 16, 18, and 28 August 1928, AAW-CF; Fred Beetson to WHH, 7 May 1925, WHP, box 27; mass mailing from Mary Caldwell, 29 May 1926, GFP, box 16. CCG believed that earlier Hays had hired AAW to write a handbook for clubwomen on cooperating with the motion picture industry. CCG to Elizabeth A. Perkins, 22 September 1930, GFP, box 83.

34. National Conference on Motion Pictures, *The Community and the Motion Picture*, 13, 64, 80–81.

35. AAW to Mrs. S. M. N. Marrs, 30 October 1929, 26 November 1929, GFP, box 17; AAW, "Women and the Motion Picture," *The Motion Picture*, n.d., GFP, box 67; GFWC press release, 9 January 1930; MPPDA press release, 14 March 1930, WHP, box 41.

36. Jason Joy to Maude Aldrich, 7 April 1925 (Aldrich to CCG attached to 5 January 1927 letter), GFP, box 81; "Minutes of the National W.C.T.U.," 18 November 1914, 60–61; 1922, 46; 17 November 1924, 33, 48, 50, 68; 1925, 192–93; 1926, 175–76; and 1927, 173–74; "National W.C.T.U. President's Address" and "National Representative at Washington," 1916, 124–25, 335; *Union Signal*, 27 January 1916, 2; 4 December 1924, 10; 29 January 1925, 8, WML.

37. FMPC Board of Directors Meeting, 12 December 1929, GFP, box 80; quotes in Maude Aldrich, "What the People Want," *Union Signal* (5 March 1925), 6, FWML; and Aldrich to Carl Milliken, 3 July 1927, GFP, box 81.

38. Jason S. Joy, "How Women Can Help for Better Films," *Union Signal* (2 June 1928), 351, WML. See also "Motion Picture Producers Adopt Policy of Support of Prohibition Law," *Union Signal* (24 July 1926), 3, WML, and Aldrich to Julia Deane, 4 January 1930, GFP, box 69.

39. "Minutes of the National W.C.T.U.," 1928, 156–59; 1929, 173–76, and 1930, 172–76, WML; quotes in unsigned to Maude Aldrich, 12 November 1929, GFP, box 69; Carl Milliken to Ella Boole, 10 July 1930; Ella Boole to Lulu Larry, 23 August 1929 and 13 September 1929, GFP, box 83; CCG to Mary Sayers, 30 September 1929; CCG to Chase, 30 September 1929; Aldrich to Mary Sayers, 28 October 1929; CCG to Boole, 4 December 1929, GFP, box 82.

40. First quote in Aldrich to CCG, 6 January 1930, GFP, box 69; remaining quotes in Aldrich to Julia Deane, 4 January 1930, GFP, box 69; *Union Signal*, 25 January 1930, 60–61, WML.

41. CCG to Ms. Dreyfus-Barney, 17 October 1929, GFP, box 69.

42. "Second Statement of the National Council of Women of the United States," August 1891; "Statement Concerning the National Council of Women of the United States," 15 December 1892; "Addresses by May Wright Sewall, President of the National Council of Women, at the Opening and Closing of the Second Triennial Session of the National Council of Women of the United States Held in Washington, D.C.," 1895, microfilm, Schlesinger Library; *Women in a Changing World: The Dynamic Story of the International Council of Women since 1888* (London: Routledge and Kegan Paul, 1966), 203–5, 165–66; quote in CCG to Chase, 12 January 1927, GFP, box 81; CCG to Mina Van Winkle, 12 March 1927, GFP, box 69.

43. Quote in CCG to Aldrich, 7 May 1927, GFP, box 81; CCG to Mrs. Howard Ben-

nett, 21 March 1927; CCG to Mrs. Neville Rolfe, 2 April 1927; CCG to Henni Forehhammer, 5 April 1927; CCG to Laura Dreyfus-Barney, 19 March 1927, GFP, box 69. On Bovey, see Ruth Bovey Stevens, "Just for Us," 1992, unpublished manuscript, MHS, 271–77.

44. Anna Garlin Spencer to CCG, 17 May 1927, 15 June 1927, GFP, box 69.

45. *The Year Book and Directory of the National Council of Women of the United States, Inc., Including the Proceedings of the Fourteenth Convention* (New York, 1928), 25–26; Kim E. Nielsen, *Un-American Womanhood: Antiradicalism, Antifeminism, and the First Red Scare* (Columbus: Ohio State University Press, 2001), 112, 119–20.

46. CCG to Anna Garlin Spencer, 15 July 1927; CCG to Dame Katherine Furse, 2 August 1927, GFP, box 69; CCG to William Chase, 14 July 1927; Chase to CCG, 19 July 1927; CCG to Mary Caldwell, 21 September 1927, GFP, box 81; "Report of the Chairman of the Motion Picture Committee of the National Council of Women," 7–17 June 1927; "Digest of Report and World Survey Made by the Motion Picture Committee to the National Council of Women," 1928, GFP, box 68; *Year Book and Directory of the National Council of Women*, 83–85.

47. CCG to Agnes Peters, 3 June 1929, 12 June 1929; CCG to Valeria Parker, 3 June 1929; CCG to Madam Dreyfus-Barney, 3 June 1929; Mabel Eichel to CCG, 11 June 1929; CCG to Eichel, 13 June 1929; National Council of Women Bulletin, 29 May 1929, GFP, box 69; CCG to Chase, 21 October 1929, GFP, box 82.

48. First quote in CCG to Don Seitz, 23 September 1929 and 2 October 1929; see also July 1929 correspondence, GFP, box 69.

49. Quotes in *Boston Herald*, 7 November 1929; *New York Telegram*, 8 November 1929; *Brooklyn Eagle*, 9 November 1929; *Christian Science Monitor*, 12 November 1929; *New York Sun*, 7 November 1929; *New York Times*, 7 November 1929; *Dayton Ohio News*, 10 November 1929, GFP, box 69; CCG to Catharine Oglesby, 21 November 1933, GFP, box 76; CCG to Congressman Grant Hudson, 11 November 1929; CCG to Congressman Smith Brookhart, 11 November 1929; CCG to James Murray, 11 November 1929; CCG to Rev. O. R. Miller, 15 November 1929; CCG to Seitz, 20 November 1929; CCG to Mabel Eichel, 22 November 1929; CCG to Valeria Parker, 22 November 1929; Eichel to CCG, 25 November 1929, GFP, box 69; CCG to Chase, 7 November 1930, GFP, box 83; CCG to Madam Dreyfus-Barney, 20 July 1931, GFP, box 70.

50. *General Federation News*, December 1928, 10, 33 and February 1929, 12–13; Mrs. Ambrose N. Diehl, chairman, "Committee on Motion Pictures," Thirteenth Biennial Council, 1929, GFWC.

51. Quote in CCG to Hilda Merriam, 12 March 1930, GFP, box 69; memo issued by the Citizen's League of Maryland for Better Motion Pictures, 29 March 1930; *Baltimore Sun*, 8 June 1930, GFP, box 63; Federal Council of Churches memo, 1925, GFP, box 15. Histories of the General Federation do not even mention the AAW movie controversy; CCG to Elizabeth A. Perkins, 22 September 1930, GFP, box 83.

52. *The Sunday Union and Republican*, 11 May 1930, GFP, box 64; *Minneapolis Star*, 9 June 1930; "Women's Clubs Thwart Censure of Mrs. Winter," unidentified local newspaper, 10 June 1930; "Mrs. Winter under Fire at Convention," unidentified local newspaper, 12 June 1930; "Film Relations Stir Club Women," unidentified local newspaper, 13 June 1930; "Thrust Aimed at Mrs. T. J. Winter Killed by Winter," unidentified local newspaper, 14 June 1930, AAW-CF; *Denver Post*, 12 June 1930; *Baltimore Sun*, 8 and 12 June 1930; Memo from the Citizen's League of Maryland for Better Motion Pictures, 29 March 1930; see also *Rocky Mountain News*, 7 June 1930, GFP, box 63; "Resolutions Opposing the

Appointment of Representative of the General Federation of Women's Clubs on the Studio Relations Committee of the Motion Picture Industry," 1930, GFP, box 67.

53. Ibid.

54. Ibid.

55. Mrs. Ambrose Diehl, "Report of the Motion Picture Committee of the General Federation of Women's Clubs, 1929," GFP, box 68; Frances Diehl, "General Federation Motion Picture Committee Report to the National Council of Women Motion Picture Chair," 14 April 1930, GFP, box 69; *General Federation News*, March 1930, Presidents' Papers: Alice Ames Winter, GFWC.

56. First quote in Virginia Roderick to CCG, 4 December 1929 (telegram and letter), and 27 December 1929; CCG to Roderick, 23 December 1929, GFP, box 82; second quote in *Parent-Teacher Broadcaster*, March 1930, 6–7, 27–28, GFP, box 68; *Woman's Journal*, February 1930, 10–12, 34; March 1930, 7–9, 45–46; CCG to AAW, 30 January 1931, 7 April 1931, 23 April 1931, 1 June 1931; AAW to CCG, 28 April 1931, GFP, box 71.

57. First quote in CCG to Langworthy, 9 January 1935, GFP, box 79; second quote in CCG to Frances Parks, 21 February 1930; Parks to CCG, 27 February 1930; third quote in CCG to Dreyfus-Barney, 17 March 1930, GFP, box 69; CCG to Elizabeth A. Perkins, 22 September 1930, GFP, box 83; CCG, "Suggestions for Action upon Federal Legislation Regulating and Supervising Motion Pictures at Their Source," May 1930, GFP, box 69.

58. "WCA Annual Reports, 1921–1929," GFP, box 48. These figures could be misleading. In 1924, the NBR filled the void created by the WCA's strategy shift by launching its own Minnesota better film committees, supported by the Woman's Club of Minneapolis. Thus WCA efforts to retain the community element of its reform program also suffered from the confusion caused by the National Board and Woman's Club intervention.

FIVE: "We Don't Want Our Boys and Girls in a Place of That Kind"

1. Information about the Gayety Theater comes from the WCA inventory cited below, and Audley M. Grossman, "The Professional Legitimate Theater in Minneapolis from 1890 to 1910" (Ph.D. diss., University of Minnesota, 1957), 85.

2. "Investigation of Gayety Theater," record number 3757, 3 November 1920; 9 November 1922; 6 November 1924; 31 January 1925; 18 November 1925; 12 October 1927, GFP, box 57.

3. "Investigation of Gayety Theater," 9 November 1922, 6 November 1924, 31 January 1925, 7 February 1925, 7 October 1925, 14 October 1925, 10 April 1925, 10 April 1926; quote in I. M. Modisttee to WCA, September 1930, GFP, box 57; Bernard Sobel, *Burleycue: An Underground History of Burlesque* (New York: Farrar and Rinehart, 1931), 244–45.

4. "Legitimate" theater referred to mainstream professional drama or musical presentations, generally excluding motion pictures and the often amateurish variety performances found on the vaudeville or burlesque stage. Quotes in Koenig to Herk, 22 February 1919, THSB , reel 3.

5. Quote in Official Transcript, "License Committee vs. Gayety Theatre, Transcript of Proceedings Held in the Council Committee Room, Court House, City of Minneapolis, on Thursday, October 25, 1928, at 2:30 P.M. by Mae E. Costello, reporter," GFP, box 57; "Old Gayety Is Purchased," 15 August 1944, unidentified local newspaper; *Minneapolis Star*, 30 June 1970, MJT; Robert Clyde Allen, *Horrible Prettiness: Burlesque and American Culture* (Chapel Hill: University of North Carolina Press, 1991), 246.

6. "Investigation of Gayety Theater," 12 October 1927, 14 January 1928, 16 March 1928, 7 September 1928, 5 October 1928, 13 and 29 September 1930, GFP, box 57.

7. "Investigation of Gayety Theater," 12 and 13 October 1927, GFP, box 57.

8. Quotes in *Proceedings of the City Council of the City of Minneapolis, Minnesota from July, 1927 to July, 1928*, 14 October 1927, 431–32; and "Investigation of Gayety Theater," 14 October 1927, GFP, box 57.

9. *Proceedings of the City Council . . . from July, 1927 to July, 1928*, 431–32, 459, 462, 502–3, 519; *Proceedings . . . from July, 1928 to July, 1929*, 436, 597, 673; "Investigation of Gayety Theater," 22 November 1928, 22 December 1928, 23 December 1928, GFP, box 57.

10. *Proceedings of the City Council . . . from July, 1927 to July, 1928*, 431–32, 462, 502–3, 519; *Proceedings . . . from July, 1928 to July, 1929*, 436, 597, 673; "Investigation of Gayety Theater," 19, 20, and 22 October 1927, GFP, box 57.

11. CCG to Estelle Holbrook, 7 May 1923, GFP, box 15.

12. "Investigation of Gayety Theater," 14 and 18 October 1927, GFP, box 57; *Proceedings of the City Council . . . from July, 1927 to July, 1928;* 14 October 1927, 431–32; *Minneapolis Tribune*, 26 October 1928.

13. "Investigation of Gayety Theater," 20 October 1927, 31 August 1932; *Minneapolis Tribune*, 12 May 1932; "Official Transcript of Public Hearing on the Gayety License Revocation" and "WCA Transcript," both 25 October 1928, GFP, box 57. The women's groups represented include: the Women's Christian Temperance Union, the Daughters of the American Revolution, the Concordia Society, and the Young Women's Christian Association.

14. Aldermen quoted in "Investigation of Gayety Theater," 11 and 12 May 1932; *Minneapolis Tribune*, 12 May 1932; I. M. Modisttee to the WCA, n.d., 4 February 1929 and 15 August 1929, GFP, box 57.

15. "Investigation of Gayety Theater," 12 May 1932; *Minneapolis Tribune*, 12 May 1932, GFP, box 57.

16. Quotes in "Investigation of Gayety Theater," 12 January 1928, 16 March 1928; theater program quoted in "Official Transcript," 25 October 1928, GFP, box 57.

17. First quote in *Minneapolis Tribune*, 1 September 1932; second quote in "Official Transcript," 25 October 1928; Evans, Carroll, and Manning quotes in "WCA Transcript" and "Official Transcript," 25 October 1928, GFP, box 57; notes from Better Movie Movement Meeting, December 1921, GFP, box 48; *Vital Movie News*, January 1944, GFP, box 8.

18. Quotes in "Official Transcript," 25 October 1928, and "WCA Transcript," 25 October 1928, GFP, box 57; Elizabeth Gilman, "Catheryne Cooke Gilman," 197; Jill Conway, "Women Reformers and American Culture, 1870–1930," *Journal of Social History* 5 (winter 1971–72), 164–77.

19. Quotes in "WCA Transcript" and "Official Transcript," 25 October 1928, GFP, box 57; and *Minneapolis Tribune*, 26 October 1928.

20. *Dual City Blue Book*, 1911–1912, 193; 1917–1918, 227. Something of an anomaly, MacGrath wrote a letter of commendation to the city council in October of 1927, thanking the aldermen for revoking the Gayety's license. One year later, MacGrath opposed revocation of the license, insisting that the shows had improved. *Proceedings of the City Council . . . from July, 1927 to July, 1928*, 459.

21. "Investigation of Gayety Theater," 11 October 1928, 23 December 1928, GFP, box 57; *Minneapolis Journal*, 16 October 1928; *Minneapolis Tribune*, 17 October 1928.

22. *Minneapolis Journal*, 15 October 1928.

23. First quote in "WCA Transcript," and "Official Transcript," 25 October 1928; "City Council Declines to Close Gayety: Aldermen at Point of Blows during Heated Debate," unidentified local newspaper article, 24 November 1928, GFP, box 57; Melaney quote in *Minneapolis Tribune*, 26 October 1928; aldermen quoted in "Investigation of Gayety Theater," 28 October 1927, 18 January 1928, 18 May 1932, GFP, box 57.

24. Quotes in *Minneapolis City Directory*, 1929, 15–16, and Rev. Marion Daniel Shutter, *History of Minneapolis: Gateway to the Northwest* (Chicago: S. J. Clarke, 1923); Charles Rumford Walker, *American City* (New York: Farrar and Rinehart, 1937), 85–86; William Millikan, "Defenders of Business: The Minneapolis Civic and Commerce Association versus Labor during W.W. I," *Minnesota History* 50 (spring 1986), 3–17; Lois Quam and Peter J. Rachleff, "Keeping Minneapolis an Open-Shop Town: The Citizens' Alliance in the 1930s," *Minnesota History* 50 (fall 1986), 105–17; William Millikan, "Maintaining 'Law and Order': The Minneapolis Citizen's Alliance in the 1920s," *Minnesota History* 51 (summer 1989), 219–33; William Millikan, "Saving Minnesota Capitalism in the Elections of 1920," *Roots: Speaking Out* 18 (spring 1990), 4–12; Carl Chrislock, *The Progressive Era in Minnesota, 1899–1918* (St. Paul: Minnesota Historical Society, 1971), 114, 127, 158–59; John E. Haynes, "Reformers, Radicals, and Conservatives," in Clifford E. Clarke Jr., ed., *Minnesota in a Century of Change: The State and Its People since 1890* (St. Paul: Minnesota Historical Society Press, 1989), 367–79.

25. CCG to Mrs. Gemmell, 8 June 1931, GFP, box 17; Pratt quotes in Grace Pratt, "The Church as a Factor in the Prevention of Delinquency," 14 September 1928, GFP, box 42; *Proceedings of the City Council . . . from July, 1927 to July, 1928*, 491; *Minneapolis Tribune*, 1 September 1932. A few businessmen did want to close the Gayety. The wife of a milliner whose shop faced the Gayety wrote the Women's Cooperative Alliance that her husband "feels strongly that the higher the moral standards of his neighborhood can be kept the better it is for business. Mr. Bradshaw employs a large number of women and girls and for their sakes he is anxious to keep that vicinity in as good moral condition as possible. He cannot see how a questionable show can possibly do business any good. Mr. Bradshaw feels that he speaks for at least some of the other business men of that neighborhood." Myrle Bradshaw to WCA, 24 October 1928, GFP, box 57.

26. "Last WCA Meeting," by Mrs. James Paige, 15 December 1932; "Women's Cooperative Alliance: Total Solicitations by Years from 1925 to 1930, inclusive," GFP, box 23; Bovey Stevens, "Just for Us," unpublished manuscript, MHS, 25, 36, 41, 138, 165, 271–77; William Solyman Coons, *Koon and Coons Families of Eastern New York: A History of the Descendants of Matthias Kuntz and Samuel Kuhn* (Rutland, VT: Tuttle, 1937); Mary Dillon Foster, *Who's Who among Minnesota Women* (Mary Dillon Foster, 1924), 33; Trimble, *In the Shadow of the City*, 16, 120–21; Albert Nelson Marquis, *The Book of Minnesotans: A Biographical Dictionary of Leading Living Men of the State of Minnesota* (Chicago: A. N. Marquis and Company, 1907), 527; William H. Bingham, ed., *Compendium of History and Biography of Minneapolis and Hennepin County, Minnesota* (Chicago: Henry Taylor, 1914), 324; Ludcke, "You've Come a Long Way, Lady!," 88; Faue, *Community of Suffering and Struggle*, 189; Maureen Flanagan, "Gender and Urban Political Reform: The City Club and the Woman's City Club of Chicago in the Progressive Era," *American Historical Review* 95 (October 1990), 1032–50.

27. Leland quoted in "Investigation of Gayety Theater," 1 September 1932, GFP, box 57, and *Minneapolis Tribune*, 1 September 1932. In a *Labor Review* editorial, Cramer insisted that "the Citizens' Alliance would like to see theatre censorship and would un-

doubtedly like to see the Gayety closed so it would throw several union workers out of jobs." Theater workers in Minneapolis were among the most successfully unionized; still, circumstantial evidence indicates that the Citizens Alliance did not necessarily want to close the Gayety. Judge Montgomery, who sided with the Gayety, received financial backing from the Citizens Alliance for his election campaign. Furthermore, the WCA received absolutely no cooperation from the Hennepin County grand jury, which was, according to Millikan, "essentially, [a] creature of the CA [Citizens Alliance]." Millikan, "Maintaining 'Law and Order,'" 221–22, 229–31; Cramer quotes in *Minneapolis Tribune*, 26 October 1928, and *Minneapolis Labor Review*, 26 October 1928, 4; "Investigation of Gayety Theater," GFP, box 57; *Minneapolis Tribune*, 20 October 1927 and 12 May 1932.

28. "WCA Transcript" and "Official Transcript," 25 October 1928, GFP, box 57.

29. Cramer quotes in "WCA Transcript," and "Official Transcript," 25 October 1928; "Investigation of Gayety Theater," 1 September 1932; *Minneapolis Tribune*, 1 September 1932, GFP, box 57. Cramer may have been referring to the implementation of the Minnesota Children's Code, a set of guidelines drawn up by the Minnesota Child Welfare Commission in 1917, and designed to provide services for "neglected children." CCG served as a member of the commission. Haynes, "Reformers, Radicals, and Conservatives," 370.

30. WCA notes refer to fishing trips that included Gayety men and aldermen. "Investigation of Gayety Theater," 20 October 1927, 7 November 1928, GFP, box 57.

SIX: "Thinking As a Woman and of Women"

1. "Women's Cooperative Alliance: A Survey of Neighborhood and School Conditions in [name blacked out]," 19 November 1920, GFP, box 60; "Typical Interview No.1," 20 February 1928; "Typical Interview No. 13," 14 May 1928; "Typical Interview No. 17," 11 June 1928; "Standard Interview No. 8," January 1928; "Standard Interview No. 2," January 1928, GFP, box 53.

2. Quotes from "Parent Education," undated newsletter, GFP, box 52, and Women's Cooperative Alliance Funding letter, 9 May 1930, GFP, box 17.

3. Jeffrey Moran, *Teaching Sex: The Shaping of Adolescence in the Twentieth Century* (Cambridge: Harvard University Press, 2000), 50–54; Gertrude Seymour to E. N. Farrington, 18 July 1918; CCG to George F. Derry, 22 February 1918, GFP, box 13; CCG to James Foster, 26 July 1917; CCG to Frank Kellogg, 5 June 1917, GFP, box 36.

4. CCG, "A Vocabulary for Family Use in the Early Sex Education of Children," and "Outline of the Principles of the Program for Early Sex Education in the Home: For the Use of Parents," both 1929; CCG, "Early Sex Education in the Home: When? How? What?" and "Description of the Program of Early Sex Education in the Home," both undated, GFP, box 35; WCA Bulletin, October 1928, GFP, box 34; "Women's Cooperative Alliance: A Survey of Neighborhood and School Conditions," 19 November 1920, GFP, box 60.

5. "Women's Cooperative Alliance: A Survey of Neighborhood and School Conditions," 19 November 1920, GFP, box 60; CCG to George H. Partridge, 2 February 1920, GFP, box 13; CCG Presentation at Child Study Conference, 22 October 1925, GFP, box 56; "Women's Cooperative Alliance Annual Report," 1925, GFP, box 34.

6. "Report of the Materials and Methods in Social Hygiene Being Used by the Women's Cooperative Alliance," 10 June 1927; Collection of Sex Education Pamphlets,

GFP, box 53; Parental Education Bulletin, 1926, GFP, box 34; "Introductory Conference Based on *Biology of Sex* by Galloway," October 1926, GFP, box 51; CCG, "An Organization to Assist Mothers in Their Responsibility for Social Hygiene Education," 1923, GFP, box 35, also published in the *Journal of Social Hygiene* 9 (October 1923), 411–21.

7. CCG Presentation at Child Study Conference, 22 October 1925, GFP, box 56; Maurice A. Bigelow, *Sex Education: A Series of Lectures Concerning Knowledge of Sex in Its Relation to Human Life* (New York: Macmillan, 1918); Thomas W. Galloway, *Sex and Social Health: A Manual for the Study of Social Hygiene* (New York: American Social Hygiene Association, 1924).

8. "Women's Cooperative Alliance," speech, undated; "Policies of the Women's Cooperative Alliance: Purpose of the Education and Publicity Department," 28 February 1921, GFP, box 23; "WCA Bulletin," September 1925, GFP, box 34; "WCA Statement to Joint Committee," January 1927, GFP, box 56; CCG to George H. Partridge, 2 February 1920, GFP, box 13.

9. "Standard Interview No. 4," January 1928; "Typical Interview No. 10," 28 May 1928, GFP, box 53. See also "Typical Interview No. 10," 23 April 1926; "Typical Interview No. 22," 16 July 1928, GFP, box 53.

10. "Typical Interview No. 10," 23 April 1926, GFP, box 53.

11. "Typical Interview," 22 September 1931; "Typical Interview No. 1," January 1928, GFP, box 55; "Typical Interview No. 9," 16 April 1928; "Typical Interview No. 10," 23 April 1928; "Typical Interview No. 6," 17 April 1928; "Typical Interview No. 10," 24 April 1928; "Typical Interview No. 25," 6 August 1928; "Typical Interview No. 1," 3 April 1928; "Typical Interview No. 22," 27 February 1928; "Standard Interview No. 1," January 1928; "Special Typical Interview," January 1929, GFP, box 53; "Women's Cooperative Alliance," speech, undated; "Policies of the Women's Cooperative Alliance: Purpose of the Education and Publicity Department," 28 February 1921, GFP, box 23; "WCA Bulletin," September 1925, GFP, box 34; CCG, "Child Study Conference," 22 October 1925; "WCA Statement to Joint Committee," January 1927, GFP, box 56; CCG to George H. Partridge, 2 February 1920, GFP, box 13; CCG, "A Co-operative Social Effort for the Prevention of Delinquency," *Health and Empire: The Journal of Social Hygiene Council* 3 (July 1925), GFP, box 35.

12. "Women's Cooperative Alliance Annual Report," 1925 and 1928, GFP, box 34; CCG's notes for Sex and Social Health Conference, 6 April 1927; quote in Sex and Social Health Conference Minutes, 27 April 1927; Introductory Conference, Session VI, with Frances B. Strain, 29 November 1927, GFP, box 54; "Project X," November 1926, GFP, box 51.

13. "Women's Cooperative Alliance Annual Report," 1925 and 1928, GFP, box 34.

14. "Notes on Practical and Theoretical Material used at Sex Education Conferences Based on *Biology of Sex*—Dr. T. W. Galloway," submitted by Elizabeth S. Monahan, M.D., Julia E. Pomeroy, B.A., Marion Bjorhus Rotnem, B.A., Avis C. Zuppann, R.N., 1926, GFP, box 53; first quote on billboard, Perrysburg, Ohio, near Highway 25 and Five Points Road, July 2001; CCG quotes in research notes, 7 October 1929, GFP, box 70; CCG to William Cox, 13 March 1935, GFP, box 72; and CCG, "Motion Pictures," undated, GFP, box 73.

15. Quote from William Chase to Frank P. Graves, 13 July 1927, GFP, box 81. See also, Martha Sprague Mason to CCG, 25 September 1933, GFP, box 72; Henry Lloyd to CCG, 12 April 1922, GFP, box 14; "Sex and Social Health Conference Minutes," 27 April 1927, GFP, box 54.

16. Quotes in "The Social Hygiene Classes of the WCA with Demonstration of Instruction," 14 February 1922, 4–5, GFP, box 52, and "Typical Interviews," 1928, GFP, box 53.

17. CCG, "Women's Cooperative Alliance, Inc.," 19 April 1921, GFP, box 5; WCA Bulletin, April 1927 and March 1928, GFP, box 34.

18. First quote in CCG's handwritten note, undated, GFP, box 15; second quote in "Parent Education—Opposition Interviews," undated, GFP, box 52. CCG offered an explanation of Sewall's attitude toward her in a confidential note affixed to this document. A Unity House social worker who employed Sewall's daughter, Eleanor, reported her to CCG "as a masturbator . . . involved with sex practices with younger boys at Unity House"; third quote in "Typical Interview No. 2," 1 March 1928; see also "Typical Interview No. 5," 19 March 1928, GFP, box 53; Women's Cooperative Alliance Annual Report, Department of Parental Education, 1926, GFP, box 34.

19. CCG, "An Organization to Assist Mothers in Their Responsibility for Social Hygiene Education," *Journal of Social Hygiene* (October 1923), 411–21, GFP, box 35; WCA Annual Report, 1925, GFP, box 34; Chloe Owings, "Sex Education for Parents: A Research in Teaching Methods and Material," *Journal of Social Hygiene* 14 (December 1928), GFP, box 59; WCA Board Meeting Minutes, 20 October 1927, GFP, box 25; CCG to Maurice Bigelow, 17 August 1928; quotes in Ralph Bridgeman to CCG, 29 June 1928; William Leonard to CCG, 13 April 1929; Thomas Galloway to CCG, 20 April 1929, GFP, box 54; and Katherine Bement Davis to CCG, 10 March 1930, GFP, box 69.

20. Correspondence File, 1947, GFP, box 20; letters to CCG from the University of Chicago School of Social Service Administration, 5 April 1929; Dame Katherine Furse, 8 April 1929; Grace Abbott, 10 April 1929; Juvenile Court, Los Angeles County, 19 April 1929; New York School of Social Work, 1 May 1929; New York Committee on Maternal Health, 13 August 1929, GFP, box 17. The Bureau of Social Hygiene funded and published an intensive study of the alliance's sex education program. See Helen Leland Witmer, *The Attitudes of Mothers toward Sex Education* (Minneapolis: University of Minnesota Press, 1929).

21. No other group duplicated the Women's Cooperative Alliance. The WCTU may have come closest, promoting "modest" sex education and supporting a two-part anti-obscenity agenda of replacing salacious entertainments with "pure" alternatives. But the WCTU did not deal in sexual explicitness. Parker, *Purifying America*, 25, 51, 72, 158–94. On William Sheafe Chase, see Chase, "Catechism on Motion Pictures in Inter-State Commerce," October 1922, New York: New York Civic League, GFP, box 65; Chase, "Why Federal Control?" *Moral Welfare* 16 (November 1924); Chase, "The Motion Picture Situation," *The Light* (July–August 1925), GFP, box 64; Chase to CCG, 27 January 1927, GFP, box 81; Chase to William Short, 6 October 1934, GFP, box 72; Anna Garlin Spencer to CCG, 17 May 1927, GFP, box 69; CCG to Ida Compton, 18 September 1934, GFP, box 78. On Mary Ware Dennett, see Constance Chen, *"The Sex Side of Life": Mary Ware Dennett's Pioneering Battle for Birth Control and Sex Education* (New York: New Press, 1996), 129–39, 171–82; CCG to Chase, 1 May 1929, GFP, box 83; CCG to Dennett, 8 April 1929; Dennett to CCG, 27 June 1929, MWD-MC, reel 21; CCG to Dennett, 26 July 1929; Dennett to CCG, 2 August 1929, MWD-MC, reel 22; Dennett to CCG, 23 September 1929, GFP, box 54; Mary Ware Dennett, *Birth Control Laws: Shall We Keep Them, Change Them, or Abolish Them* (New York: F. H. Hitchcock, 1926).

22. John Craig, " 'The Sex Side of Life': The Obscenity Trials of Mary Ware Den-

nett," *Frontiers: A Journal of Women Studies* 15 (1995), 149–52; *United States v. Dennett* 39 F. (2d) 564; Dennett to "Dearest People," 2 May 1929, MWD-MC, reel 21; Mary Ware Dennett, *Who's Obscene?* (New York: Vanguard Press, 1930), 46–47, 188–89, 195–98.

23. Fisher to CCG, 9 May 1929; Katherine Hattendorf to CCG, 7 May 1929, GFP, box 17; "Project VIII," November 1926 (uses diagrams from "The Sex Side of Life"); "Project X," November 1926 (cites and quotes Dennett), GFP, box 51; Katherine Hattendorf, "Report of the Materials and Methods in Social Hygiene Being Used by the Women's Cooperative Alliance, 1 March 1926 to 1 June 1927," 10 June 1927 (includes Dennett's pamphlet in a list of materials made available to mothers), GFP, box 53; CCG to W. R. Colby, 20 March 1934, GFP, box 77; first quote in Dudley Nichols, "Sex and the Law," *The Nation* 128 (8 May 1929), 554; second quote in CCG to Fisher, 9 May 1929, GFP, box 17. See also Katherine Bement Davis to Morris Ernst, undated, quoted in Dennett, *Who's Obscene?*, 80–81.

24. Dennett also expressed suspicion of the jury that convicted her, noting that two of the original twelve were dismissed because they admitted that they had read "a little" of the writings of Havelock Ellis and/or H. L. Mencken and that, of those chosen, eleven were middle-aged or elderly men with families. Dennett, *Who's Obscene?*, 22, 132, 194–95; "A Court Verdict for Sex Education," *Literary Digest*, 22 May 1930; "The Prosecution of Mary Ware Dennett for 'Obscenity,'" American Civil Liberties Union, June 1929, GFP, box 42; Dudley Nichols, "Sex and the Law," 552–53; Craig, "'The Sex Side of Life,'" 152.

25. As Gilman wrote to another friend, "The result of [Dennett's] trial seems inconceivable in this day and age of pornographic literature to be found on every newsstand in the country." Gilman to Mrs. Hubert Fisher, 9 May 1929, GFP, box 17. The popular press made similar comments; even the *Christian Century* made this connection, noting that "the purveyors of pornography sniggered in their sleeves when . . . Mrs. Mary Ware Dennett was convicted." *Christian Century*, 12 March 1930; CCG to Chase, 1 May 1929, GFP, box 83.

26. First quote in Dennett, *Who's Obscene?*, 69–70, 115; Chase to CCG, 6 May 1929; CCG to Chase, 22 May 1929, GFP, box 83; second quote in "Up-to-the-Minute Bulletin of the International Reform Federation: The Testimony of Dr. Howard A. Kelly of Baltimore, Md., America's Greatest Authority on Sex Problems," 1 May 1929, GFP, box 42; and Dennett, *Who's Obscene?*, 122–24; third quote in Dennett, "The Sex Side of Life," 4, 8–9, GFP, box 53; fourth quote in Dennett, *Who's Obscene?*, 116, 120; fifth and sixth quotes in "The Sex Side of Life," 8–9, 14, GFP, box 53; sixth and seventh quotes in Dennett, *Who's Obscene?*, 116–19; and Chase to the *Christian Leader*, 31 May 1929, GFP, box 83.

27. First quote in "Sex and Social Health Conference Minutes," 27 April 1927 and November 1928, GFP, box 54; Mrs. E. F. Purtill to CCG, 10 August 1933; CCG to Purtill, 31 August 1933, GFP, box 18; second quote in CCG to Fisher, 9 May 1929, GFP, box 17; CCG to E. K. Wickman, 19 June 1928, GFP, box 54; CCG, "A Vocabulary for Family Use in the Early Sex Education of Children," Women's Cooperative Alliance, Inc., January 1929, GFP, box 35; third quote in Dennett, *Who's Obscene?*, 116; CCG to Karl de Schweinitz, 19 June 1928, GFP, box 54; fourth quote in CCG to James Foster, 25 July 1917; CCG to Frank Kellogg, 5 June 1917, GFP, box 36.

28. "Introductory Social Hygiene Conference: Session I," May 1931, GFP, box 54; "To the Parent Recorder," undated WCA handout, GFP, box 51; CCG to Mrs. Chester Greene, 10 March 1932, GFP, box 84; CCG to Walter Clarke, 16 July 1929, GFP, box 36. Several of Gilman's attempts to affiliate the WCA with the American Social Hygiene Association foundered on this very issue, since the ASHA educational campaign emphasized

the very topics that the WCA downplayed—sexual dangers and venereal disease. Correspondence between CCG and Paul Popenoe, January 1920, GFP, box 36; CCG to Mrs. Rufus Gibbs, 15 December 1933, GFP, box 84.

29. "Typical Interview No. 1," 20 February 1928, GFP, box 53; "Sex and Social Health Conference Minutes," 30 March 1927, GFP, box 54; CCG to Fisher, 9 May 1929, GFP, box 17; CCG to Chase, 1 May 1929, 3 June 1929, GFP, box 83; "Introductory Social Hygiene Conference," May 1931, GFP, box 54.

30. Fisher to CCG, 7 May 1929, GFP, box 17; CCG to Chase, 22 May 1929, GFP, box 83; WCA "Typical Interviews," 1927–28, GFP, box 53; quote in "Typical Interviews No. 3 and 11," 7 March 1928, GFP, box 53.

31. Fisher to Gilman, 7 May 1929, GFP, box 17; first quote in Dennett to "Dearest People," 2 May 1929, MWD-MC, reel 21; CCG, "Outline of the Principles of the Program for Early Sex Education in the Home," WCA, 1929; CCG, "A Vocabulary for Family Use in the Early Sex Education of Children," WCA, January 1929; "Early Sex Education in the Home: When? How? What?," WCA, 1928; "Description of the Early Program of Early Sex Education in the Home," WCA, 1928, GFP, box 35; CCG to Karl de Schweinitz, 5 May 1928, 24 May 1928, 19 June 1928; CCG to E. K. Wickman, 19 June 1928, GFP, box 54; second quote in CCG to Fisher, 9 May 1929, GFP, box 17; third and fourth quotes in Dennett, *Who's Obscene?*, 97, 177.

32. First Chase quote in Nichols, "Sex and Our Children," *The Nation*, 6 February 1929, 155; second quote in Chase to the *Christian Leader*, 31 May 1929, included in Chase to CCG, 31 May 1929, GFP, box 83.

33. This rule derived from the 1868 decision in the British case *Regina v. Hicklin* and was usually interpreted as protecting the feebleminded and children. Elements of Hicklin remained pertinent in American obscenity law as late as *Roth v. United States* (1957), and even beyond in the opinion of some legal scholars. See for example, "Notes and Comments: More Ado about Dirty Books," *Yale Law Journal* 75 (1966), 1364–1405. For a sweeping and contemporarily relevant discussion of the development of obscenity law, see Donald Alexander Downs, *The New Politics of Pornography* (Chicago: University of Chicago Press, 1989); *United States v. Dennett*, 1930 U.S. App. LEXIS 4119, 76 A.L.R. 1092.

34. Hand quote in *United States v. Dennett*, 39 F. (2d) 564; *Literary Digest*, 22 May 1930; *Christian Century*, 12 March 1930, 325–26; *Commonweal*, 22 May 1929, 74–75.

35. Gilman hoped her letters "may modify [Chase] in his action. I have had a letter from him that seems to show a willingness to concede some points which his earlier communications did not indicate." CCG to Fisher, 9 May 1929, GFP, box 17. On the significance of the Dennett case, see Chen, *"The Sex Side of Life,"* 300–301; Craig, "'The Sex Side of Life,'" 158–61; Boyer, *Purity in Print*, 239–42; Walker, *In Defense of American Liberties*, 82–86; Rochelle Gurstein, "The Repeal of Reticence: The Controversy about Privacy, Obscenity, and Exposure, 1873–1934" (Ph.D. diss., University of Rochester, 1991), 164–65, 207, 372–73.

36. Dennett also continued her advocacy for birth control and wrote a book on sex education, entitled *The Sex Education of Children: A Book for Parents* (New York: Vanguard Press, 1931). See also Walker, *In Defense of American Liberties*, 82–83; Chen, *"The Sex Side of Life,"* 300–303. Witmer, *The Attitudes of Mothers;* CCG to William Cox, 13 March 1935, GFP, box 72; "Notes on Practical and Theoretical Material Used at Sex Education Conferences," 1926, GFP, box 53; WCA funding letter, 9 May 1930, GFP, box 17.

37. "Minutes of the Mayor's Committee on Questionable Publications," 29 Febru-

ary 1929, GFP, box 39; CCG to Ross N. Young, 24 March 1932; "Committee of One Thousand Resolutions," 5 April 1932; "The Minneapolis Committee of One Thousand: Original Minutes," 5 April 1932, GFP, box 39; CCG to Mrs. H. L. Wilkins, 21 April 1932; "Indecent and Obscene Publications Inventory," Record Number 5274, 6 April 1932, 40, GFP, box 57.

38. "The Minneapolis Committee of One Thousand: Original Minutes," 5 April 1932; "Committee of One Thousand Resolutions," 5 April 1932; "Minutes of the Mayor's Committee on Questionable Publications," 29 February 1932; CCG to Mrs. C. C. Dragoo, 10 February 1932; CCG to Mayor Anderson, 29 March 1932, GFP, box 39; "Indecent and Obscene Publications Inventory," 21 July 1932, 42, GFP, box 57; *Minneapolis Journal*, 30 January 1932, 20 February 1932, 6 April 1932; "WCA Semi-Annual Report," January to June 1932, GFP, box 29; CCG to Mayor Anderson, 8 January 1932, 13 February 1932, 24 February 1932, 9 March 1932, 15 March 1932; "Indecent and Obscene Publications Inventory," 36–43, GFP, box 57; Criminal Court Records, Municipal Court, City of Minneapolis, *The State of Minnesota v. Maurice Brickman*, 23 March 1932, file 30132.

39. *New York Times*, 14 January 1932, 21 January 1932, 11 May 1932.

40. CCG to Dennett, 26 July 1932, GFP, box 39; newspaper advertisements for "Crazy Quilt," *Minneapolis Tribune*, 24–26 March 1932; Earl Conrad, *Billy Rose: Manhattan Primitive* (Cleveland: World Publishing, 1968), 87–89; Stephen Nelson, *"Only a Paper Moon": The Theatre of Billy Rose* (Ann Arbor, MI: UMI Research Press, 1987), 17–20. The flop of "Crazy Quilt" brings Fannie Brice and Billy Rose together in the Barbra Streisand and James Caan Hollywood production *Funny Lady* (1975).

41. *Minneapolis Tribune*, 27 March 1932; *Minneapolis Journal*, 27 March 1932; *Minneapolis Tribune*, 28 March 1932; *Minneapolis Journal*, 28 March 1932; Hatcher Hughes to Mayor Anderson, 5 April 1932; CCG to Hughes, 23 April 1932; Hughes to CCG, 6 April 1932; CCG to Dennett, 26 July 1932, GFP, box 39; first quote in Hughes to Anderson, 5 April 1932; Hughes to CCG, 6 April 1932; Hughes to CCG, 28 April 1932; second and third quotes in CCG to Hughes, 23 April 1932, 16 May 1932; CCG to Dennett, 26 July 1932, GFP, box 39. See "Crazy Quilt" advertisement in the *Minneapolis Journal*, 24 March 1932.

42. CCG to Hughes, 23 April 1932; CCG to Dennett, 12 May 1932; Dennett to CCG, 7 May 1932, 25 May 1932, GFP, box 39; CCG to Dennett, 26 April 1932, MWD-MC, reel 35; CCG to McCabe, 2 August 1927; WCA Bulletin, May 1925, GFP, box 16; CCG to Chase, 3 June 1929, GFP, box 83. On women and jury service, see Hoff, *Law, Gender, and Injustice*, 225.

43. Gordon W. Moss to Dennett, 18 May 1932; Dennett to Moss, 25 May 1932; quote in CCG to Dennett, 26 July 1932, MWD-MC, reel 35; Hughes to CCG, 28 April 1932; Dennett to CCG, 7 and 25 May 1932, GFP, box 39. See also Elmer Rice to CCG, 30 August 1932, GFP, box 18.

44. *Minneapolis Journal*, 29 March 1932; *Minneapolis Tribune*, 29 March 1932, 30 March 1932.

SEVEN: "Sinful Girls Lead"

1. Mrs. M. J. C. Wilkin, "Written on the Occasion of the Disbanding of the Women's Cooperative Alliance, Inc.," 27 October 1932; "Women's Cooperative Alliance, Total Solicitations by Years from 1925 to 1930, inclusive"; WCA Finance Report, 1931; Corporation Meeting Minutes, 28 October 1932; letters read at last alliance meeting, 15 Decem-

ber 1932; Virginia Blythe, "The Origins of the Women's Co-operative Alliance Was on This Wise," n.d., GFP, box 23; CCG to Bovey, 24 June 1932; CCG to Mathilde Michalson, 5 January 1933; CCG to Mrs. James Paige, 14 January 1932, GFP, box 18; Final Report, WCA, 15 December 1932, GFP, box 29.

2. William Short to CCG, 11 March 1932, GFP, box 71; CCG to William Seabury, 25 May 1932, GFP, box 84; CCG to Frances Parks, 28 January 1931; CCG to Madam Dreyfus-Barney, 20 July 1931, GFP, box 70; CCG to Mrs. Bradford, 11 April 1933, GFP, box 75. Upon CCG's departure from the National Council of Women, the General Federation of Women's Clubs renewed its membership.

3. Mabel Parkhouse (Pettijohn's secretary) to CCG, 4 October 1932; CCG to Parkhouse, 17 October 1932, GFP, box 18; CCG to William Short, 18 November 1932 and 8 December 1932, GFP, box 71; CCG to Martha Sprague Mason, 7 April 1934, GFP, box 77; CCG to Mrs. Chester Greene, 5 May 1933, GFP, box 75.

4. CCG, undated and untitled address, GFP, box 73; *Variety*, 7 February 1933, 16, and 14 March 1933, 12.

5. As AAW herself noted, "Sound makes bad things worse and good things better." *Woman's Journal*, March 1930, 46. See address by Representative Hudson, "Digest of the Sixth National Motion Picture Conference, Held at the Mayflower Hotel, Washington, D.C., under the Auspices of the Federal Motion Picture Council in America, Inc.," 26–27 November 1928, GFP, box 65; *The Public Relations of the Motion Picture Industry*, 107–11; *The Churchman*, 13 July 1929, 10 August 1929, 21 September 1929, WHP, box 40; John Lord O'Brian to WHH, 8 October 1929; Frank J. Rembusch to WHH, 8 May 1929; Jerry A. Mathews to WHH, 29 May 1929; WHH to Bishop Francis J. McConnell, 20 September 1929; Plaintiff's Motion in *Motion Picture Producers and Distributors of America v. The Churchman Company*, Supreme Court, New York County, n.d., WHP, box 40; *New York Times*, 13 February 1930, WHP-MC, reel 3; *Literary Digest*, 12 April 1930, GFP, box 67; AAW to CCG, 28 April 1930; AAW, "The Fight for Better Motion Pictures," 9 June 1930; AAW, "Women and the New Code of Motion Pictures," *Motion Picture Herald*, n.d., GFP, box 71; *Woman's Journal*, June 1930, 49–50; Frank Walsh, *Sin and Censorship*, 54.

6. CCG to Rebecca Naomi Rhodes, 16 April 1930; CCG to Mrs. Ogilvie Gordon, 5 May 1930; CCG to Rachel Crowdy, 5 May 1930, 3 June 1930, GFP, box 69; CCG, "The 1930 Code of Ethics for the Motion Picture Industry," GFP, box 65; "The New Hudson Motion Picture Bill, H.R. 9986," March 1930, GFP, box 66; CCG to Editors, *Woman's Journal*, 11 March 1930, GFP, box 71; CCG to Mrs. Rufus Gibbs, 16 May 1930; Chase to CCG, 22 July 1930; CCG to Chase, 26 July 1930 and 13 October 1930; CCG to Clifford Twombly, 21 October 1930, GFP, box 83; "National Groups Endorsing Federal Supervision of Motion Pictures . . . as Provided in the Grant Hudson Motion Picture Bill, H.R. 9986," n.d., GFP, box 80; CCG to Lulu Larry, 6 May 1931, GFP, box 84; National W.C.T.U. Annual Report, 1931, 115–17, WML; *The Parent-Teacher Broadcaster*, March 1930, 7, 28; *Woman's Journal*, February 1930; *The Churchman*, 1 February 1930; *Christian Century*, 26 August 1931; *The Friend*, March and April 1930, GFP, box 68; *Union Signal*, 19 April 1930, 8, and 13 September 1930, 12, WML.

7. *Literary Digest*, 12 April 1930, 9–10; *Woman's Journal*, March 1930, 7–9, 45–46; *The Motion Picture* 6, no. 5 (1930); see AAW's monthly bulletins to the "Motion Picture Public," 1930 and 1931, GFP, box 71; "Mrs. Winter Decries Film Censorship," 20 January 1930, unidentified Minneapolis newspaper article, AAW-CF; CCG to Aldrich, 13 and 22 September 1930, 13 and 21 October 1930; CCG to Chase, 13 October 1930, GFP, box 83;

CCG to Mrs. B. S. Gadd, 21 January 1929; CCG to Elaine Goodale Eastman, 29 October 1930; CCG to Mrs. Dreyfus-Barney, 31 December 1930, GFP, box 69; CCG to F. J. Kelly, 23 January 1931; CCG to Mrs. Alfred Tyler, 28 March 1933, GFP, box 84; *Union Signal*, 14 March 1931, WML; *Christian Century*, 15 June 1932, 764.

8. Hays, *The Memoirs of Will Hays*, 437–46; Black, *Hollywood Censored*, 40, 72–74, 77–78; *Literary Digest*, 12 April 1930, 9–10; *Variety*, 29 December 1931, 5, 27; Fanny Woodson to Mrs. Ambrose Diehl, 13 June 1932, GFP, box 84; *Harrison's Reports, Blonde Venus*, 1 October 1932, 158; *Faithless*, 26 November 1932, 191; *Call Her Savage*, 3 December 1932, 194; Ruth A. Inglis, *Freedom of the Movies: A Report on Self-Regulation from the Commission on Freedom of the Press* (Chicago: University of Chicago Press, 1947), 118–19; CCG to Mrs. Bradford, 15 November 1933, GFP, box 76.

9. AAW to Madam, 21 January 1931, 20 March 1931, GFP, box 71; CCG to AAW, 30 January 1931, 7 and 23 April 1931, 1 June 1931; AAW to CCG, 28 April 1931, GFP, box 71.

10. AAW memo to files, quoted in Gregory Black, *Hollywood Censored*, 61–62; AAW to WHH, 6 November 1932; WHH to AAW, 10 November 1932; WHH to Jason Joy, 14 November 1932; Joy to WHH, 17 November 1932; Martin Quigley to WHH, 4 August 1932, WHP-MC, reel 8.

11. William Short's interviews with CCG, 3, 6, 7 July 1928; "Juvenile Protection Association and Hull House Group," 2 July 1928; CCG, "Suggestions for Conference: Columbus, OH," 5–7 October 1928; Short, "Historical Sketch"; Motion Picture Research Council Director's Report, 15 December 1928; Notes on meeting at Hull House, 11 January 1930, GFP, box 70; correspondence between CCG and Short, 1928, GFP, box 71, file 1.

12. "A Memorandum Regarding Purpose, Findings, and Plan of Action," 16 September 1931; W. W. Charters, "Outline of Research Findings," CCG's notations on "Resumés of Findings in Motion Picture Research as Reported at a Conference of the Educational Research Committee of the Payne Fund," 1931, GFP, box 70; Short to CCG, 9 August 1928, 6 June 1932; CCG to Short, 14 August 1928, 26 June 1929, 5 March 1929, 23 May 1929; Mark May to CCG, 6 June 1929; CCG to Short, 3 September 1931, GFP, box 71.

13. "Facts from Payne Fund Research," September 1934, GFP, box 74; CCG to Bradford, 8 July 1933, GFP, box 75; "Motion Pictures: Six Units for Investigation and Discussion," n.d., GFP, box 73; CCG to Carolyn Smiley, 21 November 1933, GFP, box 76. This study, conducted by Herbert Blumer, was published for the first time in Garth Jowett et al., *Children and the Movies: Media Influence and the Payne Fund Controversy* (New York: Cambridge University Press, 1996), 281–301.

14. Correspondence between Short and researchers, 7 December 1931; CCG to Short, 11 December 1931; Short to Charters, 3 May 1929, 9 and 16 October 1931, 4 November 1931; Charters to Short, 13 October 1931; Frederick Thrasher to Short, 2 November 1931, GFP, box 71; first quote in Henry James Forman, *Our Movie-Made Children* (New York: Macmillan, 1933), 214–32; CCG to Short, 19 April 1933, GFP, box 72; second quote in "Answering Objections to Patman Bill, H.R. 6097," Statement from the Texas Congress of Parents and Teachers, 1934, GFP, box 76.

15. For examples of positive reports see "Daily Report," 10, 29, 31 May 1933; 8, 12, 13, 14, 16, 17, 27 June 1933, WH-MC, reel 9; "Daily Report," 4, 9, 15 January 1934 and 7, 23 February 1934, WH-MC, reel 10. For widely ranging interpretations see *Daily Oklahoman*, 31 May 1933; *Santa Barbara [California] News*, 3 June 1933; *Sacramento [California] Bee*, 3 June 1933, excerpted in F. J. Wilstach report to WHH, 17 June 1933; *Staunton*

[Virginia] News-Leader, 1 June 1933; *Philadelphia Public Ledger,* 30 May 1933, excerpted in F. J. Wilstach report to WHH, 8 June 1933, WH-MC, reel 9; Henry James Forman, "To the Movies—But Not to Sleep!" *McCall's,* September 1932, 12–13, 58–59; CCG to Short, 3, 11, 19 and 31 October 1932, GFP, box 71. Critical reports appeared in the *St. Paul Dispatch,* 8 June 1933; *Montgomery [Alabama] Advertiser,* 5 June 1933; *Philadelphia Public Ledger,* 6 June 1933, excerpted in F. J. Wilstach report to WHH, 16 June 1933; *Kansas City Journal-Post,* 30 May 1933, excerpted in F. J. Wilstach report to WHH, 8 June 1933; *Gloversville [New York] Herald,* 5 June 1933, excerpted in F. J. Wilstach to WHH, 12 June 1933, WH-MC, reel 9. Alarmist reports can be found in Black, *Hollywood Censored,* 193, 17n; *McCall's,* September 1932, 12–13, 58–59; *New York Times,* 27 May 1933; K. L. Russell report to WHH, 10 May 1933, WH-MC, reel 9.

16. M. D. Kann (editor, *Motion Picture Daily*) to CCG, 4 August 1932; Short to CCG, 8 August 1932; CCG to Kann, 8 September 1932, GFP, box 71; K. L. Russell to WHH, "Still a 'Big Noise' (Payne Fund Study)," 27 April 1933; "Introducing the 'Big Noise' Team—Eastman and Short," 2 May 1933, WH-MC, reel 9; "Annual Report, Public Relations Department [MPPDA]," 5 February 1934, WH-MC, reel 10; "The Screen's Contribution to the Prevention of Crime," by the MPPDA, 11 December 1934, WH-MC, reel 13; Mortimer J. Adler, *Philosopher at Large: An Intellectual Autobiography* (New York: Macmillan, 1977), 192–94; Adler, *Art and Prudence* (New York: Longmans, Green, 1937); Raymond Moley, *The First New Deal* (New York: Harcourt, Brace and World, 1966), 500–501; Moley, *Are We Movie Made?* (New York: Macy-Masius, 1938); CCG to Eleanor Twiss, 25 November 1933, GFP, box 76.

17. Sophinisba Breckenridge, *Women in the Twentieth Century: A Study of Theory on Political, Social, and Economic Activities* (New York: McGraw-Hill, 1933), 51–54, 92; Martha Sprague Mason, ed., *Parents and Teachers: A Survey of Organized Cooperation of Home, School, and Community* (Boston: Ginn and Company, 1928), 114, 116, 125, 281.

18. Mrs. E. Hugh Morris, "National Congress of Parents and Teachers Plan of Work, Committee on Motion Pictures," July 1930; "Discussion of the Motion Picture Plan of the National Congress of Parents and Teachers," 24 May 1933; CCG, "Plan of Work for 1932–1934: Committee on Motion Pictures," August 1932, GFP, box 73; Mason, *Parents and Teachers,* 289; CCG to Mason, 25 May 1932; CCG to Mrs. R. A. Simons, 11 October 1932; CCG to Mrs. George Meagher, 20 October 1932, GFP, box 74; CCG to Madam Dreyfus-Barney, 3 June 1932, GFP, box 70; CCG to Short, 3 October 1932, GFP, box 71. For a state chapter perspective, see Dorothy Sparks, *Strong Is the Current: History of the Illinois Congress of Parents and Teachers, 1900–1947* (Chicago: Illinois Congress of Parents and Teachers, 1948), 78–79.

19. Quotes in Martha Sprague Mason to CCG, 12 December 1932; Mildred Lewis Russel to Mrs. Charles Remington, 22 January 1933; CCG to Eleanor Twiss, 14 November 1932; Minnie Bradford to CCG, 17 December 1932, GFP, box 74; Etta Brown to CCG, 24 June 1933, GFP, box 75; CCG to National PTA members and *Child Welfare* subscribers, 27 October 1932, GFP, box 74.

20. Martha Sprague Mason to CCG, 15 February 1933, 14 March 1933, 25 April 1933; CCG to Mason, 21 February 1933, 18 March 1933, 11 April 1933; CCG to Edith Hope, 4 March 1933; Marry Ferre to CCG, 10 March 1933; Minnie Bradford to CCG, 14 March 1933, and 12 April 1933; CCG to Bradford, 6 April 1933 (2 letters); CCG to Ferre, 25 March 1933; CCG to Mrs. Maynard Hart, 27 March 1933; CCG to Isa Compton, 28

March 1933; Ferre to CCG, 10 and 30 March 1933, GFP, box 75; Harry and Bonaro Overstreet, *Where Children Come First: A Study of the P.T.A. Idea* (Chicago: National Congress of Parents and Teachers, 1949), 205.

21. CCG, "National Congress of Parents and Teachers, Plan of Work for 1932–1934 Committee on Motion Pictures," GFP, box 73; CCG to Miss B. L. Mascorich, 20 September 1932; CCG to Mrs. C. H. Green, 8 October 1932; CCG to Mrs. R. A. Simons, 11 October 1932, GFP, box 74; correspondence, April 1933, especially CCG to Mrs. F. B. Elwell, 3 April 1933; CCG to Mrs. M. B. Lewis, 20 April 1933; CCG to Mrs. R. L. Denton, 22 April 1933, GFP, box 75; CCG to W. W. Story, 8 May 1935, GFP, box 79.

22. CCG to Mrs. John McRae, 5 June 1933; CCG to Martha Sprague Mason, 14 June 1933; CCG to Mary Langworthy, 2 August 1933, GFP, box 75. Alice Ames Winter's early communications claimed that the National PTA recognized her as its ambassador to the motion picture industry. Lillian Kelly to CCG (enclosing AAW to Kelly, 11 February 1930), 8 March 1930; CCG to Elizabeth Perkins, 22 September 1930, GFP, box 83; "A Statement Concerning the Use of the Name of the National Congress [of Parents and Teachers] in Connection with Listing and Previewing Motion Pictures," no author, n.d., GFP, box 73; *Parent-Teacher News*, 1 January 1934, GFP, box 76.

23. Etta Brown to CCG, 24 June 1933, GFP, box 75; Mary Ferre to CCG, 28 June 1933, GFP, box 72; CCG to Mary Langworthy, 2 August 1933, GFP, box 75; *Parent-Teacher Manual for Parent-Teacher Associations in Membership with the National Congress of Parents and Teachers* (Chicago: National Congress of Parents and Teachers, 1933).

24. "Annual Report, Public Relations Department [MPPDA]," 5 February 1924, WH-MC, reel 10; K. L. Russell report to WHH, 11 May 1933, WH-MC, reel 9; "Daily Report," 31 October 1933; 3, 13 November 1933; 17, 19, 23 January 1934; 8 March 1934, WH-MC, reel 10.

25. Correspondence (files 5 and 6); CCG to Mrs. Pettengill, 6 December 1932; CCG, "Informal Report of the Motion Picture Chairman," 18 September 1933, GFP, box 74; Carolyn Smiley to CCG, 12 November 1933, GFP, box 76; CCG form letter, 2 August 1933, GFP, box 75. Bureau of Mines films can be found at the National Archives at College Park, Maryland.

26. CCG to Mrs. T. D. A. Cockerell, 14 December 1933, GFP, box 76; CCG to Mrs. Bennett, 6 November 1935, GFP, box 72.

27. CCG to Miss Ruth Fox, 24 April 1930, GFP, box 69; *Daily Times* [Mamaroneck, New York], 11 January 1933, GFP, box 74; *Harrison's Reports*, 5 January 1926, 19 January 1929, 18 January 1930, 6 May 1933, 3 June 1933; Pete Harrison to CCG, 1 April 1935 (CCG's reply attached), GFP, box 79. See also CCG to Mrs. Francis Blake, 17 July 1935, GFP, box 80.

28. *Motion Picture Herald*, 30 March 1935; "SPECIAL RELEASE FROM NATIONAL CONGRESS OF PARENTS AND TEACHERS," 4 April 1935, GFP, box 79; WHH, "Motion Pictures and the Public: An Address before the Women's City Club of Philadelphia," 20 April 1925, 18, WHP, box 27; see also WHH to Jason Joy, 18 October 1922, WHP, box 18; WHH, "President's Annual Report," 29 March 1925, WH-MC, reel 21.

29. Courtland Smith to WHH, 9 August 1932; WHH to Smith, 9 August 1932; WHH to various newspaper editors, 9 November 1932; WHH to President Roosevelt, 10 November 1932; WHH to Kennedy, 20 June 1933, WH-MC, reel 9; Bert Adler to "George," 7 November 1934; *Tampa Morning Tribune*, 12 November 1932; R. H. Cochrane, Adolph Zukor, et al. to the managing editor of the *Los Angeles Times*, 14 No-

vember 1934, WH-MC, reel 13; Joseph Kennedy to WHH, 12 July 1932; C. C. Pettijohn to Editor, *Tampa Tribune*, 23 November 1932, WH-MC, reel 8.

30. *New York Times*, 30 June 1933, 23 July 1933, 1 August 1933, 3 August 1933, 9 August 1933; William Short to CCG, 21 and 22 August 1933, GFP, box 72; *Christian Century*, 20 September 1933, 1170–71; CCG to Hugh Johnson, 24 August 1933, GFP, box 75; "N.R.A. Code for Movies—Daily Report," 8 September 1933, WH-MC, reel 9.

31. CCG to Clarice Wade, 10 June 1932, GFP, box 74; CCG to Mrs. Bradford, 11 April 1933; CCG to Mrs. Pettengill, 13 July 1933, GFP, box 75; CCG to William Short, 9 May 1932; Short to CCG, 20 May 1932, GFP, box 71; quotes in AAW to WHH, 10 July 1933, WH-MC, reel 9; and AAW to WHH, 8 and 21 November 1933, WH-MC, reel 10.

32. "Statement of Will H. Hays, President of the Motion Picture Producers and Distributors of America, Inc., at the Opening of the Hearing on the Code for the Motion Picture Industry, Washington, D.C.," 12 September 1933, WH-MC, reel 9; *New York Times*, 13 September 1933; "National Industrial Recovery Administration: Hearing on Code of Fair Practices and Competition: Motion Picture Industry," 12 September 1933, Transcripts of Hearings, 1933–35, entry 44, box 219, RG9, National Recovery Administration, National Archives [hereafter RG9].

33. Ibid.; CCG to Sol Rosenblatt, 21 October 1933, RG9, box 3740; CCG to Catherine Oglesby, 21 November 1933, GFP, box 76; CCG to Mrs. Eugene White, 9 October 1933; CCG to Hugh Johnson, 24 August 1933; CCG to Mr. T. Karatz, 29 August 1933; CCG to Mrs. E. O. Uedemann, 9 October 1933; CCG to Minnie Bradford, 9 and 19 October 1933; Bradford to Eleanor Roosevelt, 20 October 1933, GFP, box 75; Consolidated Approved Code Industry File, Motion Pictures, Code, complaints, RG9, boxes 3740–44; "Annual Report of the Motion Picture Chairman of the National Congress of Parents and Teachers," June 1934, GFP, box 73; *New York Times*, 13 September 1933, 10 October 1933, 25 October 1933; *Christian Century*, 25 October 1933, 1326–28; *Harrison's Reports*, 4 November 1933, 176; Evelyn T. Patterson to Mrs. Franklin D. Roosevelt, 5 October 1933, RG9, box 3742.

34. For examples see, Margaret M. Johnson to FDR, 20 November 1933, RG9, box 3741; Mrs. J. R. A. Harriet to FDR, 9 November 1933; Mrs. L. J. Forbes to FDR, 24 November 1933, RG9, box 3740; Mrs. H. L. (illegible) and Ida M. Peterson to FDR; Mrs. Harold L. Perrin to FDR, 5 November 1933; Mrs. E. J. Payne to FDR, 6 December 1933, RG9, box 3742; Mrs. F. C. Kearn et al., petition to FDR, 24 October 1933; Mrs. R. B. Vail to FDR, 6 November 1933, RG9, box 3744.

35. First quote in CCG to Alida Bowler, 21 October 1933, GFP, box 75; CCG to Eleanor Twiss, 12 December 1933; CCG to Mrs. M. T. Remington, 15 December 1933, GFP, box 76; second quote in Abram Myers, unidentified newspaper article, n.d., GFP, box 73; *Harrison's Reports*, 9 December 1933; "Statement of Jack S. Connolly, General Manager Pathe News," *Hearing before the Committee on Interstate and Foreign Commerce, House of Representatives, on H.R. 6097*," 19 March 1934, 61–63; *New York Times*, 9 August 1933; *Union Signal*, 23 December 1933, WML.

36. Rosenblatt to Charlott W. Goux, 27 February 1934, Division 5 Day File, RG9, box 22, entry 174. Dozens of identical letters went out during January and February, 1934. Quote in Rosenblatt to Frederic A. Delano, 16 November 1933; see also Rosenblatt to Mrs. Wallace Patterson, 9 November 1933, RG9, box 4, entry 174; Rosenblatt to Mrs. C. S. White, 31 January 1934; Rosenblatt to Mrs. Frederick A. Wade, 29 January 1934; Rosenblatt to Mrs. Ford Smith, 29 January 1934; Rosenblatt to Bertha D. Geer, 6 Janu-

ary 1934, Division 5 Day File, RG9, box 23, entry 174; Rosenblatt to F. Dean McClusky, 23 October 1933, RG9, box 3742.

37. *New York Times*, 28 December 1933; Pat Casey to Maurice Mckenzie, 12 January 1934; Sidney Kent to Joseph B. Keenan, 12 January 1934, WH-MC, reel 10; Gabriel Hess to Fred W. Beetson, 28 May 1934, WH-MC, reel 11; Pat Casey to Maurice McKenzie, 9 November 1934; Irwin House to WHH, 10 November 1934, WH-MC, reel 13; quote in Rosenblatt to Mrs. Piercy Chestney, 27 December 1933; Rosenblatt to Mrs. Alonzo Richardson, 27 December 1933; Rosenblatt to Mrs. Richard Curry, 27 December 1933; Rosenblatt to Mrs. E. F. Boyce, 12 January 1934, Records of the Office of the Director of Compliance and Enforcement, Office Files of Sol Rosenblatt, 1933–1935, Division 5 Day File, RG9, box 23, entry 174. Rosenblatt telegram to Pat Casey, 5 January 1934; Rosenblatt to Mabel Kinney, 18 January 1934, Records of the Office of the Director of Compliance and Enforcement, Office Files of Sol Rosenblatt, 1933–1935, Division 5 Day File, RG9, box 23, entry 174; Pat Casey to Maurice McKenzie, 15 February 1934, WH-MC, reel 10.

38. "Code of Fair Competition for the Motion Picture Industry as Approved on November 27, 1933 by President Roosevelt," United States Government Printing Office, Washington, 1933, 244; "Flinn's Break-Down of Cases by Sections under the Code," 31 December 1934, RG9, box 16, entry 174; Louis Nizer, *New Courts of Industry: Self-Regulation under the Motion Picture Code* (New York: Longacre Press, 1935), 77–80.

39. Rosenblatt to George Schaefer, Sidney Kent, H. S. Bareford, and Felix Feist, 10 January 1934; Rosenblatt to Frederick Gamage, 10 January 1934; Rosenblatt to Gamage, 22 January 1934, Division 5 Day File, RG9, box 23, entry 174; Bi-Weekly Mail Summaries: A. R. Forbush to General Johnson, 10–12 September 1934, forwarded letter from Senator Van Nuys of Indiana; 6–8 May 1935, forwarded letter from Congressman Rogers; 11–13 March 1935, forwarded letter from Senator Joseph F. Guffey, Division 5 Reports, RG9, box 21, entry 174.

40. CCG to William Short, 17 September 1934, GFP, box 72. Emphasis added.

41. WHH "Daily Reports," 10 September 1934, WH-MC, reel 12.

42. *Minneapolis Tribune*, 6 June 1933; "Holds Public to Blame for 'Dirty' Films," unidentified local newspaper, 5 June 1933, AAW-CF; AAW, "Resume of the Best Pictures: First Eight Months of 1934," GFP, box 66; *Harrison's Reports*, 25 February 1933, 31; 13 May 1933, 75; 1 July 1933, 103; and 8 July 1933, 106.

43. Ibid., AAW to WHH, 10 July 1933, WH-MC, reel 9; AAW to WHH, 8 November 1933; AAW to WHH, 21 November 1933; WHH to AAW, 24 November 1933, WH-MC, reel 10; AAW to Dr. Wingate, 17 March 1933; Wingate to WHH, 18 March 1933, Production Code Administration Files: "The Story of Temple Drake," Margaret Herrick Library, Academy of Motion Picture Arts and Sciences.

44. *Variety*, 16 June 1931, 1, 24. The Hays Office, too, assumed that "women's pictures . . . inevitably means sex pictures." James Wingate to WHH, 28 February 1933, Production Code Administration Files: "Baby Face," Margaret Herrick Library, Academy of Motion Picture Arts and Sciences.

45. First quote in CCG to Martha Sprague Mason, 19 June 1933, GFP, box 75; second quote in Mrs. Richmond Wheeler to CCG, 10 May 1934, GFP, box 77; third quote in *New York Times*, 26 May 1934; see also "Daily Report," 30 October 1933, 3 November 1933, WH-MC, reel 10.

46. "Daily Report," 21 February 1933, WH-MC, reel 8; "Daily Report," 26 October

1933, 3 November 1933, 14 March 1933; "Daily Report," 17 November 1933, WH-MC, reel 10; *Houston Post*, 5 March 1934.

47. See "The Woman's Angle," *Variety*, 3 November 1931, 29 December 1931, 27 December 1932, 31 January 1933, 21 February 1933, 28 March 1933.

48. CCG to Robbins Gilman, 3 October 1931, GFP, box 17.

49. Quote in "Too Many Laws Passed, Mrs. Winter Claims at Federation Convention," unidentified local newspaper article, 17 June 1921, AAW-CF; CCG, "Jane Addams, The Universal," 1946, Women's International League for Peace and Freedom, Minnesota Branch, MHS, box 28; CCG to William Seabury, 25 May 1932; Seabury to CCG, 24 June 1932; CCG to Mrs. E. H. Kopplin, 8 July 1932, GFP, box 84; CCG, undated and untitled address, GFP, box 73, file 7; "Entertainment Basic Movie Rule, Woman Critic Says," unidentified and undated local newspaper article; "Mrs. Winter Decries Film Censorship," 20 January 1930, unidentified local newspaper article, AAW-CF; CCG to Mrs. Kate Bovey, 5 April 1920, GFP, box 13; CCG to Phyllis Abdullah, 14 January 1935, GFP, box 79.

50. "Club Women . . . Puritanism . . . ," unidentified local newspaper article with torn headline, 6 December 1925, AAW-CF; Elizabeth Gilman, "Catheryne Cooke Gilman," 191.

51. "Social Progress Credited to Men by Mrs. Winter," unidentified local newspaper article, between 1920 and 1924, AAW-CF.

52. Ida to Catheryne, 28 October 1914; L. Roy Woodward to Robbins Gilman, 25 December 1914, GFP, box 12.

53. CCG to Robbins Gilman, 17 and 18 September 1931, GFP, box 17.

54. CCG to Miss Sabina Marshall, 21 January 1933; CCG to Miss Elizabeth Quinlan, 26 April 1933, GFP, box 18; "Education and Publicity Department, Women's Cooperative Alliance: Instructions for the Voluntary Court Committee," November 1920, GFP, box 34; "Research and Investigation Monthly Report," published as a brochure, February 1921, GFP, box 35.

55. "Social Progress Credited to Men by Mrs. Winter," unidentified local newspaper article, between 1920 and 1924; "Sex Antagonism Denied as Plan of Women's Clubs" and "Mrs Winter Takes Issue with Dudley," unidentified local newspaper articles, 14 August 1921 and 25 November 1923, MJT, CF: AAW, MPL; Alice Ames Winter, *The Heritage of Women* (New York: Minton, Balch and Company, 1927), 7, 154, 294.

56. On CCG see *Woman's Journal*, February 1930, 10–12, 34; *The Parent-Teacher Broadcaster*, March 1930, 6–7, 27–28; *Child Welfare*, January 1933, GFP, box 68. On AAW see *Woman's Journal*, March 1930, 7–9, 45–46; *Parent-Teacher Broadcaster*, March 1930, 6, 27; "Mrs. Winter Decries Film Censorship," 20 January 1930, unidentified local newspaper article, AAW-CF.

57. Ibid., CCG to Kate Bovey, 5 April 1920, GFP, box 13.

58. "Mrs. Winter Decries Film Censorship," 2 January 1930; "City Committee on Films Picked by Mrs. Winter," 18 January 1930, unidentified local newspaper articles, AAW-CF; AAW to Dear Friends of Better Pictures, 3 May 1932; 1 June 1932, GFP, box 71.

59. AAW to Dear Madam, 20 March 1931; AAW to Dear Friends of Better Pictures, 1 June 1932, GFP, box 7; quotes in CCG to Mrs. T. D. A. Cockerell, 14 December 1933; CCG to Mrs. Bruce Smyth, 26 February 1934, GFP, box 76; *The Friend*, n.d., GFP, box 68; CCG to Mrs. R. A. Simons, 11 October 1932, GFP, box 74; CCG to Mrs. F. B. Elwell, 3 April 1933, GFP, box 75; CCG to Mrs. Kenneth Gelber, 21 January 1935, GFP, box 79; *The Churchman*, 1 February 1930; CCG, "To the Motion Picture Chairmen of the State Congresses of Parents and Teachers: What Everyone Wants to Know," June 1933, GFP, box 74.

60. Carl Milliken to "Dear Friend," 28 March 1934; Maurice McKenzie to WHH, 5 May 1934; WHH's Notes on Leaked AAW Report, 13 April 1934, WH-MC, reel 11; *Minneapolis Tribune*, 6 June 1933, and "Holds Public to Blame for 'Dirty' Films," unidentified newspaper, 5 June 1933, AAW-CF; AAW to "Friends of Better Pictures," "Resumé of the Best Pictures: First Eight Months of 1934," GFP, box 66; *Motion Picture Herald*, 31 March 1934, 13–14.

61. "Daily Reports" to WHH, 10 September 1934, WH-MC, reel 12; CCG testimony, *Hearing before the Committee on Interstate and Foreign Commerce . . . on H.R. 6097* (19 March 1934), 40–41; "Daily Reports" to WHH, 19, 22, 23, 25, 30 October 1934; 2, 5, 8, 9, 12, 13 November 1934, WHP, box 47; CCG to state PTA motion picture chairs, June 1935, GFP, box 80; *Child Welfare*, June 1934, GFP, box 73; CCG to Mrs. H. Fabry, 10 September 1934; CCG to Mrs. James Sheehan, 6 December 1934, GFP, box 78.

62. "Daily Reports" to WHH, 19, 30 October 1934; 5 November 1934, WHP, box 47.

EIGHT: "'Catholic Action' Is Blazing a Spectacular Trail!"

1. CCG to Mrs. Richmond Wheeler, 23 May 1934, GFP, box 77; CCG to Mrs. Howard Bennett, 29 March 1933, GFP, box 84; CCG to state PTA motion picture chairs, April 1933, GFP, box 75; *Union Signal*, 23 September 1933, WML, CCG to Eunice McClure, 13 December 1933, GFP, box 76.

2. CCG to Mrs. Henry Somers, 7 June 1933, GFP, box 75; CCG to Mrs. Bruce Smyth, 26 February 1934; CCG to Mrs. R. G. Williams, 26 February 1934, GFP, box 76; FMPC Minutes, 19 March 1934, GFP, box 80; McClure to CCG, 22 December 1933; CCG to McClure, 9 January 1934; CCG to Mrs. Eugene White, 9 October 1933; CCG to Edgar Dale, 9 October 1933, GFP, box 76; *Child Welfare*, May 1934, GFP, box 73; CCG to Mrs. Eugene White, 9 October 1933; CCG to Edgar Dale, 9 October 1933, GFP, box 75.

3. Mrs. Richard McClure, "Explanation of Statements in Parent Teacher Letter," 1935, GFP, box 79.

4. These accusations spread over a period of years but probably originated with Diehl. Frances Diehl to Elaine Goodale Eastman, 24 April 1932; CCG to Martha Sprague Mason, 7 April 1934; CCG to Marguerite E. Schwarzman, 12 June 1934, GFP, box 77; Diehl to CCG, 13 May 1932, GFP, box 84.

5. Fanny Woodson to CCG, 1 June 1932; Woodson to CCG, 14 June 1932; CCG to Minnie Bradford, 3 April 1934, GFP, box 77; CCG to Fanny Woodson, 8 July 1932, GFP, box 84.

6. CCG to Mrs. Hugh Bradford, 6 December 1932, GFP, box 74; CCG to Mrs. George Cole, 22 March 1933, GFP, box 75; Mary G. Hawks, "Motion Pictures: A Problem for the Nation," 7–11 October 1933, GFP, box 67; Walsh, *Sin and Censorship*, 147; Elizabeth McKeown, *War and Welfare: American Catholics and World War I* (New York: Garland, 1988); "Statement of Miss Agnes G. Regan, Executive Secretary, National Council of Catholic Women," 9 March 1936, National Catholic Welfare Conference/National Council of Catholic Women Records, collection 10, box 1, Catholic University of America.

7. "Daily Report" to WHH, 15 May 1934; Commentary on Daily Reports, 11 and 21 May 1934, WH-MC, reel 11.

8. Quote in CCG to Miss Ruth Bottomly, 13 June 1934, GFP, box 77; CCG to Mrs. Howard Bennett, 21 March 1927, GFP, box 69; *Woman's Home Companion*, January 1930, WH-MC, reel 3; CCG to Mrs. George Cole, 22 March 1933, GFP, box 75; CCG to Mrs.

Eugene White, 26 February 1934; CCG, "Churches Follow P.T.A. in Fight against In-decent Motion Pictures," undated speech, GFP, box 76; CCG to Mrs. Chester Greene, 31 May 1934, 14 June 1934, GFP, box 77; "Daily Reports" to WHH, 19 October 1934, WHP, box 47.

9. Minnie Bradford to CCG, 19 June 1934; CCG to Bradford, 6 July 1934; CCG to Mrs. David Stewart, 5 July 1934, GFP, box 77.

10. *New York Times*, 28 June 1934, 10 July 1934; Hays, *The Memoirs of Will Hays*, 450–51;Walsh, *Sin and Censorship*, 59, 82–84, 88, 104; "Daily Report" to WHH, 26 March 1934, WH-MC, reel 11; "Daily Report" to WHH, 9 July 1934; Fred Allport, "Notes on the Week's Press Items," 31 August 1934, WH-MC, reel 12; "Daily Report" to WHH, 2 October 1934; Fred Allport, "P.C.A. Reaction," 4 October 1932; Fred Allport, "Notes on the Week's Press Items," 5 October 1934, WH-MC, reel 13.

11. CCG to James Cummings, 18 April 1934; CCG to John T. McNicholas and John Cantwell, 26 April 1934; quotes in CCG to Minnie Bradford, 6 July 1934, GFP, box 77.

12. Press Release, "Statement by Mrs. Thomas A. McGoldrick, Chairman, Motion Picture Bureau, International Federation of Catholic Alumnae," 7 April 1930, WH-MC, reel 4; CCG to Elaine Eastman, 29 October 1930, GFP, box 69; CCG to Mrs. Hugh Brad-ford, 6 December 1932, GFP, box 74; CCG to Mrs. George Cole, 22 March 1933, GFP, box 75; Mary Looram, "Report of Motion Picture Bureau, International Federation of Catholic Alumnae, 1932–1934," 31 October 1934, 4, WH-MC, reel 13; Walsh, *Sin and Censorship*, 51.

13. *Christian Century*, 15 August 1934, 1037–39; "Vital Movie News: Organ of the Fed-eral Motion Picture Council in America," GFP, box 81; Eleanor Campbell to Mrs. F. H. Misner, 9 November 1934, GFP, box 78.

14. "Annual Report, Department of Public Relations," March 1926, WH-MC, reel 26; Rita McGoldrick testimony in "Hearings before the Committee on Education, House of Representatives, Sixty-Ninth Congress First Session on H.R. 4094 and H.R. 6233, Bills to Create a Commission to Be Known as the Federal Motion Picture Commission," 14–17, 27 April 1926 and 4 May 1926, 31–34; "Statement by Mrs. Thomas A. McGoldrick, Chairman, Motion Picture Bureau, International Federation of Catholic Alumnae," 7 April 1930, WH-MC, reel 4; CCG to Elaine Eastman, 29 October 1930, GFP, box 69.

15. Gilman quote in *The National Elementary Principal*, October 1934, GFP, box 68; Curley quote in "Daily Reports" to WHH, 9 January 1933, WH-MC, reel 8; "Daily Re-ports" to WHH, 21 June 1934, WH-MC, reel 12; Walsh, *Sin and Censorship*, 95–96.

16. *New York Times*, 28 January 1934, 9 July 1934, 10 July 1934; Walsh, *Sin and Cen-sorship*, 134–35.

17. Quotes in "Daily Report" to WHH, 3 October 1934, WH-MC, reel 13; and Mary Harden Looram, "Report of Motion Picture Bureau, International Federation of Catholic Alumnae, 1932–1934," 31 October 1934, WH-MC, reel 13; CCG to Madam Dreyfus-Barney, 1 August 1934, GFP, box 70.

18. *New York Times*, 9 July 1934; quotes in Joseph F. Rummel to Agnes Regan, 6 No-vember 1939, and John T. McNicholas to Rummel, 4 November 1939, National Catholic Welfare Conference/National Council of Catholic Women Records, collection 10, box 1, Catholic University of America; Walsh, *Sin and Censorship*, 138–43; *Minneapolis Jour-nal*, 31 August 1934.

19. "Daily Report" to WHH, 11 June 1934, WH-MC, reel 11.

20. William Short, director of the Motion Picture Research Council, on which CCG

served, fueled such bigotry with his compilation of anti-Semitic statements in "A Generation of Motion Pictures," *New York Times*, 9 July 1934; "Daily Report" to WHH, 20 March 1934, 26 March 1934; Louis Nizer to Stephen Wise, 23 April 1934, WH-MC, reel 11.

21. "Motion Pictures," *National W.C.T.U. Annual Report*, 1934–1938, 1939, WML; Mrs. Harry A. Ling to CCG, 19 March 1945, GFP, box 86; Lola Gentry to Jason Joy, 27 September 1927, WHP, box 35.

22. CCG to Minnie Bradford, 9 October 1933, GFP, box 75; William Short to Jesse Binford, 29 March 1934; CCG to Short, 23 July 1934; CCG to Binford, 25 June 1934, GFP, box 72; Iva White to CCG, 11 July 1934, GFP, box 77; CCG to Mrs. J. B. McCrary, 5 March 1935; Stephen Cabot to CCG, 10 March 1935, GFP, box 79; "Federal Motion Picture Council Board Meeting Minutes," 18 February 1935, GFP, box 80; *A New Day for the Movies* (New York: Motion Picture Research Council, 1934).

23. Langworthy to CCG, 11 March 1935; CCG to Langworthy, 9 January 1935 and 15 March 1935; Bannerman to "State President," 23 March 1935; Francis Culkin to CCG, 1 April 1935; CCG to Maude Joss, 7 May 1935; CCG to Martha Sprague Mason, 28 May 1935, GFP, box 79; FMPC "Board Meeting Minutes," 18 February 1935; CCG to Langworthy, 17 July 1935 and 10 September 1935; CCG to Mrs. Francis Blake, 17 July 1935; Langworthy to CCG, 2 September 1935; CCG to Mason, 10 September 1935; CCG to Minnie Bradford, 11 September 1935, GFP, box 80.

24. Chase to CCG, 24 February 1933, GFP, box 84; FMPC "Board Meeting Minutes," 18 February 1935, 10 February 1936, 30 September 1937, 10 April 1939, GFP, box 80; FMPC "Board Meeting Minutes," 29 June 1945; CCG to Eric Johnston, 27 January 1947 and 9 July 1947; Johnson to CCG, 3 March 1947, GFP, box 86.

25. "Film Shopper's Guide," *The Clubwoman*, November 1934, April 1935; "Motion Picture Work Makes Great Strides," *The Clubwoman*, August 1935; Mrs. William Brown, "Committee on Motion Pictures," *The Clubwoman*, March 1936, June 1936, September 1936, July 1937, GFWC.

26. AAW to WHH, 19 June 1934, WH-MC, reel 11; *The Clubwoman*, November 1935, May 1937, GFWC; "Mrs. Thomas G. Winter," 1935, and Winter, "Up the Ladder," 4–12 June 1935, Presidents' Papers: Alice Ames Winter Speeches, GFWC; "Films Are Clean, Says Mrs. Winter on Visit," unidentified newspaper, 20 May 1935, AAW-CF; *Minneapolis Times*, 17 November 1942, AAW-CF; *New York Times*, 17 November 1942.

27. Gerald Gardner, *The Censorship Papers: Movie Censorship Letters from the Hays Office, 1934 to 1968* (New York: Dodd, Mead and Co., 1987), 24–25, 143–47, 159.

28. Newell Edson to CCG, 14 September 1933; Martha Sprague Mason to CCG, 25 September 1933; CCG to Edson, 9 October 1933, GFP, box 72; CCG to Mason, 9 October 1933, GFP, box 75; CCG to Mrs. C. E. Sweet, 13 February 1934, GFP, box 76; CCG to William F. Snow, 25 April 1934, GFP, box 77; Walsh, *Sin and Censorship*, 153–54; McNicholas quoted in Paul Facey, *The Legion of Decency: A Sociological Analysis of the Emergence and Development of a Social Pressure Group* (New York: Arno Press, 1974), 113–14.

29. Walsh, *Sin and Censorship*, 157–58, 194–95; Black, *The Catholic Crusade against the Movies, 1940–1975* (Cambridge: Cambridge University Press, 1997), 131; CCG, "Motion Pictures, Radio, and Press in National and International Propaganda," February 1948, GFP, box 72.

30. CCG to Mrs. George Cole, 22 March 1933, GFP, box 75; Mary G. Hawks, "Motion Pictures: A Problem for the Nation," 7–11 October 1933, GFP, box 67; Walsh, *Sin and Censorship*, 147; John T. McNicholas to Joseph F. Rummel, archbishop of New Or-

leans, 4 November 1939; Rummel to Agnes G. Regan, executive secretary, National Council of Catholic Women, 6 November 1939, National Catholic Welfare Conference/National Council of Catholic Women Records, collection 10, box 1, Catholic University of America; "Daily Report" to WHH, 1 and 29 October 1934, WH-MC, reel 13; CCG notes, undated, GFP, box 73; CCG to Alice Mitchell, 18 November 1935, GFP, box 72; CCG to Mrs. Piercy Chestney, 29 November 1933, GFP, box 76.

31. Sullivan quote in "Daily Report" to WHH, 4 October 1934; "Foresees End of Block Booking, Priest Discusses Films for Adults," unidentified newspaper article, 17 October 1934; "Endorsed Motion Pictures, Published by the International Federation of Catholic Alumnae," October 1934, WH-MC, reel 13; CCG to Mrs. E. O. Uedemann, "Endorsed Motion Pictures, Published by the Motion Picture Bureau of the International Federation of Catholic Alumnae," 6 February 1933, GFP, box 75; Walsh, *Sin and Censorship*, 130; Gilman quote in CCG to Mrs. A. H. Reeve, 24 July 1934, GFP, box 77.

32. "Daily Report" to WHH, 2 November 1934, 1 and 8 November 1934; F. W. Allport comments, "Daily Report," 9 November 1934, WH-MC, reel 13.

33. "Daily Report" to WHH, 1 and 8 November 1934, WH-MC, reel 13.

34. Quoted in "Pettijohn vs. the Church Leaders," *Motion Picture Research Council Bulletin*, August 1934, GFP, box 72; *Harrison's Reports*, 28 March 1936.

35. CCG to Alice Mitchell, 18 November 1935, GFP, box 72; CCG to C. G. Dowds, 8 May 1935, GFP, box 79; CCG to Mrs. Rufus Gibbs, 1 March 1941, GFP, box 85; *Vital Movie News*, July 1945, GFP, box 81.

CONCLUSION: Anti-obscenity Reform and Women's History

1. Gilman to Eleanor Twiss, 28 July 1933, GFP, box 75.

2. The phrase belongs to Linda Gordon, "Putting Children First: Women, Maternalism, and Welfare in the Early Twentieth Century," in Linda Kerber et al., *U.S. History As Women's History: New Feminist Essays* (Chapel Hill: University of North Carolina Press, 1995), 63–86.

3. This chapter's comparisons with welfare reform draw heavily on Robyn Muncy, *Creating a Female Dominion in American Reform, 1890–1935* (New York: Oxford University Press, 1991).

4. Muncy, *Creating a Female Dominion*, 124–27.

5. Jane Jerome Camhi, *Women against Women: American Antisuffragism, 1880–1920* (Brooklyn, NY: Carlson Publishers, 1994), 101, 103.

6. Emily P. Bissell, "A Talk to Women on the Suffrage Question," reprinted in Brenda Stalcup, ed., *The Women's Rights Movement* (San Diego, CA: Greenhaven Press, 1996), 145–46.

7. Both Lathrop and Abbott respected Gilman but objected to her severe public criticism of Winter and Hays. Lathrop to CCG, 15 January 1931, GFP, box 84; Gilman note re: Julia Lathrop and motion pictures, written on League of Nations Child Welfare Committee Report, 10 April 1931, GFP, box 68; Mlle. A. Colin to CCG, 23 February 1932, GFP, box 70; Grace Abbott to Mrs. T. D. A. Cockerell, 8 November 1933, GFP, box 76.

8. Muncy, *Creating a Female Dominion*, 58, 104, 126–29.

9. Ibid., 153–56.

10. Moran, *Teaching Sex*, 227.

11. Lynn Chancer, *Reconcilable Differences: Confronting Beauty, Pornography, and the Fu-*

ture of Feminism (Berkeley: University of California Press, 1998), 75; "Talk of the Nation," National Public Radio, with Susie Bright (author of *The Best American Erotica*), and Wendy McElroy (author of *XXX: A Woman's Right to Pornography*), on National Public Radio, 18 October 1995; Tom W. Smith, "The Polls—A Report: The Sexual Revolution?" *Public Opinion Quarterly* 54, no. 3 (fall 1990), 415–35.

12. Nadine Strossen, *Defending Pornography: Free Speech, Sex, and the Fight for Women's Rights* (New York: Scribner, 1995), 177–78, 209–10.

Note on Sources

Against Obscenity grew out of research in a wide array of archival material. Most important were the voluminous personal papers of the Gilman Family (Minnesota Historical Society, St. Paul, Minnesota). This collection—nearly one hundred large boxes that Gilman saved because "some day, someone will need this material to help in the struggle against th[e] national menace" of the motion picture industry—thoroughly documents the Women's Cooperative Alliance's local work and Gilman's national motion picture reform and sex education efforts. Though biased, it introduces all of the key players in the anti-obscenity movement. The similarly extensive Will Hays Papers (Indiana State Library, Indianapolis, and on microfilm) contain correspondence and memorabilia covering Hays's twenty-three years as president of the Motion Picture Producers and Distributors of America. Other important personal collections are the papers of Theodore Hayes (Minnesota Historical Society, St. Paul); Alice Ames Winter (Hoover Institution, Stanford University, Palo Alto, Calif.); and Mary Ware Dennett (on microfilm; University of Minnesota, Minneapolis). Useful organizational records include the Woman's Club of Minneapolis (accessed by Caroline Loken, president: club members insist on accessing information for researchers); General Federation of Women's Clubs (General Federation of Women's Clubs History and Resource Center, Washington, D.C.); Women's Christian Temperance Union (Frances E. Willard Memorial Library, Evanston, Ill.); Motion Picture Producers and Distributors of America, Inc. (on microfilm, accessed by and in possession of Ruth Vasey, Flinders University, Adelaide, Australia); and the Production Code Administration (Academy of Motion Picture Arts and Sciences, Margaret Herrick Library, Beverly Hills, Calif.). The *Minneapolis Journal* and *Tribune* Newspaper Morgue (Minneapolis Public Library Special Collections) contains invaluable clipping files on important Minneapolis figures in this study; the National Recovery Administration records (Record Group 9, National Archives, College Park, Maryland) include many boxes of documents on the development and enforcement of the motion picture code; the Billy Rose Theatre Collection at the New York Public Library contains several valuable files on "Crazy Quilt"; and the National Council of Catholic Women Records (National Catholic Welfare Conference/National Council of Catholic Women Records, Catholic University of America, Washington, D.C., accessed by Kathleen Laughlin) includes a key file on women's motion picture reform in the 1930s.

Corporate newsletters, histories, and handbooks provided essential information on organizations that have received little scholarly attention, including the General Federation of Women's Clubs, National Council of Women, and National Congress of Parents and Teachers. See, *The Clubwoman*, later changed to *General Federation News; The Parent-Teacher Broadcaster; Child Welfare Magazine;* Mary Belle King Sherman, "The Women's Club in the Middle-Western States" (Philadelphia: American Academy of Political and

Social Science, 1906; rpt. New Haven: Research Publications, 1977); Caroline M. Seymour Severanc, *The Mother of Clubs* (Los Angeles: Baumgardt Publishing, 1906); Mary I. Wood, *The History of the General Federation of Women's Clubs* (New York: General Federation of Women's Clubs, 1912); Kate Louise Roberts, *The Club Woman's Handybook of Programs and Club Management* (New York: Funk and Wagnalls, 1914); Alice Ames Winter, *The Business of Being a Club Woman* (New York: Century, 1925); *The Yearbook and Directory of the National Council of Women of the United States, Including the Proceedings of the Fourteenth Convention* (New York, 1928); Martha Sprague Mason, *Parents and Teachers: A Survey of Organized Cooperation of Home, School, and Community* (New York: Ginn and Company, 1928); Anna Steese Richardson, *A Manual for Clubwomen* (New York: L. C. Smith and Corona Typewriters, 1929); *Parent-Teacher Manual for Parent-Teacher Associations in Membership with the National Congress of Parents and Teachers* (Chicago: National Congress of Parents and Teachers, 1933); National Council of Women of the United States, *Our Common Cause: Civilization* (New York: National Council of Women, 1933); Dorothy Sparks, *Strong Is the Current: History of the Illinois Congress of Parents and Teachers* (Chicago: Illinois Congress of Parents and Teachers, 1948); Harry and Bonaro Overstreet, *Where Children Come First: A Study of the P.T.A. Idea* (Chicago: National Congress of Parents and Teachers, 1949); Mildred White Wells, *Unity in Diversity: The History of the General Federation of Women's Clubs* (Washington, D.C.: General Federation of Women's Clubs, 1953); *Women in a Changing World: The Dynamic Story of the International Council of Women since 1888* (London: Routledge and Kegan Paul, 1966); and Anna Garlin Spencer, *The Council Idea: A Chronicle of Its Prophets and a Tribute to May Wright Sewall* (New Brunswick, N.J.: Heidingsfeld Co., 1930).

Published information on the Women's Cooperative Alliance's sex education program can be found in Catheryne Cooke Gilman, "An Organization to Assist Mothers in Their Responsibility for Social Hygiene Education," *Journal of Social Hygiene*, October 1923; Chloe Owings, "Sex Education for Parents: A Research in Teaching Methods and Material," *Journal of Social Hygiene* (December 1928); and Helen Leland Witmer, *The Attitudes of Mothers toward Sex Education* (Minneapolis: University of Minnesota Press, 1929). Contemporary sex education experts on whom the Women's Cooperative Alliance relied include Maurice A. Bigelow, *Sex Education: A Series of Lectures Concerning Knowledge of Sex in Its Relation to Human Life* (New York: Macmillan, 1918); and Thomas W. Galloway, *Sex and Social Health: A Manual for the Study of Social Hygiene* (New York: American Social Hygiene Association, 1924). On Mary Ware Dennett's sex education/obscenity case, see Dudley Nichols, "Sex and the Law," *The Nation*, May 8, 1929; Nichols, "Sex and Our Children," *The Nation*, February 6, 1929; "Safe Sex Teaching Needed," *Twentieth Century Progress*, July 1929; "Sex Instruction Is No Crime," *Christian Century*, March 12, 1930; Mary Ware Dennett, *Who's Obscene?* (New York: Vanguard, 1930); Edward L. Keyes, "The Trial of Mrs. Dennett," *Commonweal*, May 22, 1929; William Sheafe Chase letter to the editor, *Christian Leader*, May 31, 1929, and Mary Ware Dennett, *The Sex Education of Children: A Book for Parents* (New York: Vanguard, 1931). Two very helpful secondary sources on Dennett are John M. Craig, "'The Sex Side of Life': The Obscenity Case of Mary Ware Dennett," *Frontiers: A Journal of Women Studies* 15, no. 3 (1995), and Constance Chen, *"The Sex Side of Life": Mary Ware Dennett's Pioneering Battle for Birth Control and Sex Education* (New York: New Press, 1996).

Especially useful published primary sources on motion picture reform for this period include *The Public Relations of the Motion Picture Industry: A Report by the Department of*

Research and Education, Federal Council of the Churches of Christ in America (1931; Jerome S. Ozer, 1971); *The Community and the Motion Picture: Report of National Conference on Motion Pictures Held at the Hotel Montclair, New York City, September 24–27, 1929* (New York: Motion Picture Producers and Distributors of America, 1929); Will Hays, *The Memoirs of Will Hays* (Garden City, N.Y.: Doubleday, 1955); Louis Nizer, *New Courts of Industry: Self-Regulation under the Motion Picture Code* (New York: Longacre, 1935). The scholars who participated in motion picture studies sponsored by the Motion Picture Research Council and financed by the Payne Fund published their work in separate volumes; they include Herbert Blumer, *Movies and Conduct;* Samuel Renshaw et al., *Children's Sleep: A Series of Studies on the Influence of Motion Pictures;* Ruth Peterson, *Motion Pictures and the Social Attitudes of Children;* and Werrett Wallace Charters, *Motion Pictures and Youth, A Summary* (all published New York: Macmillan, 1933). The studies are summarized and sensationalized in Henry James Forman, "To the Movies—But Not to Sleep," *McCall's* (September 1932), and *Our Movie-Made Children* (New York: Macmillan, 1935). The motion picture industry responded to these studies with Mortimer Jerome Adler, *Art and Prudence: A Study in Practical Philosophy* (New York: Longmans, Green, 1937), summarized in Raymond Moley, *Are We Movie Made?* (New York: Macy-Masius, 1938). For a current scholarly analysis of the Payne Fund studies and a previously unpublished study, see Garth Jowett, ed., *Children and the Movies: Media Influence and the Payne Fund Controversy* (New York: Cambridge University Press, 1996).

Scholarship on the history of obscenity law and free speech provides legal and constitutional context for my work on grassroots activists. Most legal and constitutional scholars aim to discover the origins of current free speech theory and jurisprudence; as a result, their treatment of activists focuses on extremists—those who sought to pass or repeal anti-obscenity legislation—and celebrates those who championed free expression. Early works, such as Paul Murphy, *The Meaning of Free Speech: First Amendment Freedoms from Wilson to FDR* (Westport, Conn.: Greenwood Publishing Company, 1972), and Paul Murphy, *World War I and the Origin of Civil Liberties in the United States* (New York: W.W. Norton, 1979), treat World War I as a pivotal moment in the evolution of American attitudes toward freedom of speech, emphasizing the role that class, ethnic, and ideological conflict played in sparking debate over the meaning of the First Amendment. Without denying the importance of World War I as a major turning point, John Wertheimer, "Free Speech Fights: The Roots of Modern Free-Expression Litigation in the U.S." (Ph.D. diss., Princeton University, 1992), and David Rabban, *Free Speech in Its Forgotten Years* (Cambridge: Cambridge University Press, 1997), have argued for the significance of free speech radicals at the turn of the century, decades before the war, and long before free speech arguments would influence women's anti-obscenity work. In "Eras of the First Amendment," *Columbia Law Review* (1991), David Yassky links the Supreme Court's liberalizing speech trends to the 1930s New Deal, suggesting a free speech periodization compatible with the experiences of female anti-obscenity activists.

Until very recently, scholars of anti-obscenity reform have focused on the efforts of male activists to use anti-obscenity reform to exert social control over working-class and ethnic groups. The most notable are David Pivar, *The Purity Crusade: Sexual Morality and Social Control, 1868–1900* (Westport, Conn.: Greenwood Press, 1973), and Paul Boyer, *Purity in Print: The Vice-Society Movement and Book Censorship in America* (New York: Scribner's, 1968). Anna Louise Bates continues this trend, but focuses on men's control of women, in "Protective Custody: A Feminist Interpretation of Anthony Comstock's Life and Laws" (Ph.D. diss., State University of New York, Suny-Binghamton, 1990). Newer works that look beyond and complicate the social control thesis to explain middle-class opposition to obscenity include Rochelle Gurstein, "The Repeal of Reticence: The Controversy about Privacy, Obscenity, and Exposure, 1873–1934" (Ph.D. diss., University of Rochester, 1991); Nicola Beisel, *Imperiled Innocents: Anthony Comstock and Family Reproduction in Victorian America* (Princeton, N.J.: Princeton University Press, 1997); Andrea Tone, *Devices and Desires: A History of Contraceptives in America* (New York: Hill and Wang, 2001); and Helen Lefkowitz Horowitz, *Rereading Sex: Battles over Sexual Knowledge and Suppression in Nineteenth-Century America* (New York: Knopf, 2002). On the grassroots impact of obscenity law, I recommend Shirley Burton, "Obscenity in Victorian America: Struggles over Definition and Concomitant Prosecutions in Chicago Federal Court, 1873–1913" (Ph.D. diss., University of Illinois, 1991), and Elizabeth Hovey, "Stamping Out Smut: The Enforcement of Obscenity Laws, 1872–1925" (Ph.D. diss., Columbia University, 1998).

Readers who wish to know more about women's anti-obscenity reform should turn next to two outstanding recent studies: Alison Parker, *Purifying America: Women, Cultural Reform, and Pro-Censorship Activism, 1873–1933* (Chicago: University of Illinois Press, 1997), and Andrea Friedman, *Prurient Interests: Gender, Democracy, and Obscenity in New York City, 1909–1945* (New York: Columbia University Press, 2000), both of which challenge the social control thesis common in earlier work—Parker by portraying a unitary middle class regulating itself, and Friedman, a middle class at war with itself over who may wield moral authority. Parker shows how middle-class women tried to use censorship and entertainment alternatives to shape and escape a burgeoning commercial culture dominated by men. Friedman pushes the analysis further, arguing that women's attempts to exert moral influence over obscenity faltered on an emergent concept of democratic moral authority.

Some of the most exciting work being done on clubwomen focuses on black women, who appear to have played little role in anti-obscenity reform. The most promising recent work on white women's clubs compares men's with women's clubs. See Maureen Flanagan, "Gender and Urban Political Reform: The City Club and the Woman's City Club of Chicago in the Progressive Era," *American Historical Review* (October 1990), and Sara Deutsch, "Learning to Talk More Like a Man: Boston Women's Class-Bridging Organizations," *American Historical Review* (April 1992). Karen Blair remains the leading authority on white women's clubs: *The Clubwoman As Feminist: True Womanhood Redefined, 1868–1914* (New York: Holmes and Meier, 1980) and *The Torchbearers: Women and Their Amateur Arts Associations in America, 1890–1930* (Bloomington: Indiana University Press, 1994). Other useful works include Theodora Penny Martin, *The Sound of Our Own Voices: Women's Study Clubs, 1860–1910* (Boston: Beacon Press, 1987); Anne Ruggles Gere, *Intimate Practices: Literacy and Cultural Work in U.S. Women's Clubs, 1880–1920* (Chicago: University of Illinois Press, 1997), and Priscilla Murolo, *The Common Ground of Womanhood: Class, Gender, and Working Girls' Clubs, 1884–1928* (Chicago: University of Illinois Press, 1997). Many of the local studies of women's clubs that I have consulted can be found in the dissertation (University of Minnesota, 1998) on which this book is based. Because most clubwomen resist opening their records to scholars, they have written much of their own history, with results that tend to be rather uncritical and celebratory.

Important histories of the twentieth century's first so-called sexual revolution include James McGovern, "The American Woman's Pre–World War I Freedom in Manners and

Morals," *Journal of American History* (September 1968); John C. Burnham, "The Progressive Era Revolution in American Attitudes towards Sex," *Journal of American History* (March 1973); and Howard Kushner, "Nineteenth-Century Sexuality and the 'Sexual Revolution' of the Progressive Era," *Canadian Review of American Studies* (spring 1978). For more recent work that explores the role of gender, class, and sexual orientation, see Christina Simmons, "'Marriage in the Modern Manner': Sexual Radicalism and Reform in America, 1914–1941" (Ph.D. diss., Brown University, 1982); Kathy Peiss, *Cheap Amusements: Working Women and Leisure in Turn-of-the-Century New York* (Philadelphia: Temple University Press, 1986); Joanne Meyerowitz, *Women Adrift: Independent Wage Earners in Chicago, 1880–1930* (Chicago: University of Chicago Press, 1988); Kevin White, *The First Sexual Revolution: The Emergence of Male Heterosexuality in Modern America* (New York: New York University Press, 1993); Timothy Gilfoyle, *City of Eros: New York City, Prostitution, and the Commercialization of Sex, 1790–1920* (New York: W.W. Norton, 1992); Sharon R. Ullman, *Sex Seen: The Emergence of Modern Sexuality in America* (Berkeley: University of California Press, 1997); Kevin White, *Sexual Liberation or Sexual License?: The American Revolt against Victorianism* (Chicago: Ivan R. Dee, 2000); and Randy D. McBee, *Dance Hall Days: Intimacy and Leisure among Working-Class Immigrants in the United States* (New York: New York University Press, 2000).

Curiously, historians have left the history of sex education largely to specialists in education and the health sciences. See James Randall Cook, "The Evolution of Sex Education in the Public Schools of the United States, 1900–1970" (Ph.D. diss., University of Southern Illinois, Carbondale, 1971); Patricia Campbell, *Sex Education Books for Young Adults, 1892–1979* (New York: Bowker, 1979), and Michael Imber, "Analysis of a Curriculum Reform Movement: The American Social Hygiene Association's Campaign for Sex Education, 1900–1930" (Ph.D. diss., Stanford University, Palo Alto, California, 1980). An exceptional and excellent historical treatment is Jeffrey Moran, *Teaching Sex: The Shaping of Adolescence in the Twentieth Century* (Cambridge, Mass.: Harvard University Press, 2000).

Issues of children and sexuality continue to receive a great deal of attention in today's national media, where debates have become even more polarized than those that defeated Gilman's anti-obscenity/sex education agenda in the 1930s. Recent examples of books that lump sexually explicit materials together, arguing not only that all are protected under the First Amendment but that they should be available to children, include Marjorie Heins, *Not in Front of the Children: "Indecency," Censorship, and the Innocence of Youth* (New York: Hill and Wang, 2001), and Judith Levine, *Harmful to Minors: The Perils of Protecting Children from Sex* (Minneapolis: University of Minnesota, 2002). In *A Return to Modesty: Discovering the Lost Virtue* (New York: Free Press, 1999), Wendy Shalit offers a radically different perspective, arguing that children should be shielded from all sexual explicitness. A much more sophisticated and nuanced treatment is Heather Hendershot, *Saturday Morning Censors: Television Regulation before the V-Chip* (Durham, N.C.: Duke University Press, 1998); Hendershot includes the history of a women's group, Action for Children's Television (ACT), founded in 1968, that, like Gilman and her colleagues, differentiated carefully between commercial and educational sexual material for children.

A number of general histories on women and politics provided a foundation for *Against Obscenity*. The best synthetic piece is still Paula Baker's "The Domestication of Politics: Women and American Political Society, 1780–1920," *American Historical Review* (June 1984). I also recommend Nancy Cott, *The Grounding of Modern Feminism* (New Haven: Yale University Press, 1987); Suzanne Lebsock, "Women and American Politics,

1880–1920," in Louise Tilly and Patricia Gurin, eds., *Women, Politics, and Change* (New York: Russell Sage Foundation, 1990); Anne Firor Scott, *Natural Allies: Women's Associations in American History* (Chicago: University of Illinois Press, 1993), and Melanie Gustafson, Kristie Miller, and Elisabeth Israels Perry, *We Have Come to Stay: American Women and Political Parties, 1880–1960* (Albuquerque: University of New Mexico Press, 1999).

I have drawn heavily on the concept of "maternalism" developed chiefly by historians of women and the American welfare state. See especially Linda Gordon, ed., *Women, the State, and Welfare* (Madison: University of Wisconsin Press, 1990); Theda Skocpol, *Protecting Soldiers and Mothers: The Political Origins of Social Policy in the United States* (Cambridge, Mass.: Harvard, 1992); Seth Koven and Sonya Michel, eds., *Mothers of a New World: Maternalist Politics and the Origins of Welfare States* (New York: Routledge, 1993); Molly Ladd-Taylor, *Mother-Work: Women, Child Welfare, and the State, 1890–1930* (Chicago: University of Illinois Press, 1994); Linda Gordon, *Pitied but Not Entitled: Single Mothers and the History of Welfare, 1890–1935* (New York: Free Press, 1994); Estelle Freedman, *Maternal Justice: Miriam Van Waters and the Female Reform Tradition* (Chicago: University of Chicago Press, 1996), and Robyn Rosen, "Federal Expansion, Fertility Control, and Physicians in the United States: The Politics of Maternal Welfare in the Interwar Years," *Journal of Women's History* (autumn 1998). Regarding different types of maternalism espoused among middle-class female welfare reformers, see Elizabeth J. Clapp, *Mothers of All Children: Women Reformers and the Rise of Juvenile Courts in Progressive Era America* (University Park: Pennsylvania State University Press, 1998).

Battles among women over suffrage and prohibition presaged and paralleled many of the anti-obscenity debates that divided women. See Jane Jerome Camhi, *Women against Women: American Anti-Suffragism, 1880–1920* (Brooklyn, N.Y.: Carlson Publishing, 1994); Thomas Jablonsky, *The Home, Heaven, and Mother Party: Female Anti-Suffragists in the United States, 1868–1920* (Brooklyn, N.Y., Carlson Publishing, 1994); Susan E. Marshall, *Splintered Sisterhood: Gender and Class in the Campaign against Woman Suffrage* (Madison: University of Wisconsin Press, 1997); Elna Green, *Southern Strategies: Southern Women and the Woman Suffrage Question* (Chapel Hill: University of North Carolina Press, 1997); David Kyvig, "Women against Prohibition," *American Quarterly* (1976); Katherine Harris, "A Study of Feminism and Class Identity in the Women's Christian Temperance Union, 1920–1979: A Case Study," *Historicus* (fall–winter 1981); Kenneth Rose, *American Women and the Repeal of Prohibition* (New York: New York University Press, 1996); and Catherine Gilbert Murdock, *Domesticating Drink: Women, Men, and Alcohol in America, 1870–1940* (Baltimore: Johns Hopkins University Press, 1998).

Several books have traced a decline in women's political efficacy following enfranchisement, linking it to a variety of factors internal and external to women's organizations, including ideological disagreements, short-sighted suffrage movement strategies, inattention to women's institutions, professionalization, efforts to remain nonpartisan, entrance into partisan politics, lack of an ongoing movement base, the demise of Progressivism, the first Red Scare, and the growing hegemony of American business. See William O'Neill, *Everyone Was Brave* (New York: Quadrangle, 1969); Dorothy Johnson, "Organized Women as Lobbyists in the 1920s," *Capitol Studies* (spring 1972); J. Stanley Lemons, *The Woman Citizen: Social Feminism in the 1920s* (Chicago: University of Illinois Press, 1973); Estelle Freedman, "Separatism As Strategy: Female Institution Building and American Feminism, 1870–1930," *Feminist Studies* (fall 1979); Nancy F. Cott, *The Grounding of Modern Feminism* (New Haven: Yale University Press, 1987); Michael McGerr, "Political Style and Women's Power, 1830–1930," *Journal of American History* (December 1990); Robyn Muncy, *Creating a Female Dominion in American Reform, 1890–1935* (New York: Oxford University Press, 1991); Kristi Anderson, *After Suffrage: Women in Partisan and Electoral Politics before the New Deal* (Chicago, Ill.: University of Chicago Press, 1996); Sara Hunter Graham, *Woman Suffrage and the New Democracy* (New Haven: Yale University Press, 1996); Jo Freeman, *A Room at a Time: How Women Entered Party Politics* (New York: Rowman and Littlefield, 2000). For a slightly more optimistic version see Felice Gordon, *After Winning: The Legacy of the New Jersey Suffragists, 1920–1947* (New Brunswick, N.J.: Rutgers University Press, 1986), and, for a critical discussion of earlier interpretations, see Nancy Cott, "Across the Great Divide: Women in Politics before and after 1920," in Louise A. Tilly and Patricia Gurin, eds., *Women, Politics, and Change* (New York: Russell Sage Foundation, 1990). Peggy Pascoe finds a similar downward trajectory for female reformers in the American West (who won the vote long before their eastern sisters), but attributes it to dynamics unrelated to women's enfranchised politics: *Relations of Rescue: The Search for Female Moral Authority in the American West, 1874–1939* (New York: Oxford University Press, 1990).

Politics intersects with popular culture in several other useful books, each of which examines how women as consumers, performers, producers, or scriptwriters used motion pictures and burlesque theater to acquire power, express themselves, and subvert class or gender hierarchies. See Kay Sloan, "Sexual Warfare in the Silent Cinema: Comedies and Melodramas of Woman Suffragism," *American Quarterly* 33 (fall 1981); Miriam Hansen, *Babel and Babylon: Spectatorship in American Silent Film* (Cambridge: Harvard University Press, 1991); Lizzie Francke, *Script Girls: Women Screenwriters in Hollywood* (London: British Film Institute, 1994); Lauren Rabinovitz, *For the Love of Pleasure: Women, Movies, and Culture in Turn-of-the-Century Chicago* (New Brunswick, N.J.: Rutgers University, 1998); Nan Enstad, *Ladies of Labor, Girls of Desire: Working Women, Popular Culture, and Labor Politics at the Turn of the Twentieth Century* (New York: Columbia University, 1999); M. Alison Kibler, *Rank Ladies: Gender and Cultural Hierarchy in American Vaudeville* (Chapel Hill: University of North Carolina Press, 1999), and Susan A. Glenn, *Female Spectacle: The Theatrical Roots of Modern Feminism* (Cambridge, Mass.: Harvard University Press, 2000). Another book that includes useful information on working-class women and movies is Steven J. Ross, *Working-Class Hollywood: Silent Film and the Shaping of Class in America* (Princeton, N.J.: Princeton University Press, 1998).

The best general works on motion picture reform and industry self-regulation (1910–1940) include Lary May, *Screening Out the Past: The Birth of Mass Culture and the Motion Picture Industry* (New York: Oxford University Press, 1980); Leonard Leff and Jerold Simmons, *The Dame in the Kimono: Hollywood, Censorship, and the Production Code from the 1920s to the 1960s* (New York: Grove Weidenfeld, 1990); Lea Jacobs, *The Wages of Sin: Censorship and the Fallen Woman Film, 1928–1942* (Madison: University of Wisconsin Press, 1991); Robert Sklar, *Movie-Made America: A Cultural History of American Movies* (New York: Vintage Books, 1994); Janet Staiger, *Bad Women: Regulating Sexuality in Early American Cinema* (Minneapolis: University of Minnesota Press, 1995), Frances Couvares, ed., *Movie Censorship and American Culture* (Washington, D.C.: Smithsonian Institution Press, 1996), and Ruth Vasey, *The World According to Hollywood, 1918–1939* (Madison: University of Wisconsin Press, 1997). On Hollywood in the 1930s, see Tino Balio, *Grand Design: Hollywood As a Modern Business Enterprise, 1930–1939* (New York: Scribner's, 1993); Colin Shindler, *Hollywood in Crisis: Cinema and American Society,*

1929–1939 (New York: Routledge, 1996); Giuliana Muscio, *Hollywood's New Deal* (Philadelphia: Temple University Press, 1997), and Thomas Doherty, *Pre-Code Hollywood: Sex, Immorality, and Insurrection in American Cinema, 1930–1934* (New York: Columbia University Press, 1999). On Catholic motion picture reform see Robert Janes, "The Legion of Decency and the Motion Picture Industry" (M.A. thesis, University of Chicago, 1939); Paul Facey, *The Legion of Decency: A Sociological Analysis of the Emergence and Development of a Social Pressure Group* (New York: Arno Press, 1974); James M. Skinner, *The Cross and the Cinema: The Legion of Decency and the National Catholic Office for Motion Pictures, 1933–1970* (Westport, Conn.: Praeger, 1993); Gregory Black, *Hollywood Censored: Morality Codes, Catholics, and the Movies* (Cambridge: Cambridge University Press, 1994), and Frank Walsh, *Sin and Censorship: The Catholic Church and the Motion Picture Industry* (New Haven: Yale University Press, 1996).

Several books that examine the development of business associations and their connections to reformers have helped me to understand the role of the Minneapolis Citizens Alliance network in this story. They are David Horowitz, *Beyond Left and Right: Insurgency and the Establishment* (Urbana and Chicago: University of Illinois Press, 1997); William Millikan, *A Union against Unions: The Minneapolis Citizens Alliance and Its Fight against Organized Labor, 1903–1947* (St. Paul: Minnesota Historical Society Press, 2001), and Sven Beckert, *The Monied Metropolis: New York City and the Consolidation of the American Bourgeoisie, 1850–1896* (Cambridge: Cambridge University Press, 2001).

The feminist sex wars of the 1980s inspired this book. The best published primary sources for the subject include Carole Vance, ed., *Pleasure and Danger: Exploring Female Sexuality* (London: Pandora Press, 1984); "Notes and Letters," *Feminist Studies* (spring 1983, fall 1983); Varda Burstyn, *Women against Censorship* (Vancouver: Douglas and McIntyre, 1985); and Andrea Dworkin and Catharine A. MacKinnon, *Pornography and Civil Rights: A New Day for Women's Equality* (Catharine A. MacKinnon and Andrea Dworkin, 1988). For secondary works that favor the feminist anti-censorship position, see Lisa Duggan and Nan D. Hunter, *Sex Wars: Sexual Dissent and Political Culture* (New York: Routledge, 1995); Alice Echols, *Daring to Be Bad: Radical Feminism in America, 1967–1975* (Minneapolis: University of Minnesota, 1989); and Jane Gerhard, *Desiring Revolution: Second-Wave Feminism and the Rewriting of American Sexual Thought, 1920–1982* (New York: Columbia University Press, 2001). More balanced treatments can be found in Donald Alexander Downs, *The New Politics of Pornography* (Chicago: University of Chicago Press, 1989); Lyn Chancer, *Reconcilable Differences: Confronting Beauty, Pornography, and the Future of Feminism* (Berkeley: University of California, 1998); and Ruth Rosen, *The World Split Open: How the Modern Women's Movement Changed America* (New York: Penguin, 2000).

Finally, this book benefited enormously from feminist theorists' work on essentialism and identity politics. See especially Elizabeth V. Spelman, *Inessential Woman: Problems of Exclusion in Feminist Thought* (Boston: Beacon Press, 1988), and Barbara Ryan, ed., *Identity Politics in the Women's Movement* (New York: New York University Press, 2001).

Index